THE AUTHOR DISCOVERED THAT GATHERING MATERIAL FOR AN EXOTIC BOOK ON COOKERY WAS PLEASANT AS WELL AS TECHNICALLY INFORMATIVE

The Gentleman's Companion

VOLUME I

BEING AN EXOTIC COOKERY BOOK

OR, AROUND THE WORLD WITH KNIFE FORK AND SPOON

By *Charles* H. *Baker, Jr.*

INCLUDING:

A Company of *Hand-Picked Receipts,* each one *Beloved & Notable in its Place,* collected faithfully on *Three Voyages & a Quarter Million Miles around the World, & Other Journeys.*

NOT FORGETTING:

Certain *Valuable Words to the Wise, Gleaned* from Divers Chefs *in Many & Strange Places;* & the *Home Formulae for Construction of such Intriguing Exotics* as *Hell-Fire Bitters, Key West Old Lime Sour, Herb Vinegars;* to Say Nothing of Various *Strange and Delicious Sauces & Bastings for Fish, Flesh, Fowl, & the Wilder Games.*

Martino Publishing
Mansfield Centre, CT
2013

Martino Publishing
P.O. Box 373,
Mansfield Centre, CT 06250 USA

ISBN 978-1-61427-445-2

Cover design by T. Matarazzo

Printed in the United States of America On 100% Acid-Free Paper

The Gentleman's Companion

VOLUME I

BEING AN EXOTIC COOKERY BOOK

OR, AROUND THE WORLD WITH KNIFE FORK AND SPOON

By *Charles* H. B*aker, J*r.

INCLUDING:

A Company of *Hand-Picked Receipts,* each one *Beloved & Notable in its Place,* collected faithfully on *Three Voyages & a Quarter Million Miles around the World, & Other Journeys.*

NOT FORGETTING:

Certain *Valuable Words to the Wise, Gleaned* from Divers Chefs *in Many & Strange Places;* & the *Home Formulae for Construction of such Intriguing Exotics* as *Hell-Fire Bitters, Key West Old Lime Sour, Herb Vinegars;* to Say Nothing of Various *Strange and Delicious Sauces & Bastings for Fish, Flesh, Fowl, & the Wilder Games.*

The Derrydale Press
New York
1939

DEDICATION

Contrary to current routine this volume is not dedicated to Publisher, Wife, Friend, Mistress or Patron, but to our own handsome digestive tract without which it never could have seen light of day.

"GENTLEMEN," said Mr. Peregrine Touchwood, "Man is a Cooking Animal; & in whatever Situation he is found, it may be assumed as an Axiom, that his Progress in Civilization has kept exact Pace with the Degree of Refinement he may have Attained in the Art of Gastronomy. . . . From the Hairy Man of the Woods to the Modern *Gourmet,* apportioning his Ingredients & blending his Essences, the Chain is Complete!"

Introduction to:
The Cook & Housewife's Manual,
Med Dods,
Edinburgh, A.D. 1826

CONTENTS

A FOREWORD

It was all of fourteen years ago during a first adventure around the world that we made the agreeable discovery that all really interesting people—sportsmen, explorers, musicians, scientists, vagabonds and writers—were vitally interested in good things to eat and drink; cared for exotic and intriguing ways of composing them. Diplomats and colonial officials were pungent gourmets.

We soon discovered further that this keen interest was not solely through gluttony, the spur of hunger or merely to sustain life, but in a spirit of high adventure. It was intrigue of the unexpected in herb or spice or sauce; the titillating savour of exotic ways of putting flesh to fire or greens to bowl.

Sportsmen boasted of a new Malay curry as proudly as they would pelt a ten foot tiger. Explorers took the same agreeable thrill in discovering a succulent *Calalou* as in sourcing the Congo.

Diplomat, artist and scientist beamed on a special Black Sea *Bortsch* from Odessa as he might on an international pact; a Brazilian basket of deep fried whole shrimp became as vital as a tube of madder lake to painting a Rio beauty's shawl; a Tahitian fish salad with lime and coconut dressing took rank with making health contagious instead of grippe.

But most important of all, ***these people who cared for superior food were equally interested in the history of those exotics, their traditional background, their romantic origin!***—something this volume has endeavoured to possess.

That was all we needed to start us on this pleasant madness of receipt collection. Being a passionate collector of divers and amazing addenda from all over the world, it was a relatively simple matter to hang a field note book and pencil among other burdens as we threaded our way from bazaar to eating house to bistro to coffee shop.

Thus an agreeable and mounting collection has lived with us faithfully three voyages and a quarter million miles around the world, across Europe; in Asia, Africa, the British and Dutch East Indies; the Philippines, Hawaii and the three Americas. It has snupped Bahamian and other island dishes through the whole sweep of the West Indies, and various coastwise Americana through ten thousand additional sea miles sailing our own deep water ketch *Marmion* from Key West to New England's north shore. We eagerly delved back into bygone years in canoe and under tent among the Florida Keys, the river and lake region of central Florida. We recorded a few choice memories from twenty-five years spent in the deep south: Florida, Virginia, South Carolina, Tennessee.

This initial volume—barely half the collected list!—represents our final selection of exotic savouries. Each one is beloved and notable in its place and, something not yet found in parallel efforts—lists ingredients which at most can take no longer than seventy-two hours to possess in any part of America. In moderate proportion it is a collection of lusties. Certain dishes do appear to list many ingredients, but if readers will take pause to note each of these, a vast proportion are found on any sanely stocked kitchen shelf.

IN A WAY this collection was begun for fellow men, by a man. Having traveled far too much for our own good we had come to indorse womanhood mainly for her beauty, grace, discretion and charm. Having lived in many cities we had learned to flee from Women-with-Brains, Women-who-Did-Things; had learned to cleave, rather, to thoughtful young eyes and lovely smiles who sat back quietly and let us talk and prove ourself to be a monstrous clever fellow. Owning every book on cookery extant in English—and a few in foreign tongue—right from the golden age of Louis XV, through the cooking renaissance of Brillat-Savarin and clear up to our present incomparable Henri Charpentier, there had been a score of immortal chefs. Yet with possible exception of the late Madame Poulard, French sorceress of the omelette pan, what now remembered woman had ever dared create anything beyond the already written word of former male cookery masters? What delectable dish had even been named for a woman, except those by a man chef for some lovely and famous patroness?

Yes, it terrified us to think what might happen if we surrendered our collection of stout dishes for a squad of critical female readers to compare to their own floating islands or quaint tapioca affairs. Away with floating islands, a pox on sago depressions! And by gad sirrah we didn't need any pink paper panties on our roast fowl either. No sir. This exotic cookery business of ours wasn't to woo any promoter of strawberry socials, women's auxiliary luncheons, or the demure young bride. Our mission was not promoting fancy pastries for profitable sale, coy desserts for diverting the attention of brides. All these questionable depravities had already been done only too well by every woman's cook book in Christendom.

In our lawless way we doubted if any lady would give a rusty bobbie pin if we had eaten South India curry in Trichinopoly, *enchilladas* in Taxco, corned beef and' in Dinty Moore's in Shanghai. Or what did they care if we had gorged on *arroz con pollo* in Barranquilla, a lordly *rijstafel* in Soerabaja, beefsteak and kidney pie in St. Albans, or earthenware bowls of scalding and immortal onion soup at L'Escargot in its sixteenth century spot near Les Halles, Paris' vast central markets?

Why should any nice lady care if we'd consumed small Korean shrimp in Seoul, bird's-nest soup in Formosa; sampled frozen coconuts in Bangkok or sat crosslegged in Kyoto during the cherry blossom festival eating *sukiyaki* and sipping endless thimblefuls of hot saki served by laughing dolls in bamboo patterned kimonos? What weight could it possibly carry in the world of women that we had explored twenty-one courses of a Mandarin dinner—including hundred-year-old eggs, candied duck, *Fishes Dipped in the Six Perfumes,* and a huge Mandarin host who could belch louder than Sir Walter Raleigh—across the narrow Pearl River channel from Shameen, in Canton? It certainly wouldn't matter a jot that we had been introduced to *blinis* and sour cream with good black Russky caviar shipped in via Harbin, while we sat across from a Manchu princess of the blood who smoked funny long White Russian cigarettes, sat between red lacquer columns of Erik Nyholm's Buddhist *Temple of the Propitious Pearl* which broods on the very top of Western Hills—has brooded there in fact for five hundred years—sat there sipping chilled chablis and eating *blinis* and watching the steel coin of Old Buddha's summer palace lake while the dying sun lashed Peking's stark Tartar Wall through her eternal age-old haze of red dust—when Peking *was* Peking.

What would they care about things consumed on the terrace in front of the nipa-thatched Manila Polo Club, when the peak of Mariveles stood notched and black against the afterglow? Or about the time our bride and I sat until the small hours before dawn with Walter Spies, watching the legong dancers, listening to the gamelans, and running through his own harmonizations of Balinese music for five pianos—and consumed mild Bali curry of cucumbers and eggs and eggplants, sprinkled with freshly grated coconut and crumbled Bombay duck, which last is no duck at all, but an odd dried species of Indian fish which for reasons not pertinent to mention rises to the nets of dark strange fishermen of the Malabar coast near Goa?

Why should we fancy up a volume for this drove of feminists whose whole day was spoiled, setting sun of which found them unpossessed of some new disguise for bread pudding when—but how could *they* know it?—any male with the digestion of a titmouse would rather top off a good dinner with a sound spot of Stilton cheese-and-port than the duckiest little prune whip born of egg whisk?

No, to our wry and ungarnished male mind it seemed high time some loyal brother actually did something for his random fellow man.

Then a perfect howl went up. Widely scattered lady acquaintances told us, rather bluntly we thought, just where we rated in the family of reptiles. Our friend Coe Glade, leading contralto for Chicago and San Francisco's opera, first viewed us coolly through improbable huge dark eyes and tartly informed us that she owned national renown for composing Sunday morning breakfasts. Another cool lady volunteered advice that she had just completed a three months' course at *Le*

Cordon Bleu in Paris, and she guessed we hadn't troubled to do that! Ernest Hemingway's wife Pauline proved to us how beach birds should be stuffed.

Then came climax. A very handsome girl advertising genius, who had resided fourteen years in Havana, fastened on our lapel in the Stork Club and supposed all the way through a six course meal that we knew all about *Moros y Cristianos*—Moors and Christians, or black beans and rice. That we had included *Pollo Piña, Camagüey*—which was fowl of discreet age and rearing after being smothered in sun-ripe pineapple pulp, the peel of small green limes, raisins and a gift of white rum. She imagined that our knowledge of muskmelons impregnated with *Anis del Mono*—which is Spanish anise liqueur of the monkey head label—and chilled colder than cold, would fill a whole chapter. How about *langostinos* boiled in sea water the way they did them out Matanzas way with a green sauce of mayonnaise, lime, garlic salt and Nepal pepper? . . . Well, and so we were getting up a man's cookery book were we. And what now, precisely, did we intend doing about it? Furthermore, because of our questionable stove-side conceits for male *amateurs* she imagined all smart American women from Seattle to Key West now had to put on sackcloth and ashes, admit gullible feminine mediocrity, and bow down forever to pink quivery things that leer out of ice boxes at you and taste like pink soda pop with a dab of vanilla cotton batting on top. So, and so, and so! . . .

Our head was bloody but unbowed. We hung on grimly, waiting for the bell—and the check—when a great light exploded across our groping brain. We suddenly realized that *all* America was seething in a thumping renaissance of good cookery, master and mistress alike. In spite of prohibitions and depressions, wars and rumours of wars; in face of rubber stamp personal mediocrity with which all ruling gentlemen seemed bent on moulding their citizens, this slow rebirth in one of the truly fine arts quickly became the most cheerful and tolerant gleam on the whole current horizon.

Why, now, when we really stopped to think of it, the entire American scene was fairly waving with grills, salad tongs, coffee biggins and duck presses! Ladies had sloughed off gardening gloves for asbestos grilling gauntlets. Perhaps the base betrayal of the prohibition era had blessed us in disguise, spurring all men and women into knowing what *was* fit for primate nourishment and thirst! No longer would it be smart to boast ignorance in proper food and wine. Strong men openly strutted their pet species of crêpes suzettes, and other strong men clapped them on the back.

It was incredible. It was like wrist watches. Before our naive entry into the last European war any American gentleman caught wearing one of those useful time pieces was in danger of audible ridicule in company, suspect, if not in bodily peril. A scant dozen years back any Yankee male friend guilty of tossing salad, poaching a filet of sole or whipping up a deep dish apple pie was in contempt—held to be a hair different from his normal fellow; a foppish gazing-stock, an irregular queer fish whom all orderly men looked upon with that mortified disbelief they would feel should a favourite maiden aunt remove her upper plate at a White House banquet.

Dark eyes so charmingly opposite us had caused the light to break—that ladies as well as gentlemen at last were racing into this new and healthful sport of random cookery. This combined battle of the pots was why American shops were designing, discovering, infinitely smarter and more colourful utensils; why the once-trite corner grocery was fairly burgeoning with bayleaf, soya sauce and basil. No local yokel stared now when asked for mango chutney, wild rice or tarragon vinegar. We bet that even those dwelling in truly isolated sectors could post a letter to the nearest city and get our hickory salt and Nepal pepper within a couple of days.

Mentally we started waving the star spangled banner for this national rebirth of good taste. Our mind's eye saw a vast and orderly company, men and women, marching rank on rank with grilling racks at shoulder arms. It all made us feel very proud and confident and homey. We sipped a leisurely dry Amontillado sherry to the brown eyes opposite. We were very proud of our countrymen, but especially so of our countrywomen—woman. We raised the thin stemmed crystal. Then just as we were going to speak of all this the waiter stood between us and thrust menus at us, with the gift only waiters seem to have.

But our feminine gourmet of the dark eyes didn't even glance at it. She smiled up at the waiter with more charm than the situation called for and said, "Bring me a prune whip, please. With lots and lots of nice thick cream on top. If you haven't got one tell them to make one!"

Then she looked back at us blandly. "Now," she said, "remember you were going to tell *me* things about all kinds of strange things to eat."

THIS VOLUME, then, is a company of hand-picked receipts we have met during world wanderings, or which have been added to the collection through grace of friends and correspondents with dilatory or permanent domicile in odd and intriguing spots of the globe. Although we don't list the eternal Frenchman's live snails, or hundred-year-old eggs, or sea-slugs—*bêche de mer*—or bird's nests of swallow spittle, or deep fried octopus, or creamed rattlesnake, or alligator tail, we have at one time or another and for one reason or another eaten all of these.

In this primary volume it seemed more neighbourly to cleave those select exotics that have most appealed to the American side of our palate; those which require ingredients neither rare nor too difficult of source. In this process half were rejected. All the residuary list has been eaten with gusto by ourselves. Each has stood the test of time *in situ,* and we can affirm that none is any chancey addendum supplied by some local armchair explorer whose travels abroad have taken him as far toward the mysterious East as Coney Island.

We therefore invite you to cruise with us on the magic carpet of your own kitchen saucepan, and share the rare flavours from many far off places. It is our further earnest hope that such trusting and gustatorial readers will find half as much pleasure in recreation of these dishes as we had in their original consumption!

The Gentleman's Companion

AN EXOTIC COOKERY BOOK

CHAPTER I

A DESIGN *FOR* COOKERY

Relating where *Imagination & Daring* take Their Part; why *Suspect the Lean & Hungry Chef;* & brief Instruction on *Measurements & Heats;* & finally an *Invitation to The Blender.*

CREATION of an Exotic Cookery Book of this sort presupposes not only the ability to read on the part of its readers, but the additional attributes of intelligence, imagination and a hustling spirit of adventure.

With bookshop shelves groaning beneath their burdens of routine cookery books there can be no place here for formulae or instruction on such items as the making of brown or white foundation sauce; what basting is; what is meant by marinate, lard and score; just as we assume vocabulary including such essentials as au gratin, brochette and sippet; or truss, toss and skewer; or when we say "faggot" no bundle of inflammable dry twigs is indicated but a clutch of sweet herbs. With a selected list of exotics having already cut down original strength by half through lack of space, it would not be reasonable to bleed elected receipts further by inclusion of elementary matters of this type. And in passing it is profitable to note that, besides the host of books on general cookery compiled for housewife or amateur, there are several small limply bound volumes for the professional chef, dealing tersely with hundreds of sauces, egg dishes in 1000 ways, the chef's reminder, and so on.

This then is solely a book of succulent exotics easily created from basics buyable in any man's home town, not a general primer on making raw food palatable.

FROM the start every amateur chef might do well to approach his kitchen with a gleam of imminent adventure in his eye! Preparation of a fine exotic dish can be exactly like a latter-day Columbus sailing to new and unknown worlds. It required imagination to make Queen Isabella part with her jewels. It took daring to sail westward in those top-heavy high-pooped sailing ships, equipped with doubtful compasses and having no valid assurance what lay before them; or what mysteries and thrills hid behind that setting sun.

There can be the same adventure in cookery, explorations of a milder and more healthful sort. Preparing a worthy dish is like painting a fine portrait, composing a nocturne or setting down a sonnet. There is constant chance of putting something *individual* into the deed, letting the chef dominate the receipt.

The herb shelf is a three-manual pipe organ, the sauce cabinet is a palette of varied colour, a simple black pepper handmill can be an unpurchasable violin of overtone. No reader should be too bound by the written word. Take the essentials, then set sail on private adventures of amateur cookery common to no one. With a very little experience we can vary any receipt this way or that, to reflect our own personality, taste, or climate.

The best exotics all over the world are not found in any cookery books. The Hawaiian, Javanese, Spaniard or Russian who first did them well had never even heard of cookbooks; in all probability could not read one if he had. Time and later chefs caught up the original dish, garnished and improved it. Tribes and provinces approved it. It became individual, and in its own peculiar way brushed with immortality. The trouble with too many chefs, amateur and professional, is that they forget that every elaborate salad came from green shoots; that larded pheasant was first grilled on a sharpened stick. In other words, there is a limit to fancy trimmings. It takes no biochemist to mark this dead line. *It comes when the trimmings become so pungent that they confound the worthwhile flavour of the basic dish.* And especially in delicate fine items like small game, fish, shellfish and certain inner quadruped importances like sweetbreads, too much fancying up is likely to approach debacles we too often find abroad—like drowning a brace of partridge in vast seas of red sauerkraut!

Receipts here should be followed in basis, then slightly varied to suit the vagaries, whims and moods of the chef. Toss in a spoonful of vanity to impress the lovely audience of the moment, a dash of daring, a pinch of conservatism and a cup of confidence. And so, fellow adventurers in gastronomy: Good hunting!

JUST WHY the LEAN & HUNGRY CHEF IS SUSPECT

". . . *Beware the lean and hungry chef,*" is an old proverb, and nothing could be more true. In other words when cooking any dish: Taste, *taste, TASTE!*

No chef, male or female, amateur or professional, can ever create without tasting his way through the dish so as to catch and preserve each little nuance of flavour, bouquet, texture, piquancy. No professional worthy of his basting spoon can taste his way through life without building up certain comfortable and ample layers of *en bon point* around the equator. Sometime explore the kitchen of any truly fine restaurant and ask to see your chef; or aboard a fine ship, or in a southern plantation house. A lean and hungry chef cannot be plying his craft and the truth is not in him.

DISREGARD the CULT of MYSTERIOUS BOASTERS

But this chef inspection must not be permitted to cast the amateur down. Just like plumbers, ship navigators and professional hunting guides, all professional chefs dearly love to twine an aura of mysterious and solitary knowledge about their work. Both God and the prophets are on the side of their own private kettle! Your hesitant questions will fetch evasive answers. You will be left feeling of somehow having violated one of the more important social niceties in the mere process of asking—of being guilty of being a mental pygmy, an amateur childishly poking its untutored nose into the affairs of elders. This, dear reader, is—if we may be pardoned the idiom—a clutch of horsefeathers.

Nonsense! It took us twenty-five years to learn that navigating a small ship—or a large one for a' that—was a matter of arithmetic, trigonometry and horse sense; not one of the black arts. It took us thirty to discover that any citizen with brain enough to hurdle grammar school can, with a little imagination and gambling spirit, turn out as good or better food in limited quantity at a time than the average professional chef. And one of the main reasons is that he cooks for fun, not for pelf. It is a high spot in the week when all the blackamoors depart and we have kitchen and grills to ourself. It is a joy, not a grim profession. The amateur is not frayed with the burden of daily routine. It is far easier for him to conjure up that slight *Umph!* which can salvage an average dish from its mediocrity and enshrine it among the company of the culinary elect.

WITH IMAGINATION RELY on FOUR BASIC PRINCIPLES in COOKED DISHES, & REMEMBER to KEEP THEM HOLY

Proper and accurate measurements.
Proper cooking temperatures.
Proper length of cooking time.
Proper time for serving.

It is amazing how often we catch ourself being careless with measurements; have oven or water too hot or cold; produce food inaccurately timed, or see it served dreadfully warm when it should come sizzling directly from broiler. . . . *Have hot foods hot as hades; cold foods arctic cold!*

A FINAL PLEA for the AMATEUR NOT to ATTEMPT too many DISHES at a GIVEN TIME, SINCE a FEW THINGS of MERIT CAN OUTSHINE a PLATOON of MEDIOCRITY . . . and a WARNING on LIABILITY of GUEST-HELPERS

It took us years of good-natured misjudgment to learn that few guests are worth their blasting powder in kitchen. Most of them seek only the easy and amusing tasks, dirty endless tools and merely succeed in delaying matters. Especially women with a little knowledge are a major cross. Give them a copy of the Old Testament to run through. It will engage their attention, keep them silent, improve the mind.

From many years' trying experience take warning from us, and assume from the start that if things are going to taste right and come out on time, *we must do the whole show without help or interference.* It is wiser to attempt a one- or two-dish meal of importance, than a seven course affair which not only will prove mediocre nourishment but a fair ticket to the booby hatch.

The elder Strauss certainly never tried setting down three or four Viennese waltzes at the same time, and most certainly didn't have a duet of well-meaning ladies jot his notes down for him if he had! Be firm on this and in the end such a routine will be recognized as just and right, and command due respect.

TEMPERATURE CHART for the OVEN and DEEP FAT KETTLE

This is important, especially when roasting large meat and poultry items, or deep frying items of some size which tend to cool boiling fat. Oven thermometers come with all good stoves these days, and an accurate deep fat thermometer is very easily found in any decent hardware store.

Very Slow Oven	250° Fahrenheit
Slow Oven	300° Fahrenheit
Medium Oven	350° Fahrenheit
Medium Hot Oven	375° Fahrenheit
Hot Oven	400° Fahrenheit
Very Hot Oven (mainly for wild ducks)	450° to 500° Fahrenheit

Certain technical institutions list more heats than this, but no chef born of man could use them due to variables: Temperature of meat when put in oven; efficiency of oven in question, as no two are exactly alike. If the temperature needle swings a few degrees over those given here, don't let it spoil the fun. We aren't running a high tension chemical laboratory anyway. Preparing pleasant dishes is 80 per cent sanity and 20 per cent technicality, after all.

TELLING OVEN HEATS without THERMOMETERS of any SPECIES

An English friend discovered this for us, and in England they still do many things the old way, and not one family in a dozen has anything like a cooking thermometer in the house.

Simply put a piece of white paper in oven.
Look at it in 5 minutes.

Slow Oven: Paper golden brown in 7 minutes.
Medium Oven: Paper golden brown in 5 minutes.
Hot Oven: Paper dark brown in 5 minutes.

TIME TABLE for COOKING MOST MEATS

Beef: Rare, 15 minutes per pound; well done, about 20 minutes.
Fowls: 20 minutes per pound on the average.
Lamb: 30 minutes per pound.
Pork: 30 minutes per pound.
Veal: 30 minutes per pound.

DEEP FAT KETTLE COOKING TEMPERATURES

Food	*Time to Cook*	*Temperature*
Doughnuts, crullers, fritters & small mixes	3 to 5 minutes	370° Fahrenheit
Fishballs, oysters, croquettes & uncooked things generally	1 to 2 minutes	395° to 390° Fahrenheit
Chops & cutlets, breaded	5 to 8 minutes	400° to 390° Fahrenheit

SEASONING, a PLEA to MAKE IT LIGHT at the OUTSET of a DISH

This is a thought so obvious that many an amateur chef has ignored it to his shame, and straightway become hoist by the petard of his own salt shaker. For Einstein in all his glory, nor the combined genius Edison and Steinmetz, could never lift over-salting out of a dish once ruined. . . . And this applies ***especially to liquids which are to be*** *boiled down, reduced, for quite a while in their cooking.* A dish of black bean soup may be mildly salt at the outset, but when thick may taste like the Dead Sea.

Countless experienced and otherwise sound cooks still make this mistake.

The same caution applies to pungent peppers, sauces and herbs in cooked dishes. It is so easy to add the needful dash just before serving, so impossible to subtract an overdose when once in, or to dilute with additional raw materials and still have the dish be recognized by its own author, when done.

HERBS in HOT and COLD DISHES

We have found that herbs, dried herbs especially, may be used at least three times as freely in a chilled, uncooked dish like salad, as can be used in cooked affairs. Heat extracts the volatile oils and flavours from the herb leaves. Overseasoning results from too generous herb donation to soups, roasts, and the dressings of fowls; whereas in a French dressing the taste is so slightly drawn out by the liquids that quite a lot makes only a reasonable flavour difference in final estimate by taste.

A WARNING on the USE of WINES in COOKERY

Nothing adds such delicate zest to many soups, fish, shellfish, crustacean and amphibian items, as a little wine. But except for white or red *unfortified* wines actually used in cooking, poaching or basting food, *NEVER ADD to the COOKING DISH until JUST BEFORE DISHING up at TABLE.*

This means sherry, port, Madeira and Marsala—*ALL FORTIFIED WINES, whether DRY or SWEET!*

Why? . . . Well, a fortified wine means one which has been raised in alcoholic content through later addition of suitable amounts of brandy—which last of course runs far higher than wine in proof—around 35 per cent alcohol, against from 10 to 15 per cent. . . . Under any heat this alcohol vanishes in steam, takes most of the taste and lovely aroma with it. What remains in the cooked dish is most depressing. It tastes like dregs from an old cask boiled down with a raccoon pelt, and has never been known to endear any chef to a gourmet's heart.

A FINAL DUET of ADVICE, concerning the VIRTUES of USING BUTTER & SUGAR in COOKERY

Here too is an ancient secret, ignored by too many chefs of all degree—probably by its very obviousness. Butter added to all sorts of fish, flesh, vegetables and sauce picks up the basic nature of the whole dish and endows it with an additional richness which we've found improbable in any other fatty agent. It is not economical in pennies, but if an amateur chef's reputation isn't worth thirty cents worth of dairy butter every other Thursday we had better go back to some other and more balanced form of indoor amusement.

When we said sugar in cookery we did not limit ourselves merely to obviously sweet dishes, but to many, many others. The ancient Chinese have always recognized this virtue and although we cannot over-eat their candied Peking duck we render credit where credit is due on other things. As a strict matter of fact there was no civilized cookery anywhere in the world until the middle of the 18th Century—except in China. . . . A little sugar on steak to be broiled, on pork; in the boiling water for the tenderizing of green peas, corn on the cob, carrots, lima beans; in green salads—but here have a care that the dressing is not made to taste sweet, a common American fault by those who should be advised. Sugar is something for each amateur to experiment with. It has the fine faculty of amplifying and framing the main delicate flavour of certain foods, much as odd products of a non-scented nature are used to fetch out the true worth of a fine perfume essence.

HEAVEN'S GIFT to the AMATEUR CHEF—the *WARING BLENDER*

The world is so full of indirect commercialism in these civilized days that many publishers of standing actually hesitate to mention a thing of merit by name, for fear of being thought a sponsor with a material interest in the item involved; or for fear of giving offense to some other lively manufacturer producing something of similar nature.

We debated the question all through composition of this volume, and of *The Exotic Drinking Book*, and have decided to speak our own mind without fear. Certainly no one hesitates extolling genius in Alexander Graham Bell, Simon Lake or Dr. Alexis Carrell, for their telephones and submarines and antiseptics, and we fail to see why Mr. Fred Waring should be ignored in these pages when his contribution to food and drink preparation is just as vital in its own especial way as the previous three gentlemen have been to a very testy and bewildered world.

Mr. Waring has always appeared to us as a gentleman, a scholar, probably the best golfer in modern musical circles, and a maestro of a cleverly melodic musical school all his own which many other internationally known bandsmen and radio staffs have flattered through out-and-out imitation, without too much credit to the originator. Besides these minor talents Mr. Waring proved himself a still more able citizen by pouncing on an invention designed primarily to agitate fluids and ice—with a nicely controlled violence and centripetal activity which does things in sixty seconds to a Daiquiri which it took Messrs. Harry Stout and Jennings Cox (originators of this peerless drink) five or six minutes of progressive effort and fatigue to produce.

But what it was able to do to food was something we wager even its parent never dreamed of at the start. For reducing green groceries such as spinach, carrots, celery and the like, to health-giving pulps or vitamin drinks for aged and young, it has no peer. For purees or any fine blending it is a pearl beyond price.

Wherever our antique English or French cookery books coyly say, "Rub through sieve," or "Pound fine in a mortar," we turn a superior shoulder and toss the whole assembly in the Waring Blender, and presto, the job is done—if not to complete fineness at least to a point where final putting through sieves and other reducers is simply a matter of gentle gravity aided by a helpful spoon, and not a major muscular task. To get what we mean we can only suggest rubbing a gallon of our Barranquilla Black Bean Soup through a sieve, then next time turning the whole puree problem over to the rapidly turning blades of Mr. Waring's brain-child, and draw personal conclusions as to whether labour has been saved or not.

Of course, this Blender is too well known to all American hosts to need either explanation or introduction, but for benefit of new arrivals to these relatively free and lucky shores we submit the following non-technical information.

There is a metal covered, liquid-proof, non-tarnishing chromium base of decent modern line and sound electrical engineering, which houses a motor with vertical spindle, of high rpm, and requiring rare and modest oilings in well indicated spots.

The top half of the Blender is a strong heavy glass mixing unit of 32 ounce working capacity, resembling a four-leaf clover in cross section, and which is in fact like a big sloping sided tumbler or bar glass. This whole unit lifts off base for pouring.

Through the Blender bottom runs a special high speed bearing and a short vertical spindle on which triple tempered steel blades are mounted. The lowest pair drive substances upward; the center pair are actually knives and do much of the cutting up; the top pair draw the substances down into the whirling blades again—like a miniature airplane propeller. When glass mixing unit is set on base the motor shaft automatically engages the base of Blender spindle.

This Blender is no toy. It is made for heavy and constant usage. Clubs and hotels toss in jiggers of spirits, juices, big lumps of ice, and away she goes. No damage to anything. It makes fruit pulp and puree and mixes all sorts of things from shrimp cocktail dressing to tropical Daiquiri Cocktails until—if so desired—the latter may be dished out with a spoon like snow from a Sun Valley ski-run. There is, literally, nothing else remotely like it.

Since Mr. Waring is a gentleman of shy and retiring demeanor, we will not attempt to agitate his nervous sensitivities by frequent allusion to this speedy labour saver by its usual family surname, but simply by the two-word title *The Blender*. And those who read, mark, learn and inwardly digest its uses will call us thrice blessed for time and labour saved, entirely aside from any mechanical thoroughness in the job it does.

BASIC STOVE-SIDE MEASUREMENTS to REMEMBER

1 Pinch or a few Grains	:	Slightly less than 1/8 Teaspoon
2 Teaspoons	:	1 Dessertspoon; 1/3 Oz. Avoirdupois
3 Teaspoons	:	1 Tablespoon; 1/2 Oz. Avoirdupois
2 Tablespoons	:	1 Oz. Avoirdupois
8 Tablespoons	:	1 Gill; 1/2 Cup; 4 Oz. Avoirdupois
16 Tablespoons	:	1 Cup; 1/2 Pint; 8 Oz. Avoirdupois
4 Cups	:	1 Quart; 32 Oz. Avoirdupois

DON'T FORGET the OLD, OLD RULE

1 Level Tablespoon: ½ Oz. of Butter, Milk, Salt, Sugar or Water. Plenty accurate enough for average usage.

A COMPLETE TABLE of WEIGHTS & MEASURES GIVING WEIGHTS in OUNCES and CORRESPONDING MEASUREMENTS MAY BE FOUND in the *APPENDIX* on PAGE 209, together with OTHER PERTINENT LORE.

Due to many old English receipts, and in fact many old-time American cookery notes, diaries and the like, listing proportions in ounces this table has been included for readers who wish to explore such green pastures.

SYMBOLS of MEASUREMENT USED in this VOLUME

1 tsp	:	1 Teaspoon
1 tbsp	:	1 Tablespoon
1 pt	:	1 Pint
1 qt	:	1 Quart
1 gal	:	1 Gallon

ALL MEASUREMENTS in this VOLUME *ARE LEVEL*

CHAPTER II

HORS d'OEUVRE & CERTAIN FIRST COURSE IMPORTANCES

Eighteen, or so, *Exotic Whets both for Pre-Solid & Pre-Liquid Use* which Can Cause One to be Honoured Among Men; A brief *Dissertation on the Regal Caviar;* West Indian Sauces for *Cocktails of Seafoods;* together with a *Brace of Stiffeners* for the *Failing Spine.*

SCHOLARS eagerly inform us that the French word "hors d'oeuvre," literally translated means "outside the work;" but like most scholars and literal Gallic translations this weighty disclosure leaves much to the imagination. As near as we can learn it probably was idiom for certain dishes which, by character or type of service, were more or less apart from the main routine of a meal.

An appetizer, or whet, is anything that inspires a desire or relish for food. The amateur should hold this thought constantly in mind in order not to be gradually drawn in to the mounting wave of questionable taste now sweeping America—that of stuffing guests with ten times more hors d'oeuvre, canapes and the like than he should have, and sending him brimming with cocktails and with all appetite quit, to face the really important thing of the evening: dinner.

An hors d'oeuvre which in quantity or type destroys appetite or dulls the delicate taste buds is a mischievous thing, the enemy of all fine gastronomy, and should be smitten hip and thigh. Do not let us be deceived in this thing. No matter a host's wealth, rank, manners or morals; in spite of all excellence in materials served, the truth is not in him if either through solid or liquid whets he destroys appetite.

The grand pre-revolutionary Russian, our modern Dane, Swede or Norwegian, will muster an array of hors d'oeuvre, or smörgåsbord, in variation and tonnage to preclude all hint of their being appetizers as we think of the word. Hors d'oeuvre to these gentlemen meant many tasty dishes to compose a major part, and often all, of any given meal. As such it has its own virtue and tradition, being a definite section of the meal, not just an appetizing first course.

After considerable dining abroad we have definitely come to the conclusion that the American host tends to burden his hors d'oeuvre tray too heavily, and also is leaning more and more toward that risky piece—the canape. Either go whole hog or none; either trot out the whole gamut of smörgåsbord table and make dinner a slight minor addition to the feast, or serve barely enough fresh, smart, piquant and daintily garnished appetizers to titillate the appetite into a small frenzy for courses to come.

In conception and purpose the canape is a pretty little item but, being married as it is to odd bits of bread or toast foundation the very construction of the thing makes its virtue almost impossible except when guests are quite few in number. During recent years our house seems to have instituted a Christmas afternoon business where people drop in for carols, wassail bowl—hot and cold—and other seasonable thoughts. It has gradually amplified in scope; and starting harmlessly enough we found ourselves last year confounded by a list of one hundred invited, and nearer two hundred arrived. So this last Christmastide we prepared. Allowing five average varied canapes per guest, that made an even thousand to compose. Professional sources tend, we had found, toward fancy colours and all the crisp flavour of cotton petit point, with three Filipinos working, by the time the last canape was ready the toast under Number I was already soggy and tough as saddle leather. It just cannot be done in quantity unless a whole platoon is flung into the work. With so many frantic varieties extant, we dodge them.

One thing worthy of remembrance is that hors d'oeuvre of all kinds should, in all ways possible, be pleasing to the eye as well as the palate. A few brightly garnished, fresh, crisp appetizers are worth a burden of hours-old, drab, careless affairs—regardless of merit in raw materials. And in this connection may we add a single re-emphasis on the old truth: *Serve hot dishes hot, and cold dishes cold.* Lukewarm items lose all charm and character.

The most civilized thought in liquid accompaniment to such dishes leans always toward the dry type of cocktail, or fortified wine. Our true gourmet will accept the briefest course of hors d'oeuvre, accompanied by not more than two dry cocktails, or vermouth, vermouth and bitters, or dry sherry, and *no tobacco at all if his will is valent.* He will view costly additional outlay on tray after tray of needless canapes with a wistful air, willing by whatever gods he may afford that the tariff of all this costly display of extra provender might reasonably be applied against a bottle or two of truly fine vintage instead of the good—but seldom exceptional—wine American hosts usually choose.

This then is our earnest prayer:

> In serving hor d'oeuvres, make them few; make them good. Make them hot or make them cold. And finally, make them attractive to the eye.

It is all so very simple, yet like most simple and virtuous matters we find it constantly being neglected for more mediocre, costly and indiscreet practice.

> WORDS to the WISE, No. I: On the Validity of spelling 'Recipe' 'Receipt.'
>
> There are already enough pink ribbons tied around cookery terms without giving the French every credit for fair cookery routine. It may be Palesteen or PalesTINE; quinneen or quinNINE, but dwelling as we do in an English-speaking country it is only just to adopt the Anglicized formation of the word. We have a volume dated just after 1650 calling it 'receipt.' What was good enough for Charles I, is good enough for us!

FIRST COMES IMPERIAL CAVIAR, the Grandest of Them All, Being the Salted Eggs of Russian Sturgeons

Various nations and places have their own special whets but there is only one caviar. Gourmets, without urging either of themselves or the sturgeon, all agree upon this. Caviar, regardless of rarity or price has stood the test of time against all and sundry comers.

There are two general types: Red and black—the former usually being salted eggs of salmons or other fishes, and lacking in aristocratic merit. In turn the black kind, which is made from eggs of the Russian sturgeon, is prepared in two ways: Fresh, and canned or extra salt.

Fresh caviar has relatively large, resilient, pleasant-appearing eggs; while the so-called salted—canned—type is usually made up of smaller eggs packed together in a more or less wilted and unhappy mass. Actually all caviar is salted but the fresh is not salted so strongly; eggs are firmer and each more or less individual and separated from its neighbour. Its high tariff, especially during recent times, is due to two reasons: the world at large is becoming conscious of its merits; and fresh caviar must be kept refrigerated *at all times* to prevent deterioration. This means by ship, train or plane; and it is a fair journey from the Volga to America.

CONVEYING the THOUGHT that DRESSING up CAVIAR IS FAR WORSE than GILDING LILIES

Except with traditional sour cream—*smetana*—as given elsewhere in the Chapter, *caviar should never be mixed with any sort of dressing agent.* By this we mean fresh caviar when served *as caviar* for hors d'oeuvre—not casual salt caviar used as flavour or trimming for some other food item.

Mayonnaise, for instance, on fresh Mallosol or Beluga caviar is in exactly the same taste as painting a picnic scene on Mr. Heifetz' pet Stradivarius. Caviar is its own excuse, has its own flavour, its rare delicacy. Clouding the pungency of that flavour with other dressings immediately alters the picture. A fine thing is fine, for and of itself. To the gourmet rarity or high price never enter the picture. Ostentation with caviar, trimming it up with fancy blendings, brings a slight shudder.

THERE ARE FIVE RULES about CAVIAR, which ARE JUST as EASY for Us as for the ROYAL CHEF to the LATE TSAR

1. All caviar must be very, very cold; not merely cooled. *Chill directly on ice for at least three hours.* Chill it in its dish of service; packing the

latter in fine ice when fetching to table or buffet. Never turn well-chilled caviar into serving dish at room temperature.

2. Serve it with quartered lime or lemon on one side, a teaspoon or so of *finely* chopped onion on the other. Persian limes, now visible on many good fruit counters, are much the best. They are very delicate, large, void of seeds. If not available locally, just write any friend in southeast Florida, as they bear the year round.
3. Please don't do elaborate things with accompanying bread. Just have thin, crisp, dark brown toast with crusts trimmed off before putting to fire. A little butter is optional, and sweet butter is always best. Butter may be sweetened by working regular butter between thumb and fingers under cold faucet to reduce salt. Press out between palms or butter paddles to extract surplus waters.
4. To our palate Mallosol or Beluga caviar averages best, seems to ship best. Prefer large black eggs, moist-appearing, each grain undamaged and undefiled, round and solid looking. . . . However the smaller grained canned caviar is far better than no caviar, and the red type is also good—actually being preferred by several friends. . . . We also have friends who prefer the works of Mr. E. Phillips Oppenheim to *Seven Pillars of Wisdom.*
5. Never allow metal to touch fresh caviar for longer than a moment. Handle or mix with wood, glass or ivory tools, serve from china or crystal—*never silver.*

THE USE of GRATED or CHOPPED EGG with CAVIAR Is of DOUBTFUL PROFIT, but CONSIDER a TRIFLE of GRATED *FRESH* COCONUT

No addition to caviar of this kind can be anything more than a colourful trimming, for certainly egg yolk and white has nothing caviar hasn't. It cannot add or bring out one iota to the sturgeon eggs. . . . We found finely grated fresh coconut meat served by the smartest hostesses in the tropical ports of the East. We use it here when we afford caviar, and find the delicate oily taste seems to point up the caviar a trifle. Fresh coconuts are found everywhere in America these days. It's merely a suggestion.

CAVIAR SERVICE IS a HAPPY CHANCE for ARTISTIC GESTURE

Here is the real chance for the artist with hot stylus and block of clear ice! What could be more ravishing than a fine crystal bowl nesting on a fish of ice; a turtle. Or fill the large pan beneath the freezing space in a refrigerator; add colouring matter, blossoms, glass coloured fish, and what not; then freeze. We've seen sculptured eagles, baskets, ships, animals, fish, and flowers, with caviar bowls enthroned therein in chilly magnificence.

CAVIAR, *MID-OCEAN COUNTRY CLUB,* BERMUDA; an Exotic from the Gulf Stream

During an article-seeking voyage to this pleasant island we became involved in one especially memorable dinner, by friends, after eighteen holes of golf in a half gale of wind, and some excellent dry Amontillado sherry. . . . Simply fry out large rounds of bread in very hot olive oil—deep fat kettle is best. Drain on paper and spread on a thick layer of chilled caviar; season with lime and a dash of Mr. McIlhenny's immortal Tabasco Sauce or Hell-Fire Bitters, noted on Page 28, and affix thereon a *very thin* slice of mild Bermuda onion trimmed to exact size of toast. Grate fresh coconut on top, and serve. . . . Those we first found had crossed anchovies as a penthouse touch, but this last was sheer swank, adding nothing to the caviar itself.

CAVIAR with *BLINI,* or RUSSIAN PANCAKES, *ERMITAGE RUSSE,* PARIS

Blini differ from the usual American product of Aunt Jemima for two principal reasons—they are made to rise with yeast overnight, and usually contain a trifle of buckwheat flour; their small size—2½" to 3"—and composition marry perfectly with caviar and sour cream. *Blini* by seven, mix before eleven! We first discovered really fine blini at Ermitage Russe, in Paris one spring. They probably weren't much better than any good *blini* in any good Russian spot; but it was spring and the horse chestnuts had lighted their white candelabra, and we were very much in love. And when Rumanian—they would import a Rumanian into a Russian place!—Dino Ionesco played minor things on his czimbalom our hearts tore apart, and there we were drinking cold Krug *'19*, and in love and eating the best *blini* and caviar in the whole beautiful world!

TO MAKE the *BLINI*, that WAY

Soften a cake of yeast with 2½ cups of warm milk, stir in 2 cups sifted white flour and work smooth. Stand in even warm temperature for 8 hours, then work in 2½ cups buckwheat flour. Break two eggs, separate whites. Beat yolks and first work in 4 tbsp butter, then add to flour; donate ¼ tsp salt, ½ tsp sugar, and let stand 3 hours longer. Finally work in beaten egg whites, pause another 15 minutes, then pour batter off top without stirring again. . . . *Blini* must be delicate and thin, so batter should be consistency of cream.

BLINI with CAVIAR & *SMETANA, ERMITAGE RUSSE*

Brush *blini* with a little hot butter. Serve one to each guest, heap with good black caviar, and cover the succulent little black mound with a double tablespoon of *smetana*, or sour cream, first chilled and whipped for a moment to keep from straying away.

BLINI ROLLS, *au CAVIARE, à la KASBEK*, from PARIS in 1926

Paris again, but this time at Kasbek over in the Montmartre direction and in a dim cave with red checkered tablecloths lighted through the wooden tops, from underneath. Music again with the Caucasian girls singing and dancing, and a seven-stringed Russian guitar played by a man who used to play for Nicholas in the grand gone days in St. Petersburg. . . . Brush *blini* with butter, then sour cream, then spread with caviar. Roll and skewer with toothpicks every inch and cut across with sharp knife, showing caviar in spiral layer. Lemon and a bit of onion pulp were the side additions, and a fine still white Burgundy—Bâtard Montrachet *'11*, and the same girl who sang *Brown Eyes* for them in English to the Russian guitar. Heigh ho!

THOUGHTS on the SOURING of CREAM not yet HAVING ATTAINED that SOMETIMES DESIRABLE STATE

The souring process may be aided and abetted. Simply heat cream or rich milk very slowly until it barely starts to simmer. Then just before cool stir in a little vinegar or cream of tartar. It thickens promptly. We prefer lime or other citric juice due to the more delicate flavour. A tiny bit of salt is optional.

POACHED EGGS STUFFED with CAVIAR, *à la MOSCOW*

Here is a swank dish which can be an hors d'oeuvre, *served hot* or a fine entree. This receipt was brought to us by a friend who was for three years stationed in Russia, through causes not connected with cookery, and has proven a scholarly dish. . . . Poach eggs, chill well. Prick yolks and drain out soft part. Stuff yolk cavity with caviar, then roll carefully in flour, then lightly beaten egg, then fine dry bread crumbs. Fry to delicate golden brown at 380° in lots of deep fat in kettle or skillet. Garnish with deep-fat-fried fresh parsley—which *only takes a few seconds* to cook; and garnish with quartered lime or lemon. . . . Delicious! And must be served sizzling.

CANNIBAL CANAPE, a REFUGE for the LISTLESS and LUSTLESS

Here is something suitable for certain bachelor, or other, crises when the soul and frame lie supine, like a fine fruit withered on vine; sparkless, without virtue or activity. Served with, let us say, The *Maharajah's Burra Peg,* Peking *Tiger's Milk,* or Wilson's *South Camp Road Cocktail* from Jamaica—all evident in *The Exotic Drinking Book*—a gentleman even in this sorry plight might again be able to hold up his head among the rugged.

So: dice a little cold *lean* beef very fine indeed, touch with lime or lemon juice; with salt and plenty of tabasco or cayenne, to taste. Cut rye bread rounds, thin, and toast dry. Brush lightly with garlic or cut onion. Spread toast with sweet butter, add meat. Consume.

AULD KILKENNY *PICKLED EGGS,* from an ANCIENT IRISH RECEIPT

This piquant variation of trite hardboiled eggs should be revived oftener. It makes a good hors d'oeuvre, is delightful with cold fowl or joint, summer cold cuts and for garnishing a fine salad. Alternated with pickled walnuts, beside meat, they are especially delicious.

To 1 doz freshly created eggs we need 3 cups vinegar, 2 tsp ground ginger, 1 tsp of allspice broken with spoon; 2/3 tsp broken peppercorns, ½ tsp or so of salt. . . . Hardboil eggs for 20 minutes; peel shells. Mix vinegar and spices and boil slowly for 15 minutes. Fill mason jars with *entirely cold* eggs, pour pickle liquor over them. Screw on tops and stand for 4 weeks or so. But remember, gentlemen, the eggs *must* be fresh, really fresh. Pickling a storage egg is chemically impossible as, for example, a 1920 vintage flapper.

BARBADOS PICKLED FISH, from the British Windward Islands

This tasty was gathered into the fold during a cruise through the West Indies in 1929, and was produced by the smart wife of a resident British official living in Bridgetown. It made a fine appetizer, and would garnish any exotic green salad, or even a pick-me-up similar to Tahiti's own fish salad addition, *I'a Ota,* via Charles Nordhoff from Papeete, West Indian *Conch Salad* or *Souse,* all noted in the Index.

To a couple of pounds boned boiled fish we pour over the following marinade: Enough vinegar or lime juice to cover fish, and liquid put in saucepan. Toss in 6 or 8 whole cloves or 3 pinches ground; 2 pinches ground ginger, ½ tsp mace, ½ tsp hot dry mustard, 3 bayleaves crushed between the palms; 2 finely chopped onions, salt and hand-ground black pepper to taste. Then a dash or two of Angostura bitters. . . . Bring this marinade to a slow boil, simmer 20 minutes, turn over cooked fish. Stand in refrigerator 3 hours. . . . A little Key West *Old Lime Sour,* Page 169, is our favourite addition for a true West Indian touch.

SMOKED SAILFISH, Smoked Marlin Swordfish & Kingfish: Smoked Eels, Geese & Turkeys

All these smoked delicacies, sliced thin, and served as is, add an exotic touch to the hors d'oeuvre tray. The first three may be had through correspondence with any friend in southern Florida, the last is a new revival of a fine old Colonial whet; the other two hail from Germany, and are imported by some of the finer shops in cities. The first three are quite modest in tariff.

SPANISH *GAZPACHO,* a POTENT GARLIC SPREAD which MAY BE DARED in COMPANY with TRIED & TRUE FRIENDS, ALL of WHOM ARE GUARANTEED to STAY PUT for the EVENING, a SPECIALTY of SPAIN & CUBA

One afternoon we motored around the bay at Gibraltar to Algeciras for a little variation of native food after the fairly awful choice available in Gib itself. Here before the recent revolution everything was at peace; the little old town went along about its business as it had for centuries. We dined on a terrace with the sun at our back, and lighting the Rock, while files of stately white herons flew eastward toward some unknown destination. *Gazpacho* came first, with thimbles of *Anis del Mono,* or "Anise of the Monkey Head." We were among friends who did likewise. We later found it in Havana, too. In Mexico.

Actually this garlic spread is much like other Latin things under different names. The only hard-to-get item is a little cumin seed, and a few days notice with our druggist will do this. . . . Toss the following into a mortar, for two persons: 2 cloves garlic, 2 pinches salt, hand-ground black pepper, 2 pinches cumin. Pound until garlic is crushed into paste, then olive oil is worked in until we have a smooth cream. . . . Spread this on slices of peasant bread, cover then with a thin layer of imported canned tomato paste or pulp—*not* canned tomatoes of usual type—and on top of the whole a couple of tbsp of finely chopped pimentos. A little vinegar, lemon juice, or water is often sprinkled on to help in softening the bread. Serve in a dish nested in finely crushed ice as it should be served very, very cold indeed.

VIRGINIA HAM WHETS, OUR OWN GIFT to the GOURMET WORLD ABROAD

Even in a book of exotics we have to list outstanding Colonial masterpieces of gastronomy; and Virginia Ham, especially the peanut fed variety from the Smithfield region are honoured abroad as jewels of price. Our first introduction to Virginia Ham was attending school near Charlottesville; hams smoked on the neighbouring farms. In later years sailing north and south on *Marmion* we never missed going into Pender's store in Norfolk, and picking out a squad of big black mellow hams, with the peanut oil fairly blooming out of them!

Cut cooked ham into paper thin rosy curls and serve with no further garnishment. Another way is to chop ham fine, mix with grated egg and a little good mayonnaise, and stuff into tender celery.

VIRGINIA or WESTPHALIA HAM, Simla Style, from an Indian Adventure

Simla is a hill station where certain lucky folk, officers' wives, and young gentlemen with fierce and predatory glances, go during the hot rainy Monsoon season of India. Life is quite gay through varying reasons, and many smart hostesses try out new and varied touches of exotica at the dinner table. Once during a bridge and poker adventure small rounds of butter-fried toast surmounted with round-cut wafers of ham, and spread over with good fine-cut mango chutney, were introduced. It made an instant success, and as good chutney is buyable in any good small town grocery these days, we include it here. Virginia Ham is by far the better.

Oddly enough this delicious ham, avocado pears, turkeys, grapefruit, dried beef, yellow rat cheese and canvasback ducks, form a septet of strange bedfellows—but here are about all the credits your European high-toned chef will grant the States!

KIPPERS in BLANKETS for HORS d'OEUVRE, a Grand Breakfast Enlivener, or a Midnight Snack

This was snupped from a famous London Snack-Bar in Piccadilly during a recent summer spent in England. . . . Trim kippered herrings into neat strips about 1″ wide and as long as width of two bacon rashers. Wrap with thin sliced smoked bacon, or curls of Virginia

Ham, pin with toothpicks and grill until bacon curls. Serve on hot buttered thin toast, crusts trimmed off, and the upper side rubbed slightly indeed with garlic. Garnish with finely snipped parsley.

MUSHROOMS, *SMETANA,* or MUSHROOMS in SOUR CREAM, *HOTEL MAJESTIC,* SHANGHAI; another HOT HORS d'OEUVRE

Those of us who weep for the Shanghai that was will remember the Majestic, originally a palace created for a fabulously wealthy Chinese; later adapted to a small hotel. We remember having missed ship once in Shanghai, and after Martinis in the little cocktail lounge that was hand-painted like a trellis beneath a deep evening sky winking with electric stars, we went in to a superb meal. Out of deference to a White Russian member of our little group the host commanded this dish, which was noted down for later investigation.

Take 1½ lbs small mushrooms, cut them up and brown them carefully in 3 tbsp butter. Next mince 2 fairly large onions finely and cook gently until clear brown in another tbsp butter. Add salt and cayenne to taste. Warm 1½ small cans of beef bouillon in saucepan, turn in everything, and simmer slowly until mushrooms are very tender. . . . Take a little of the hot juices, work in 2 tbsp flour until smooth as cream, stir into the rest. Add 2 cups sour cream and simmer 5 or 6 minutes longer. Serve quite hot.

A *DAUSSADE,* or *PAIN DAUSSÉE,* BEING A LUSTY ONION WHET from MARSEILLES

Both onion and garlic are used far more generously abroad than here, and for better or worse we list this onion specialty which is so good alone, or served along with soup. . . . Take one of those round crusty French, Italian or Mexican loaves; cut it in the longest slices possible. Freshen some butter and spread. Slice a big mild onion and rub through coarse sieve—or put in The Blender—with a little sour cream, a tsp or so of tarragon vinegar, hand-ground pepper to taste, and plenty of salt. Work into a smooth heavy cream, spread on buttered slices, and cut these into crosswise fingers ¾″ wide.

The Marseilles *Anchoïade à la Provençale* is a similar process using a little onion pulp, a few boneless anchovies, 2 tsp tarragon or red wine vinegar, a crushed small garlic clove and cayenne to taste. Add 2 tbsp or so olive oil and work through sieve or make smooth in The Blender, or pound in a mortar. Spread the result on slices of peasant bread and grill under broiler until edges of bread start to brown. Must be served sizzling.

PORK SKIN SNACKS, *à la VEDADO CLUB, HABANA*

As far as we are concerned Cuba has some of the finest chefs in the western hemisphere. Like the cookery of Mexico, New Orleans, and other once-Spanish possessions, succeeding creole chefs have built local refinements and trimmings on the parent root—resulting in many exotics both unexpected and piquant. . . . This Pork Skin Snack is one of the most amazing. We ran onto it the other year when our friend Gardinar Mulloy was winning the tennis championship of Cuba. . . . Just have your pet butcher trim off an area of fresh pork skin and thin layer of fat attached to same,—no meat at all!—cut it into 1½" squares and brown in deep fat at 370° Fahrenheit. Serve like potato chips and you have a new taste thrill. A great favourite at the very swank Club Vedado. Used mainly as a pre-liquid whet. The Cubano name is *chicharronés.*

GARLIC POPCORN, *HABAÑERO*

We carry along with garlic up to a certain point, for no cookery worth a passing glance can possibly ignore that ancient and valuable lily. Ancient Chinese, centuries before Christ, prescribed it for high blood pressure, and our finest modern specialists have fallen into line three or four thousand years later! If used properly its aroma is not dangerous. There is nothing quite like it for pointing up certain basic flavours in a dish. . . . First pop the corn, or get it *freshly popped,* and undecorated with ancient heated butters from the gentleman on the corner. To 1 cup butter allow 1 finely chopped garlic clove. Simmer these two *very gently* for 5 minutes, put through fine sieve to eradicate the chopped lily, then pour the aromatic fluid over our bowl of fresh popcorn, tossing diligently the while to insure equitable distribution. . . . Fine for soup croutons, but be sure and administer to soup at moment of service, or they will be soggy and tough. Also a smart pre-liquid thirst producer.

SARDINES *à la RUSSE,* being an HORS d'OEUVRE from MAISONETTE RUSSE which Is in PARIS

Not too long ago it was the thrill of a lifetime to take a smart and veiled lady to places with an air of intrigue and vague mystery. We hope that some of our readers with romantic leanings have not forgotten Maisonette Russe, on Rue Mont Thabor. Here the lighting was dim enough to suit any minor connivance, the food was expensive but good, the music swooning and packed with the plaints of sobbing lovers of the tragic and departed day of old Imperialistic Russia. With our chablis, then, came the following:

Prepare fairly thick golden toast with crusts trimmed off. Mount sardines on top, brush with lime or lemon juice, sprinkle with finely grated yellow orange peel, and broil under fierce heat to do the job promptly. Another touch is a pinch of caraway seed added to each portion. The quicker the job the crisper the toast.

SARDINES, *à la SRINAGAR,* or *à l'INDIEN*

One trip out to India we stayed a while with a college mate, Byron Spofford, who was American Commercial Attache for India, Burmah and Ceylon under Hoover. Spofford's houseboat in the Vale of the Kashmir was something to fire the spark of envy in any man's heart, drifting from Srinagar down the lotus-starred reaches of Dal Lake in the cool clear July air, with the three-mile-high peaks soaring above everything; lazing in the Shalimar Gardens built for the pleasure of a Mughal Emperor three hundred years ago! Cocktails and pale hands in the violet dusk, while the Kashmiri boys sang in the cook-boat trailing aft. . . . An especial favourite appetizer was: Pound sardines and mango chutney in ratio of 2 to 1, rub through sieve to extract coarse portions. Grill squares of trimmed white bread, and spread. May be served hot or cold; hot is rather the best, we found.

SPOFFORD'S COPENHAGEN CANAPE of SALMON, from DENMARK

After leaving India Spofford went with American Minister Ruth Bryan Owen to Denmark where appetizers are a major event in everyone's life. The following is a great favourite there for small cocktail parties. . . . Cream equal amounts of butter and *freshly* grated horseradish. Cut graham bread thin, trim into size 1″ x 2″. Spread well, establish thereon a pair of narrow strips smoked salmon, then 4 short ones laid across. Spot a caper in each enclosure thus formed and bestrew edge with finely chopped parsley.

SEAFOOD WHETS of MISCELLANEOUS & DIVERSE CHARACTER

Voyagers to the volcanic island of Martinique will remember the street vendors of Fort de France, usually negresses with brilliantly coloured head kerchiefs, who sell those small white-hot cooked tidbits called *Bouchée*. Martinique is a torrid spot requiring torrid foods, and there it was we found this.

A *BOUCHÉE* of CRABS, SHRIMPS, LOBSTERS or any FINELY CHOPPED MEATS, *MARTINIQUE*

Take cooked, minced, meats and moisten with lime juice. Season with salt, dry mustard, 2 dashes Angostura, pinch of grated nutmeg, and as much tabasco or Hell-Fire Bitters, noted below, as the palate can take. Next fry some fine crumbs in very hot olive oil, and mix with seasoned meats, 1 part to 3. . . . Cook in either of 2 ways: Hollow out soft rolls, leaving crust and thin layer of white; brush with olive oil, brown in hot oven. Then pack with meat, cover with curry or cream sauce, dust with crumbs, dot with butter and brown again. . . . The street vendor often sells them this way: Form into small balls, dip in batter, then crumbs, and brown in deep fat at 370° Fahrenheit.

NOW the FORMULA for the JUSTLY FAMOUS "HELL-FIRE" BITTERS from the STRANGE BRITISH ISLAND of TRINIDAD, sometimes CALLED "CAYENNE WINE"

This valuable English receipt was, to our knowledge, first recorded by Dr. Kitchiner in 1817. It is to be found in some slight variation throughout the British Colonial world, and on the tables of canny gourmets who had tasted the condiment, and took the formula home with them. We found it in Port of Spain on a West Indian cruise down to South America in 1929. We find that by adding a certain amount of strained lime or lemon juice, and allowing the business to ferment, that the mixture gains charm in the seasoning of food.

Cut up as many round red bird pepper, or hot red pod peppers, as is necessary to fill a pint bottle loosely. Over this pour as much sherry, brandy and strained lime juice, as the vacant air spaces will take. Donate 1 scant tsp of salt, and ½ tsp quinine powder. Now stand for 2 weeks on kitchen shelf, uncorked. It is then ready for use. Some stout boiler-plated Britishers even put a dash or 2 in their gin and bitters! The original British mixture used the wine-brandy blend, but ignore the citric fermented juice. . . . Cayenne Wine: means the result of substituting 2 tsp—about ¼ oz—of Cayenne pepper for the fresh red peppers, in the above routine, omitting the quinine.

SIMILARLY HOT SEAFOOD ITEMS of CRABS, SHRIMPS & the LIKE—or BEEF TONGUE, or MEATS—CALLED *EMPAREADADOS,* GUAYMAS, MEXICO

We have two different friends recently fishing out of Guaymas for striped marlin and other large and ill-tempered fishy citizens. They fetched back photographs of swordfish enough to satisfy anyone, and one or two notes on food from a vast *rancho* where they visited, rode, hunted and explored, in Sonora. Among them is this characteristic appetizer, which can vary with larder and taste. Seasoning may be mild or torrid. . . . These also can vary with type of bread used, and the chef's imagination. Slice bread thin, trim to 1½" squares or rounds; dry but do not brown in oven. Dip these quickly in milk, spread on any finely ground, well-seasoned *cooked* filling such as crabmeat, shrimp, pork, beef, lobster, or *Tongue;* and the latter can be in a single slice. Cap with another cut of bread; press together; dip in lightly salted batter. Place carefully in wire basket and fry in deep fat at 370° to a tempting golden brown. Serve sizzling. They always draw forth exclamations of delight.

AND, FINALLY, We Present a Brief Company of Five Exotic Seafood Cocktail Sauces from Here & There: & in the Last, a Brace of Liquid Stiffeners Calculated to Rectify the Frail & Failing Spine

SAUCE No. I, *à la MARMION;* Being Our Own Pet Origination

If all the seafood hauled in over *Marmion's* rail were laid end to end, it would reach quite a distance; and in all the varied preparation and consumption several original items have stood the test of friends and time. . . . To ½ cup chili sauce add 2 tbsp tarragon vinegar, ½ tsp paprika, 1 cup mayonnaise, ½ tsp hot mustard, ¼ tsp celery salt, tabasco to taste and a speck of crushed garlic with husks removed. Toss into The Blender, or beat with fork until well mixed. If garlic vinegar is on hand, don't add fresh garlic pulp. Chill well.

SAUCE No. II, Sea Island Georgia Style

Sailing south in the Fall of 1935 in *Marmion* we flirted with the edge of a November hurricane, crossed the bar at Fernandina with waves breaking in 23 feet, and coasted up back of a friend's dock on Cumberland Island, in the Andy Carnegie estate, and found notable bourbon, a half acre mint bed, and many fine fresh shrimp in the tide creeks just waiting for our 5 foot cast net. Served chilled, this local sauce went instantly into the log. . . . Sour cream, 4 tbsp; ½ cup mayonnaise, 2 tbsp chili sauce, lime or lemon juice, 3 or 4 tsp; rub in a little sweet marjoram between palms. Put in The Blender or use egg beater. The sour cream adds the "touch;" marjoram points up the delicate whole. . . . Excellent for cold boiled fish.

SAUCE No. III, from PORT of SPAIN TRINIDAD, *au Angosture*

The British Island of Trinidad is known for its perpetually renewing lake of asphalt called La Brea, and as being fountainhead of immortal Angostura Bitters, invented to ward off fever in 1824 by Herr Doktor Johann Gottlieb Benjamin Siegert—one time army surgeon under Bluecher. The secret formula is alleged to have passed into the hands of only seven human beings. Correct or not—we list on Page 152 of *The Exotic Drinking Book*, a formula which has been known in England for many years which does well enough—it is only natural that this Trinidad Cocktail Sauce should include these famous bitters. It was brought to us by a pilot who flies the big Brazilian Clipper for Pan-American Airways and who always just manages to spare our chimneys when setting the big 40-passenger ship down into a northeast breeze here after her run from the Caribbean.

To the juice of two large limes add paprika to colour, 2 dashes Hell-Fire Bitters or tabasco, 2 tsp *freshly* grated horseradish, ½ tsp worcestershire, ½ cup ketchup or chili sauce; then add salt and Angostura until highly noticeable. . . . Especially good with oysters. Mix and chill well.

SAUCE No. IV, being the TASTIEST POSSIBLE EXOTIC from FARAWAY SEOUL, KOREA, where WE VISITED in 1932 & 1931; and which MASTERPIECE WAS DOUBTLESS THOUGHT up by a CUNNING JAPANESE CHEF

This delicate sauce is a marvel for cold lobster, shrimp, boiled salmon, crabmeat and the like. Take some really good mayonnaise and with a *wooden* fork crush up enough pickled walnut to suit personal taste. Metal forks tarnish in the astringent walnut juices. Rub through a sieve of coarse mesh; add paprika for colour if desired. Incidentally the Japanese are wizards at preparing any sort of fish or seafood, we've found. Chill well.

SAUCE No. V, from the DAY BOOK of a ROVING BRITISH ARTIST FRIEND who WANDERS about the WORLD on SMALL SHIPS in SAIL

This gentleman we met just before his last voyage on an old Maine gaff-headed schooner from here to Tahiti, the Fijis, Dutch East Indies and Philippines. This sauce he noted down in Apia, British Samoa. It sounds whimsical but is a new taste thrill, so fear not the spiritual addition at the end!

To 1 cup mayonnaise add ½ tsp worcestershire, 1 tbsp lime or lemon juice, ¼ cup chili sauce, dash tabasco, sour cream 2 tbsp, salt to taste and lastly *1 tsp gin per serving portion!* A dash of Angostura is optional.

TWO STIFFENERS for the BREAKFAST, or OTHER, ZERO HOUR

To extract the juices from clams, conchs, and other allied shellfish proceed as follows: *Hard Clams* or *Quohaugs*—pronounced *Ko-Hogs* down east, please!—or soft clams, known also as "steamers." . . . Cover clams with water—that will run about 6 cups per peck. Cover tightly and steam slowly. When clams are open the job is done. Needless to say we must use scrubbing brush and clear water first—removing all sand and other flotsam. This makes strong juice; salt and dilute to taste, if need be.

For *Conchs*—simply cut up skinned conch white meat; cover with water, boil 20 minutes or so; drain off juice; salt.

TO CLARIFY CLAM or CONCH BROTH

First strain broth through cloth, then stir in either: a little lightly beaten egg white, a handful of chopped *lean* raw beef, or crushed *washed* egg shells. Put on stove, whisk well. When boiling 15 minutes, skim again; let cool, then strain again—being careful not to agitate sediment in bottom of saucepan. . . . Now for the *Clam Juice Stiffener, No. I:*

We take equal parts clam and tomato juice, and to each 1 qt mixture add: small bit crushed garlic, 2 tsp scraped onion pulp, ½ tsp celery salt, 2 tsp worcestershire, 1 tbsp lime or lemon juice, 2 tsp freshly grated horseradish; dash tabasco, dash Angostura, 1 tsp sugar. Whip well or turn into The Blender; rub through coarse sieve. Chill well on ice, or shake with ice in cocktail shaker.

CLAM JUICE STIFFENER, No. II, Culled, Oddly Enough, from a North Cape Cruise—and, of all Things, Norway

To 3 cups clam broth add 1½ to 2 tbsp lemon juice, 1 tsp fine confectioner's sugar, ¼ cup ketchup or chili sauce, 1 tsp worcestershire, 2 tsp finely and freshly grated horseradish and the same of onion pulp. Salt to taste, and at the last sprinkle on a pinch to each glass of pounded caraway seed. Turn into The Blender with a handful of ice, or whip well to blend before chilling on ice.

> THE *STOMACH* is the Mainspring of our *SYSTEM*—if it be not sufficiently *wound up* to *warm* the *HEART* & *support* the *CIRCULATION,* the whole business of *LIFE,* will, in proportion, be ineffectively *performed.* We can neither *think,* with precision,—*walk* with vigour,—*sit down* with comfort,—nor *sleep* with tranquility.
> *Ancient Proverb*

CHAPTER III

SOUPS *FROM* FAR & WIDE

Being Fifteen Exotic Soups, both Delicate & Virile, Ranging from an Enchanting Thing of Mallorcan Almonds, spiced, with Cream; through a Grecian Soup of Amiable Fowls with Eggs, Sour Cream & White Wine; to a Succulent Portuguese Affair of Shrimps & Things called *Sopa de Camarão, á Portuguesa.*

FOR CENTURIES soups have made the reputations of chefs; ever since chefs came into kitchens from camps. Kings have bestowed titles, treasure and broad acres because of soups. Men have come from half around the world to eat a certain soup in a certain place.

Unfortunately, until recent years, most decent soups meant hours slaving with the stock pot. In Europe and other lands where labor is cheap and through other household duties a fire is constantly burning in stove, home made soups from home made stocks were tasty and thrifty at the same time. But thanks to Brillat-Savarin and immaculate American industry we can purchase at any small store bouillons or consommes of beef, veal or chicken at tariff which, from a plain matter of budget, make the time and trouble of stock making both needless and unprofitable. Only in making certain soups of delicate fish, or in poaching fish, is anything like the old methods made necessary.

After virtually paddling our way around the world with a soup spoon we have discovered one worthwhile fact about foreign practice that America might note to her profit: granting good raw materials in each case, American failure in comparison with exotic chefs lies in a very simple factor—our seasoning with spices, herbs and other products strikes too much of a level. We season very delicate soups too much with tastes other than the one main ingredient; in hot or spicy or highly seasoned soups we strike too low a note, being afraid to risk the original. Also it is possible that we forget that sugar is a seasoning as well as sweetening; and once again we mildly suggest that our wide fear and ignorance of garlic and onion—a ridiculous state of affairs caused by careless chefs who fail to discard solid parts of the lily after flavour is extracted—finds us at sorry disadvantage through granting this handicap to foreign technique.

And here again, in Soups, the unpardonable sin after tastelessness is that of mediocre heat. A hot soup must be steaming; a cold soup—of which we list two, and which America neglects to her sorrow—must be chilled as thoroughly and carefully as we would a fine champagne. A lukewarm fluid in plate is the brand of a mischievous cook and careless host; a dual condition which is both signal insult to guest intelligence, and to the good foodstuffs being spoiled.

SOPA de ALMENDRAS, á MALLORQUIÑA, being a Fine Thing of Grated Almonds, Herbs & Spices in Cream, from Valldemosa in the Island of Mallorca

The use of almonds in the cookery of southern Europe is something worth remembering here where we consume them mainly in salted state, for their flavour under heat becomes notable. This soup was discovered on our second visit to the Spanish island of Mallorca, and while on pilgrimage to secure some Seville orange seeds from the tree in the monastery garden where George Sand and Chopin passed a season long ago, in Valldemosa.

Take 2 cups of blanched almonds and put 1½ cups of them through fine blade of food chopper; turn into mortar, add 2 tbsp icewater to keep oil from forming. Work to smooth paste, reserving ½ cup in chopped form. . . . To 1 qt—4 cups—chicken or veal broth add 1½ tbsp *finely* chopped lean ham, 2 pinches powdered clove, ¼ tsp mace, ¼ tsp nutmeg, salt and cayenne to taste. Add bouquet of bayleaf, stalk celery with leaf left on, a sprig thyme and the same of basil—all tied with thread; or use 2 pinches each, powdered herbs. . . . Simmer slowly 20 minutes; strain through fine sieve. Add pounded almonds, simmer 20 minutes more. Lastly stir in ½ cup reserved chopped almonds, boil up once, stir in 1 tbsp sherry and serve very hot with big tbsp cold whipped cream on top.

WORDS to the WISE, No. II, on the VIRTUES of CAYENNE in ALL WHITE CREAM SOUPS

The finest chefs ignore black pepper in white cream soups. The flavour often does not agree with the tempo, and the resultant black specks of pepper, they feel, lowers the visual attractiveness of the dish. The same applies to delicate bisques of shrimp or tomato.

ANDALUSIAN COLD "SOUP-SALAD," or *SOPA-ENSALADA FRIA á ANDALUZ*

We consider this one of the best dishes in this whole volume. We find it pleasantly startling to discriminating guests and the best hot-weather soup we've found anywhere in the world. Oddly enough instead of coming to us via Ernest Hemingway or our bull-liquidating friend Sidney Franklin, or from some other Spanish habitué, it is from memory and pen of Tom Davin—formerly head of the American Museum of Natural History publications and now book editor for Sheridan House.

1 qt tomato juice, or the sieved pulp of fresh or canned tomato
Enough croutons, or sippets, of butter fried bread
2 or 3 hardboiled eggs
1 small fine minced cucumber
1½ tsp worcestershire
1 mild onion chopped very fine
1 tsp dry mustard
1 lime or lemon sliced thin
1 clove well crushed garlic
1 lemon or 2 limes, juice
2 tbsp olive oil
1 sweet green pepper chopped fine
1 dash or so tabasco
Salt & hand-ground black pepper

Work egg yolks and olive oil into smooth paste in wood salad bowl. Add crushed garlic, seasonings, lemon juice; then work tomato pulp in, add cucumber, green pepper. Stir briskly. Chill on ice 3 hrs. . . . Cut egg whites into strips, put on bottom soup bowls with chopped pepper, thin slice lemon and possibly 3 strips scarlet pimento. Pour in soup, *add 2 ice cubes to each bowl;* dust on hot croutons. Consume with dry white, chilled wine.

RUSSIAN CROUTONS, Eminently Suitable for Many Soups

Our Russki chef, instead of frying these in butter as the Frenchman does, slices bread thin, trims crusts, brushes with melted butter and sprinkles with *a little very sharp* grated cheese. He then browns in hot oven. The slight tang of cheese points up the soup taste.

GARLIC POPCORN, Noted under Hors d'Oeuvre on Page 25, & Served Hot & Crisp just before Fetching to Table, Is also Pertinent & to be Admired for Soup Trimming

AND NOW a POLISH COLD SOUP of TART APPLES, Claret, Lemon Rind & Currant Jelly

This exotic chilled companion dish was brought to us by a much-travelled friend who motored through Poland. . . . Slice 8 *tart* cooking apples, cover with cold water; add yellow rind 1 lemon cut into fine strips, ½ tsp cinnamon, 1 to 1½ tbsp sugar, 1 or 2 pinches powdered clove and a little salt to taste. . . . Simmer slowly until apples are tender and rub through sieve.

Put on ice and chill 3 hrs. Then add chilled *strained* juice of 2 average small limes or 1 lemon, and a bottle of *chilled* claret or still red Burgundy. Melt 2 tbsp currant jelly and stir in rapidly just before serving, again with 2 ice cubes in each plate. Dust with fine toasted breadcrumbs. Lovely when the mercury climbs!

BLACK BEAN SOUP, Barranquilla, which Is in Colombia

Colombia means emeralds, mahogany, coffee, gold and oil. And up the Magdalena River the white men who seek those things, and others, built the amazing modern city of Barranquilla huddling among the foothills beside an old Spanish city. We found this black bean soup in a small restaurant in Old Town. It ranks close to being among the first six soups in the world, to our notion.

To 1 cup black beans soaked in water overnight and drained, add a fresh qt slightly salted water, a hambone or chunk of smoked hock,

4 bayleaves, 4 whole cloves, ¼ tsp celery seed, 2 coarse celery stalks chopped fine—leaves and all; a big red Spanish onion and 1 clove garlic—these last fried gently first in 1 tbsp butter or olive oil until tender. . . . Start all these to simmering, then point up the torridity with ¼ tsp dry mustard, 1 tsp chili powder, and 2 dashes tabasco. Discard bone and celery leaves. Put in The Blender or rub through sieve. Then serve piping hot in plates first garnished with 2 slices cold hard egg; and 2 slices lime or lemon, cut thin. If more thickening is wanted, melt out 1 tbsp each of butter and flour, work smooth with some of the hot soup, then stir in. . . . This black bean soup varies in all Spanish settled countries. It can easily make a one-dish meal, served with coarse bread and a big green salad. A spoon whipped cream and 1 tsp sherry is optional, as a final garnish.

BAHAMA CONCH CHOWDER, *à la CAT CAY,* as First Prepared for Us by That Colorado Claro Gentleman, Jim Arañha, of Bimini on Board Good Ship *MARMION,* Circa 1933

We rate proper conch chowder as third best soup in the world, with Green Turtle 1st, and Parisian Onion Soup tied with Petite Marmite for 2d place! In fact if any forthright French chef ever got his hands on a sweet-meated Bahama or Florida Keys conch they would be shipped to Paris every trip the *Normandie* made, in dry ice! Yes, these succulent shellfish are the tenants who vacated those lovely pink shells our dear old Aunt Euphorbia Fittich used to hold open the parlor door, or to center up the mantel between glass domes of wax flowers. To serve eight hungry mariners cruising any of these warm tropical waters; for a one-dish meal:

12 conchs, skinned, pounded like veal with mallet, cut 1½″ sq
3 big mild red or white onions
Piece salt pork 1½″ x 2″
Salt & hand-ground pepper
2 tsp sugar
4 cups milk, fresh or evaporated
¼ cup sherry, Madeira or Marsala
2 small sweet peppers
4 bayleaves
1 tsp thyme
3 cups cooked diced potatoes
2 tbsp each, flour & butter
1 clove garlic, crushed

Cook onions and pork until former are tender; discard pork. Cover conch meat with water then add everything *except* milk, potato, thickening of flour-butter, and the wine. Simmer until sweetly tender, add milk and diced potato, stirring latter in gently; thicken with butter-flour roux if desired, adding wine at the last. Serve with pilot biscuit, dried in oven.

This chowder must be tried to be appreciated, and every yachtsman coming to Florida should read, mark, learn and inwardly digest conchs in all forms. Jim Arañha has for some years been our bait cutter, chef, entrepreneur, mentor and shoal-water guide. He not only put on a performance of Hamlet for us, being head of the Bimini library and culture society, but uses longer words than Bernard Shaw, and was assistant lightkeep at Great Isaac Reef as well as at Great Stirrup Cay. Look him up in our name.

A GRECIAN SOUP of MATURER FOWLS, Eggs & Lemons, to Say nothing of Wine & Other Substances: Snared in Athens in 1931 & Rejoicing in the Title: *SOUPA AUGHOLEMONO,* as near as Our Quaint Spelling Can Make It

We had occasion, once, to look up a favourite female cousin who was ratting around in Ur of the Chaldees, and then became placed in some shared authority in Greek Archeological Museums. This soup not only finds outlet for fowl of an age discouraging to patience, teeth and digestion, but strikes a totally new note in the realm of chicken soups. Further, at the Hotel Grande Bretagne it mighty nigh saved our miserable life after a freezing, snowy day prowling the Acropolis, in company with a young, tireless, handsome, agile and elusive lady from Greenwich, whose name and genius it is not pertinent to mention.

Cut up the oldest, fattest hen available, cover with cold water and fetch *very slowly* to the boil, meanwhile contributing 2 bayleaves, a pinch each of thyme and basil; and half a lemon rind, a clove of garlic, a modest dose of salt and cayenne. While gaining heat search kitchen and add anything like 2 small onions, a clutch of celery stalks,

2 carrots, and 1 tsp sugar. When meat falls from bones put through sieve, but while at boil adding a bit of water as needed from time to time to keep a good strong broth. Now put strained broth in saucepan, add ¼ cup dry rice, juice 1 lemon, simmer until rice is quite soft; also point up with salt and cayenne as needed. Stir in two beaten egg yolks, evenly. Serve at once, floating 1 tbsp sour cream on top, dust with croutons and pinch nutmeg at the last.

A SOUP of PLUMP & GENTLE FOWLS of DISCREET AGE, and Red *RIPE* Bananas, *à SANTIAGO*

Proceed as in the Grecian dish, and when broth is done and you have a qt proceed as follows: Reserve breast and trim into shreds the size of matchsticks, cutting with the grain. To the rich broth add 2 red bananas, stood in sun until well ripened; simmer 10 minutes slowly, and rub through sieve or put in The Blender. Serve hot with a pinch of nutmeg on top.

This number was collected during a visit to Santiago and subsequent to an afternoon's visit to the factory of Bacardi, being escorted thither by a late member of that illustrious family. It was, all in all, a memorable day. For several reasons.

A FINE RICH SOUP of CALVES' KIDNEYS, from the Threshold of the Algaur Alps in Bavaria, and Known as *NIERENSUPPE*

This unusual thought came from Oberammergau, home of the famous Passion Play and the Anton Lang Christus. It is a lusty of fine seasoning and full flavour. . . . Slice a pair of calves' kidneys into small bits; remove any useless sections. Chop 3 spring onions fine and brown gently in 3 tbsp butter. Contribute 2 bayleaves, and a pinch each of thyme, marjoram and rosemary—all rubbed between palms. Add chopped kidneys, ¼ tsp mace, and smother. When light brown add 2½ tbsp flour worked smooth with juice; toss until flour is lightly brown. . . . Turn into saucepan, add 4 cups beef broth or stock, salt and pepper to taste, simmer ½ hr until good and rich. Now beat yolks 2 recent eggs with ¼ cup sour cream. Draw pot off stove and when it stops simmering stir in this egg-cream mix thoroughly to bind; then at last 1 tbsp sherry or Madeira. . . . Garnish with chopped parsley and butterfried bread cubes of ¼″ size.

AND NOW the ONE & ONLY ONION SOUP from L'ESCARGOT, on RUE MONTORGUEIL, near *LES HALLES*—PARIS' 12th CENTURY MARKETS

This truly fine restaurant was administered, during our last stay in Paris, by M. Lespinasse, once chef to Baron G. de Rothschild, and the King of Egypt. There is more atmosphere compressed into its small space than almost any other spot in all Paris—right from the clean sawdust-covered floors, the big gilt carved snails affixed at the doorway, and the painted ceiling, we were reverently informed, had once been property of their late beloved client the immortal, the divine, Sarah Bernhardt. Great men of all nations beat a pathway to its doorway, and Onion Soup there is something to mention in low, respectful tones. The atmosphere here is completely different from the neighbouring dives and "atmosphere" spots where slumming fancy gentlemen and fancier ladies rush in to rub elbows with labourers and stallkeepers from the abattoirs and markets. And so, *bon chance, mes amis!*

WORDS to the WISE, No. III, on the IMPERATIVE NEED for NUMEROUS ONIONS of PROPER SIZE & TYPE for THIS MASTERPIECE

American chefs are so hoist by the bootstraps of economy that Onion Soups they father are puny, watery, emasculated affairs not worthy of the name. Even Onion Soup in cans is better. Here in America we have gone, on urging of friends, to find similar dilute apologies in restaurants whose products they spoke of in bated breath. . . . To our modest mind any soup tied for second choice out of all the world, deserves decent treatment. THEREFORE: *USE RED ONIONS: USE EIGHTEEN to SERVE SIX!* Discard extra pulp if need be, but gain essence through strength.

MOST ONION SOUPS ARE RUINED through FIVE MAJOR SINS

1. We use entirely too few onions; should use big red onions.
2. We forget olive oil, substituting butter. Incorrect.
3. We use too much salt entirely. Spoils flavour.
4. We omit sugar entirely. And this is a real secret!
5. We use pre-grated, stale rank Parmesan cheese; not freshly grated from a hunk on our kitchen shelf.

THEREFORE to SERVE EIGHT:

Start 8 cups or so of rich beef broth to heat in saucepan. Slice from 14 to 18 red onions thinly; on bias, to avoid rings. Cook cut onions *very gently* in 1/4 cup French olive oil and when getting clear and tender, add 4 tbsp butter. Onions must never be brown, black or crisp—but limpid as a maiden's eyes, tender as her generous heart! . . . Season now with salt, pepper, sugar; the last a good 2 tbsp.

Meanwhile trim bread rounds to fit heated earthenware casseroles, toast lightly. Portion out onions and their succulent juices equitably among the 8 casseroles; almost fill with stock. Then like a miniature, pungent raft float on the toast, load it with a big tablespoon of grated fresh Parma cheese. Put on covers and pop in oven for a quarter hour at 375° Fahrenheit; and serve sizzling.

A LUSTY RED ONION SOUP from OUR OWN PUERTO RICO, with an ENHANCING TOUCH of EGG BINDING, and VINEGAR—merely a TOUCH—SPICED with TARRAGON

To serve 8 proceed exactly as above, ignoring casseroles and toasted bread floated atop. . . . When onions are tender, add stock, simmer up in saucepan. Now beat up four fresh egg yolks with 2 tsp tarragon vinegar, and stir briskly into the fragrant pot to thicken. Dish out of tureen with ladle, and use olive-oil-fried bread sippets or croutons on top—no cheese. A wonderfully rich and satisfying one-dish meal, this.

WORDS to the WISE, No. IV, BEING a PLAINTIVE URGE to PRIME WEEK-END GUESTS with EITHER of these ONION SOUPS, *for SUNDAY MORNING*—or other—*BREAKFAST*

There is something about soup made from this invaluable lily that cools the blood, eases the mind, fetches body and soul within nodding distance once more. Try it. We have seen more than one house party salvaged from certain disaster by homely wisdom of this sort!

A SOUP of OYSTERS from ST. JACQUES CAP FERRAT, which Is NEITHER in NICE, VILLEFRANCHE, nor MONTE CARLO, but between and adjacent to THEM ALL

One brightly enameled blue-sky day we wound up the Grand Corniche drive to tarry with an Editor Friend who, for reasons of his own, saw fit to engage a villa and other useful equipment in this charming spot—the whole thing hanging like a pretty swallow's nest not too high above the incredible blue of the Mediterranean. Among this villa's useful equipment was a *Niçoise*—a plump, merry chef no higher than a fence picket. And he afforded oyster soup, and we whose oyster experience was more or less limited to Grand Central Station, and our Atlantic and Pacific Coast gamut of milk stews and pan roasts, found in the dish good reason to take pause.

Choose small sweet oysters similar to our southern coast, rather than grand ones. The touch of garlic is unexpected and new, the clove picks up the brisk aria and the grand finale comes through the hint of tart dry white wine. It makes a meal for two diners, as meals right well should, on occasion.

Lightly brown a crushed garlic clove and 2 minced medium onions in 3 tbsp butter; discard garlic husks. Put 1 qt rich milk into double boiler to heat, add onions and cook until very tender and put oysters liquor in a saucepan to heat, together with a little salt, cayenne, and a bayleaf. Just *before* oysters are curled turn into the milk-onion pot. Stir in ½ cup dry white wine. Cook oysters a minute longer and serve with a ring of fine chopped parsley on each plate, with scarlet petals of paprika in center. No worcestershire!

AN INTRIGUING SOUP of SHRIMPS, CALLED *SOPA de CAMARÃO,* from the ANCIENT & ROMANTIC PORT of LISBON

Portuguese cookery of seafood ranks among the first four schools in the world, yet it is virtually unknown to America. Actually they discovered the salt codfish long before any Gloucesterman sailed out to the Grand Banks, and have dozens of ways for preparing it. It is similar to Spanish cookery, yet subtly different, although come of Spanish root. Portuguese adventurers were the first importers to Europe of Brazilian coffee, coconut and bananas. They carried their own ideas to the Far East before the British or Dutch were known out there. Even the Hindustani word for bread *pão,* or "pan" as it is pronounced; and Japan shrimp "tempura" style is a Portuguese inheritance. Rice is beloved still by Portuguese who fetched it in via the Orient; and other variations come from the Moorish invasion of Spain to Portugal. The main thing to remember is: Use olive oil, not butter, for the Lisbon touch. This will serve four.

1½ lbs uncooked *fresh* shrimp
1 crushed garlic clove
1 lemon or 2 limes, juice
2 or 3 bayleaves
½ cup dry white wine
8 tbsp olive oil, ½ cup
1 big mild onion, red is best
Dash tabasco or hot pepper
A little flour & butter
½ cup tomato pulp
Salt, to taste, put in last

First boil shrimp gently, starting in *cold* slightly salted fresh water, enough barely to cover. Remove heads and shell; reserve heads. Remove dark vein in tail. Fry out garlic and minced onion until tender; discard garlic. Now add tomato pulp, and all seasonings except wine and salt. Saute 5 minutes, then add shrimp stock. . . . While simmering pound up heads and shells, put in potato ricer, wet with stock and squeeze every drop of rich juice out. Repeat twice. Add this juice to pot, simmer until good and strong. Strain into saucepan, rub all pulps through sieve; add white wine; thicken to taste with a little flour browned in butter—equal amounts. Now salt, to taste. Boil up once more; serve with sippets of fried bread.

WORDS to the WISE, No. V, on the WISDOM of SALTING SOUPS NEAR TIME of SERVICE, rather than at the OUTSET

As mentioned elsewhere this thought is doubtless a needless caution, but we still have to remind ourselves now and then to observe it! Salt, once in, cannot be removed except by a miracle. A soup that tastes just salty enough at the start can, when reduced in quantity by boiling, be bitterer than the dead sea. Water boils away, salt remains.

A NATIVE TURTLE SOUP from MEXICO, GULF of CAMPECHE STYLE, or *SOPA de TORTUGA, á GOLFO de CAMPECHE*

Here is another exotic fetched to our verandah by one of those calm, cool-eyed gentlemen who tool the big Pan-American clippers this way and that over the blue Caribbean, Central and South America. This dish is pungent, and a veritable soup-stew adapted to a notable one-dish meal. Green turtle is best, of course, but failing a supply of this rarer species, either the loggerhead common to the American littoral from Georgia Sea Islands around the whole Gulf Coast to South America, or the hawkbill—the tortoise shell turtle—are fine. It will serve four well.

Take 4 lbs turtle meat, any small *hot* pepper, a clove of crushed garlic, small minced red onion, 4 chopped carrots and 4 stalks chopped celery, a little salt. Smother gently in lard or olive oil for 10 minutes. Then add quart of cold water and simmer until meat is very tender—not forgetting 4 bayleaves, pinch of thyme and 2 of basil. . . . Add 2/3 cup any red wine except port. Salt finally to taste. Serve with thin slices green lime, or lemon, cooked turtle eggs, or sliced hard eggs in plates. A little diced calipee, or yellow, lower-shell turtle fat, simmered in soup first, adds character. Hell-Fire Bitters will do as well as hot pepper pod. . . . *Basil is a tradition with cooked turtle dishes.* Green turtle meat is available in most large cities in America.

A DEEP SOUTH FRESH WATER TURTLE SOUP-STEW KNOWN as *CALIPASH*, & Easily Possible Anywhere on Lakes, Streams or Ponds in South Carolina, Georgia, Florida, Alabama, Louisiana or Texas, *à la SUSAN RAINEY*

Susan Rainey came into our plantation family life down in Central Florida when we were six or seven, and ruled the kitchen for fifteen years. Susan was South Carolina "Geechee," or descendant of field-hand slaves in the huge Gulla Country plantations of rice and indigo. She was very black, and muttered invocations against this threat or that, wore charms against bad luck, rheumatism, faulty teeth, snakes, corns and additional offspring. Her husband was local African Baptist shepherd of a flock of holy black sheep who could time the end of our Sunday chicken dinner to a split-second. Susan's ancestors, for two generations of po' times after de wah, had been forced to live off the land: Possums, coons, rabbit, doves, soft shell turtles and "cooters" —those striped headed hard shell turtles seen everywhere—all went into the cook pot. Armed with a vast iron stew kettle, and wearing a pair of our own abandoned tennis shoes properly razor-cut for toe-ease, she officiated at many strange, highly seasoned and tasty dishes when "dem fancy no'thern Yankee folks, he and she, done gawn up deah away fum we-all."

Ever since then we have marveled at white-man ignorance of such delicacies as cow peas, pigeon peas, turtle *Calipash,* Pine Bark Stew, and similar Afro-American carry-overs from African tribal days. The word "exotic" means, according to people who write dictionaries, anything "foreign or strange." That is why we list Susan's *Calipash* here. . . . Oddly enough the very word is exotic, from American Indian corruption of the Spanish *carapacho,* meaning the carapace or rounded shell of turtles; hence any stew cooked in the upper shell of terrapin or turtles. . . . It used to be a famous dish at our house, and the Pittsburgh Laughlins and the Chicago Piries used to come on state occasions to consume this dish.

Two average turtles will serve six. They should—for aesthetic reasons—be guillotined out of sight, let bleed, then with hatchet make a horizontal incision both sides between feet, to separate top of shell from flat lower portion. Reserve eggs, if any—and some of the fat. Scald feet to skin, using pliers for this operation to save temper. Put in kettle, cover with cold water, salt lightly, and add 8 or 10 cloves, 1 hot pepper pod or 3 dashes tabasco, ¼ tsp mace, ½ tsp allspice. Simmer slowly and when tender trim off bones, dicing meat cross-grain to avoid strings. . . . Fry out, meanwhile, 1 medium diced onion, speck crushed garlic, in 1 tbsp butter. When tender add to meat and rich stock. Melt out 2 tbsp flour with same of butter to make brown roux, work smooth with soup, then stir well into the pot. The stew should be like heavy cream.

Meanwhile have upper shells scalded and neated up. Pour in stew, salted to taste. Add pinch sweet basil to each, 1 tbsp sherry each, same with 1 scant tbsp lemon juice and a trifle of grated yellow rind. Spread sliced turtle eggs, or hard chicken eggs, on top. Cover with any good pastry dough, prick to permit steam exit, and brown in oven at 350° Fahrenheit, brush with a little milk during last 10 min to glaze. Serve with any good white wine, chilled. Here's a deep south touch for any plantation owner!

A STUTTGART HOT SOUP of WINE & SNOWY EGGS, CALLED *SCHNEEKLOSSCHEN, à la THEODORE* of the *S. S. RESOLUTE* GRILL

Long before the ascendancy of Austrian paperhangers we made two trips around the world on German *schnelldampfers*. Much of the cuisine was heavy, all was nourishing, and some was amazingly and refreshingly delicate—of which this slightly sweet and snowy soup is a typical example. . . . Make a gentle white roux of 1½ tbsp each butter and flour—do *not* brown. Work in a little milk to make smooth as cream. Stir into double boiler with 2¼ cups tart white wine of Rhine or Moselle type. Add 4 pinches cinnamon, the yellow peel ½ lemon. Cook 20 minutes, stir in beaten yolks 3 fresh eggs. . . . Meantime whip 3 egg whites with 2½ tbsp sugar until stiff. Ladle into hot plates, float meringue on top in a snowy drift, dust with 1 tsp confectioner's sugar on each, and finally dust with pinch of cinnamon per serving. This is especially welcome to the invalid or convalescent weary of the usual. More white roux makes it thicker if that is the wish.

> "Don't give we-all no fancy sto'-boughten cookin book, Ma'am. Jes' han' me good vittles and turn me loose on a good stove—Ah said a *GOOD* stove!"
>
> From the *Kitchen Sayings* of *Cook Susan Rainey,* Zellwood, Florida, *Circa,* 1907

CHAPTER IV

FISHES *FROM THE* SEVEN SEAS

Swimming an Exotic Gamut Involving Fifteen or so Piscatorial Denizens Prepared in Fashion both Savoury & Tantalizing, such as a Bretonese *Brandade* of Salted Cods, Fishes Dipped in the Six Perfumes from Chinese Canton, Baked Snappers in the Manila Fashion with Chopped Cashews, and the Persuasive Way a Russian Prince of the Blood might Deal with a Dish of Tender Trouts. . . . To say nothing of Ten Discreet Companion Sauces.

IT HAS always found us a trifle sad that America, with inland and coastal waters teeming with a variety and excellence of fish denied Europe, should find foreign chefs taking far greater pride in its preparation. No country in the globe can show all the coral reef fishes of our Florida coast, which are parallel to identical species in the South Seas, and the whole spread from there to the salmon of Maine and Alaska, the rainbow and brook trout of our northern streams.

Yet in our fish cuisine, barring the lusty originality of certain thrifty New England chowders, the Afro-American tradition of Charleston, and the Creole inheritances of New Orleans, we simply fry, boil, bake or broil, squirt on a dash of lemon, cream or tomato sauce, and let it go at that.

By this we do not contend that any fish unaccompanied by sliced truffles and a ten-ingredient fancy sauce is invalid, but we do suggest that America should realize that lemon treatment is far more valuable *before* cookery than after, that piquant thoughts in basting or dressing can take a mediocre weight of edible fish and transform it into something men can write poems about.

We, through disposition of fate, have had a great deal to do with fishes—both in their capture, their culinary transformation, and their consumption. It began too many years ago when our male parent came barging out of a placid retirement addicted to botanical and literary pursuits, to re-enter the field of engineering in co-charge of Camp Four, on Upper Matecumbe Key, when the railroad was extended over those coral islands to Key West. In one of Kirk Munroe's Canadian sailing canoes we made daily excursion to the Great Barrier Reef where we took varied loot in the form of brilliantly coloured reef fish, stone crabs—the king of all crabs!—conchs, and Florida lobster. We have fished fresh water lakes and streams from Florida to New England, to British Columbia, and during later years have fished for big tuna and marlin and other game fishes both here and off Bimini and Cat Cay.

On trips around the world we have always been especially eager to try exotic ways of fish preparation. We've eaten deep olive oil fried squid in Naples, *bêche de mer* in Hongkong, skates in Nice—and avoid such marine diablerie in this account. We do, however, set down a chosen band of exotics out of thrice that total collected—each notable for some virtue or succulence.

BACALÃO á BILBAINITA, being a MOST SUPERB DISH of SALTED CODS in the FASHION of SPANISH BILBAO, on the BAY of BISCAY

To fellow patriots assuming that the salted codfish was exclusively part of the sacred Bostonian crest, let us hasten to explain that sturdy, hard-fisted sailormen from Bilbao, from Lisbon, and from French St. Malo—to say nothing of God knows how many Norse folk—sailed their craft to the Grand Banks of Newfoundland long before Pilgrim Fathers knew of their existence. In whatever land the Portuguese or Spaniard conquered, the salt cod—or *bacalão* in Spanish—swam merrily after. They have taken this rigid, unprepossessing fare and transformed it into a kingly dish. To those of us knowing dried cod in the form of fishballs we present a lusty exotic for that special Sunday morning breakfast.

3 lbs dry salt codfish
4 big red or white onions
2 small cloves garlic
1 to 1½ cups bread crumbs
Hot peppers, or tabasco; to taste
6 or 8 sweet peppers
4 lbs tomatoes
2½ cups olive oil
2 slices soft bread
3 bayleaves, tied together
1 cup flour

First the puree sauce. Brown 1/3 of the onions, tomatoes and minced peppers gently in 2/3 cup olive oil then simmer covered for 45 minutes. Rub through sieve, or put in The Blender. Keep hot. . . . Brown fish soaked overnight in a little olive oil and dredged in flour, until pale amber. Now brown remaining onions and peppers in rest of olive oil, when onions are tender add tomato reserved; also bayleaf and crushed garlic; add puree to this. Season to taste. Simmer 10 minutes longer. . . . Arrange baking dish as follows: First a substratum of puree and vegetables, then the *bacalão,* then the rest of the sauce. Cover with bread crumbs dotted with butter and brown in hot oven around 400° Fahrenheit.

A *BRANDADE,* which Is a Bretonese Classic also Composed of Salted Cods Creamed with Shallots, Parsley, Lemon, Truffles & Varied Spicings

The Breton fishermen besides being notable for their red sailcoth trousers, have many typical dishes, and like the Spanish and Portuguese to the south'ard, know how to do things with salt codfish. This dish was discovered by us personally in 1926 during a trip into France. At risk of censure for showing two dishes of the same type of fish, we present the *Brandade* as something typically French as onion soup, for instance.

1 lb salted codfish
½ to ¾ clove garlic
¼ tsp nutmeg
Hand ground black pepper
2 tsp parsley
3 cups thick cream
¼ cup olive oil; 1 scant cup same
1 tbsp lemon juice
1 tsp grated yellow rind
3 tbsp chopped truffles, or mushrooms
Rounds of fried bread

Choose a fine lusty bit of fish. Soak overnight in milk. Drain, break in flakes, put in cold water and poach 20 minutes, timing from first boil. Drain again, skin and bone. . . . Now heat the 1/4 cup olive oil in saucepan. When smoking toss in flaked fish, crushed garlic. Stir vigorously with *wood* spoon until finely shredded. . . . Now warm the scant cup olive oil; and cream. Stir oil into fish one spoon at a time. When like stiff paste start adding cream same way. Final dish should be like a very heavy puree. Stir in spices, mushrooms already cooked, and lemon additions. Serve in timbale garnished with triangles of butter-fried bread, and pointed up with whatever sea fare the larder affords: Bits of shrimp tail, lobster, small lightly poached oysters and the like. Utterly delicious.

WORDS to the WISE, No. VI, PUBLISHING the VIRTUES of MILK rather than WATER BEING the PROPER OVERNIGHT BATH for SALTED CODFISH or HIS HALF-BROTHER, the FINNAN HADDIE

Milk, or half milk and water, seems to extract the saline content from such species of fish far better than water alone. And where the latter is used it is wise to change it now and then while the soaking process obtains.

FISHES DIPPED in the SIX PERFUMES, being a NATIVE CHINESE DISH from CANTON-SIDE

Exactly thirteen happy years before Canton knew the terror and the death that rained from the skies, we went there by steamer from Hongkong—the Hongkong, Canton & Macao Steamship Company—up through the Tiger's Mouth into Pearl River where literally millions of Chinese are born, live and die on their small river craft. Five hours from the formal British Colony of Hongkong to the heart of Mother China where human beings were crowded 35,000,000 to a single province. We stayed in Shameen through hospitality of a Shanghai-met French gentleman in the Cantonese silk business, and through him stumbled upon this dish in a Chinese Club on the other side of the river, where also tiny sing-song girls entertained us with what they quaintly contend to be singing, and we smoked our first and last five pipes of poppy dreams.

Cut up two pounds of fine white fish into average pieces. Dip first into lemon juice, and set to marinate in a little salted water containing 1 tbsp onion pulp, for 2 hours. Drain and reserve liquid; dust with a *little* powdered anise seed (from the drug store), then with cayenne, dip in lightly beaten egg and brown golden in lots of hot butter. Put on hot platter; take 3 tbsp butter, add to marinade, 5 tbsp soya sauce, ½ tsp sugar. Thicken with a little cornstarch, working in with hot liquid to avoid lumps. Simmer, pop in fish for 2 minutes, put sauce into boat and serve separately. Soya sauce may be increased or decreased, to taste. Mace in powdered form can substitute for anise, if latter is inconvenient. An odd taste thrill.

BAKED or ROASTED FISHES, being the Grandest Possible Way of Presenting a Noble Specimen of the Snapper, Kingfish, Wahoo Tribe; or other Large Mackerels

This generation of ours being considerably after the day of miracles, let us earnestly counsel amateur chefs that no fish from any sea can baste himself, and without basting the finest red snapper can become a tasteless unprofitable thing offering all the juicy flavour of a wad of cotton batting. When the unproven chef announces baked fish, all true gourmet's tremble for the dish! Therefore, to keep a fine five pound fish from drying in pan:

1. Grease pan well with olive oil or butter.
2. Dredge fish with a little flour.
3. Place not less than 4 slices salt pork or *fat* bacon over fish—and more are better.
4. Bake in medium oven around 350° to 375° Fahrenheit.
5. Baste every 10 minutes *without fail*. If still too dry add ¼ cup butter or olive oil as additional basting.
6. Baste, *baste, BASTE!* And one of those self-basting double roasters is a help, only keep oven heat nearer 375° if this is used, browning uncovered at the last.

BAKED FISH, MANILA STYLE, EMBRACING CHOPPED CASHEWS, LIMES, CHEESE of MILD DISPOSITION, NUTMEG, SHERRY & other ADMIRABLES

After a Sunday afternoon with Monk Antrim at the cockfights—and more of this gentleman later!—a quartet of us went over to the Polo Club, after two Quarentine Cocktails from hand of Monk's own priceless Chino bartender at the huge Manila Hotel. There, with chilled Chilean *Undurraga Rhin* in brown squatty saddlebag-fitting bottles, we had the following masterpiece, involving a fish much like our own southern coast red snapper. It would be equally suitable for pike, bluefish, a big rainbow trout or black bass.

A fine 5 lb fish, red snapper best	3 cups cashew nuts, chopped
1 cup grated *mild* cheese	3 limes, juice; or 1½ lemon
1 cup milk	1 cup bread crumbs, dry, fine
6 tbsp butter	½ tsp grated nutmeg
¼ cup sherry or Madeira	1 small onion, scraped pulp
1 small garlic clove, crushed	2 bayleaves, rubbed fine

One secret is that fish is painted inside and out with lime juice, salted lightly, and iced that way for at least 4 hours before cooking. Take *well* greased baking dish; dispose fish on bottom. Mix chopped nuts with cheese, garlic pulp and onion, moistening with milk to make stiff paste. Salt and cayenne to taste, and all seasonings. Then spread your fish with this toothsome blanket, and cover with dry fine bread crumbs. On this put generous walnuts of butter and brown in medium oven around 350° to 375° Fahrenheit, basting well. . . . Chopped almonds, Brazils, hazelnuts or pecans do equally well, but the cashew is traditional in the Philippines.

WORDS to the WISE, No. VII, concerning the VIRTUES of BAYLEAF in COOKING FISHES, ESPECIALLY THOSE BAKED or ROASTED

No chef has stood eye to eye with any fish about to be baked which would not gain character from addition of a bayleaf or two, both in stuffing and in basting liquid; and the same for fish chowders of every type.

A *PULAO* of PIECES of FISH, or SHRIMPS, which WE FOUND JOURNEYING from the GULF of MANAAR, on the NORTH COAST of CEYLON, to VISIT the WEIRD TEMPLES of MADURA, TANJORE & TRICHINOPOLY

This exotic will be found listed under Shrimps, where it justly belongs, under Chaptering for *SHELLFISH, CRUSTACEA, FROGS & TURTLES,* Page 80.

A MARTINIQUE *PIMENTADE* of FISHES, which HAS BEEN DESCRIBED as HOT as LOVE, FIERCE as the MAW of PELEE, TASTY as a YOUNG MAIDEN on a FLOWER-DRAPED BALCONY. From a VOYAGE to FORT de FRANCE in 1929.

Like Martinique *Bouchées,* listed under *Hors d'Oeuvres,* this dish varies with raw materials and the case-hardening of guest palates. . . . First marinate fish in lots of slightly salted lime or lemon juice, for at least 4 hours. Cover head, tail and trimmings with cold water, a pinch each of usual sweet herbs, speck garlic, bayleaf, couple of small onions, and stalk of celery. Simmer up slowly for 15 minutes. Strain off this court bouillon, put in fish. Add from 2 to 3 small round red bird peppers, or pointed pods, or several dashes tabasco. Add lime marinade liquid; poach fish slowly until tender. Keep warm and make sauce by reducing part of stock with ¼ cup tart white wine. Garnish with quartered green limes or lemons. Onion may be omitted; but garlic, never.

WORDS to the WISE, No. VIII, on the KINDLY OFFICES of LIME or LEMON JUICE in PREPARATION of *ALL* FISHES for COOKERY

Either of these juices applied to fish removes strong scents and actually starts to tender the tissues through "cooking" action of citric acid. The trouble with America is that we too often apply citric juices to fish *after* cooking when it is far more valuable *before* cooking. . . . Add a little salt to marinade, let fish stand from 2 hours to overnight. . . . Refer to *I'a Ota,* Tahitian Fish Salad, from the notebook of Charles Nordhoof.

A WORD on the DELICACY of BOILED FISHES, and What Is Poaching

If fine baked snapper is the most regal fish dish, the most delicate invite boiling or poaching. Here again amateur chefs have been left on a limb by the printed cookery word. The result in corrupted sea-food is a crying shame; the discouragement to the amateur, worse still. The rules are few but *rigid*.

1. Don't try to boil any good fish in kettle. Fare forth to any decent household supply store and purchase a regular Fish Boiler. . . . Don't be parsimonious or crippled by false economy—*GET a BIG ONE*. For a large fish cannot go into a too-small Boiler, while a small fish is finely treated in a big Boiler. . . . Such a Boiler permits fish to be boiled whole; has a perforated shelf-like support holding fish off bottom.
2. Remove with infinite care when done, so fish does not break up. Delicate fleshed fish should be wrapped in cheesecloth to hold together.
3. *NEVER* let simmering stop once started, regardless whether water or Court Bouillon is used. Latter best.
4. Where we read receipts calling for a little vinegar in the fluid, substitute about ⅛ more of lime or lemon juice and forget the vinegar entirely. Much more delicate flavour.
5. Fish to 1 lb take 10 minutes; from 1 to 1½ lbs, 15 to 18 minutes; 1½ to 3 lbs, 18 to 28 minutes; 3 to 5 lbs, 28 to 40 minutes; 5 to 8 lbs, 40 to 60 minutes. . . . Bigger fish require more time, naturally. Done when meat leaves bone—but be sure about this for few things are more depressing than undercooked boiled fish!

POACHING FISHES, what IT IS

Chefs will vary in opinion here, but reduced to legible English Poaching means simmering *very* gently in any fluid elected, in a covered pan rather than a big boiler or kettle; preferably with a domed and tight-fitting cover so that steam may rise, collect and drop down—automatically basting fish. Liquid may be water, wine, milk, court bouillon. Poaching usually employs somewhat *less* liquid than boiling. It may also be done in a shallow pan.

It is, of course, done without cover in certain cases. The process actually is boiling, of course, but usually involves smaller, tenderer fishes, or smaller cuts of large fishes. We often poach trouts, or filets of sole, but never boil them.

A RUSSIAN DISH of BOILED FISHES INVOLVING also SHRIMPS, MUSHROOMS, BAYLEAF & SOUR CREAM

In 1926 we discovered Maisonette des Comediens Russes, on the Rue Vivienne. It is rather amazing, being operated by White Russian officers, and not only affording just about the finest Russian cooking anywhere in Paris, but with really Russian music, no swing or any of the varied abortions French or other foreign gentlemen quaintly assume to be American jazz; no dancing. Just Russian gypsy music, with a touch of Hungarian concertina work thrown in. It is very gay, especially after midnight. It made us very sad and sorry about the whole Revolution business, and those wonderful madly gay, fantastic days of the Tsar's court.

3 lbs fine fish fillets	1 cup cooked shrimp
½ lb chopped mushrooms	4 tbsp butter
4 bayleaves, tied together	2/3 cup sour cream
1 bunch beet or turnip greens	1 to 1½ tbsp flour
½ cup lime or lemon juice	Salt and cayenne to taste

Mix juice with another ½ cup salted water and marinate fish for an hour. Meantime cover greens with water, a little salt, bayleaf and cayenne. Boil 10 minutes, then put in fish and poach slowly. When tender put on hot plate. While fish poaches make sauce: Chop mushrooms fine; if they are large, peel off the top skin; and where there is a choice prefer the button type. Fry out in 3 tbsp butter. When tender melt out remaining tbsp butter with flour; work smooth and add to mushrooms. Next stir in sour cream. Simmer up once more. . . . Serve fillets on platter surrounded with shrimp, and mask with sauce. Be careful greens do not cling to fillets. Thin sauce with a little stock if too thick. A very delicately flavoured dish indeed.

WORDS to the WISE, No. IX, EXTOLLING the NEED for SAUCES other than the USUAL CREAM TYPE for BOILED FISH—MAINLY *MOUSSELINE* & SAUCE *PRINCESSE,* which ARE ESPECIALLY PLEASANT.

Mousseline is one of the immortals. No finer sauce exists for a delicate boiled fish. Simply mix 2 parts good Hollandaise Sauce with 1 part whipped cream. May be hot or cold.

Sauce *Princesse* is especially equitable with boiled salmons. It requires 1 cup Hollandaise, ½ tsp beef extract, 6 oysters poached in own liquor until edges curl; then minced. Mix well.

SARDINES or PILCHARDS, COOKED FRESH from the SEA, *à la MARMION*

Two summers ago we were fishing tuna with Ernest Hemingway in Bimini, and we gave Tommy Shevlin a bachelor party on *MARMION*. So next day we were tired and didn't go fishing, and Carlos, Ernest's *Cubaño* head gaffer on *PILAR,* threw a cast net over the side of the dock and hauled it in packed with about two bushels of wriggling silver sardines, and gave us a bucket full. And there was our breakfast! Small fishes like these abound from Maine to the Argentine, and just why men wait until some Norwegian cans them in olive oil to eat them has always escaped us, for when cooked fresh they may be eaten bones and all like smelts. . . . Simply scrape with back of knife—one stroke each side, and scales are gone. Toss a garlic clove in a skillet full of olive oil. When smoking hot either brown, lightly salted, as-is; or dip first in salted milk, then egg, flour, then brown. Serve sizzling.

ROASTED SHADS, *á SEVILLANA,* or as the SPANIARD DOES

An itinerant female cousin addicted to roving in far countries and doing water colours of what she sees, fetched this back to us scribbled on the back of a bright sketch of the chef! To us, American baked shad was delicious, but still a plain baked fish. For those who wish to voyage into the unexpected let's consider the combined taste advantages of wine, olive oil, a trifle of mushroom, and the liver of the fish itself.

1 3-lb shad, or 2 of 2 lbs
2 bayleaves, broken up
Salt & cayenne, to taste
¾ cup tart white wine
1½ limes, or 1 lemon, juice
1¼ cups finely minced mushrooms
2½ tbsp olive oil
2½ tbsp butter
Reserve shad livers from market

Score fish lightly on both sides to permit sauce to penetrate. Brush with juice and let stand 2 hrs. Then brush with oil, season well. Grease pan with butter, and any surplus oil. Brown in medium oven around 350° Fahrenheit for 25 minutes or so. Baste well. . . . Meantime chop livers, parboil, and rub through sieve. Same with chopped mushrooms, cooking in reserved liver broth. Mix liver puree and mushrooms, add white wine, turn into pan about the fish, ten minutes before done—basting constantly. Use this reduced wine-liver-mushroom basting for sauce.

A FAIRLY FANCY, yet EASY, RUSSIAN WAY of FRYING SMELTS, which WILL BE a DELIGHT to the EYE & a FILLIP to the JADED PALATE

Here is another from Maisonette Russe, in Paris. To us to whom a smelt was merely a small totally consumable fish, fried either in or out of batter, it opened our eyes to the possibility of fancy trimmings on certain occasions, with gourmets visible.

2 lbs fresh smelts, large as possible
18 to 24 shrimp, depending on size
2 tsp mushroom or walnut ketchup
1½ tbsp butter
1½ tbsp flour
1 cup flour, for added duty
2 tbsp fine dry breadcrumbs
3 cups veal stock
2 tbsp lemon or lime juice
½ tsp dry hot mustard
Salt & cayenne, to taste
3 beaten egg yolks
½ small clove garlic
2 tsp chopped parsley

Large smelts are essential, as they have to be filleted with razor-sharp knife, and bone taken out. And the piquant frying sauce is what makes this dish; additional seasonings are up to the chef. . . . First melt out the butter and brown the crushed garlic gently; discard latter. Work 1½ tbsp flour into a smooth roux, add to heated stock. Chop up shrimp into lemon juice and add to stock. Put in all seasonings and the added 3 tbsp butter. Simmer very slowly for 15 minutes. Keep this rich sauce in reserve; chill well then paint fillets thoroughly, skewer together with short bits of toothpick to make like whole fish. Dip first in flour then in beaten yolk, and fry in deep olive oil or other fat (except butter) at 370° Fahrenheit. Serve the remaining sauce in a silver boat, heated well, for those who wish it.

FILET of SOLE, *HABAÑERO,* a DELICIOUS SOLUTION for POACHING FILLETS of any SWEET & TENDER FISH, a CLASSIC from the HABANA YACHT CLUB that WE DISCOVERED in 1930

Poach fillets in half tart white wine, half lightly salted water. Brush with lime juice mixed with onion pulp, ½ cup to 1 tsp latter. Brown fine-chopped almonds in a little butter. Season fillets, spread on chopped nuts evenly and thinly. Brown under quick broiler flame. Dust with chopped parsley and a trifle of fresh grated Parma cheese. Serve with dry white wine of the Rhine or Moselle type; with Undurraga *Rhin,* or better still, with still white Burgundy.

CHINESE FRIED TROUTS, or "THE SMALL WATER ANGELS of SOO-CHOW"—BEING a COMPOUND of WHITE WINE, GINGER, EGG BATTER, and the JUICE of LEMONS or LIMES, from the BEAUTIFUL LAKE CITY of the SAME NAME, where DWELL the LOVELIEST CHINESE MAIDENS in the WHOLE WIDE WORLD

May we repeat the fact that long before our European ancestors stopped wearing bear skin kimonos the Chinese had an intricate and civilized cookery? In the white race the first civilized cookery was in Italy; then France. Many Chinese culinary dishes startle the western eye and palate. Maybe they are right; maybe we. However, besides the American born Chop-Suey which is unknown as a native Chino dish, there are many receipts worthy of our attention as exotics—as this one.

Take 6 small trout, properly drawn. Dry with a cloth; brush with lemon juice mixed with onion pulp and a *trace* of crushed garlic. Make batter of 5 egg whites, ½ cup tart white wine—using Japanese *saki* if no Chino rice wine handy, for they are much the same—½ tsp sugar, salt. Beat stiff. Roll lightly seasoned fish carefully and brown golden in deep lard or olive oil at 370° Fahrenheit. The final exotic touch is a slight dusting with ground ginger just before service.

HOW a RUSSIAN PRINCE of the Blood Once Cooked a Dish of Small Trouts, with White Wine, Very Old Rum Indeed, Sweet Herbs, a Few Shrimps, & a Touch of Sherry or Madeira

This is a very old receipt from St. Peterburg before the fall of the Tsar, and when food was something besides basic nourishment under five year, or other, plans. It is fancy but delicious, and all ingredients are easily found, provided we have the necessary 1 doz trout! . . . Take fish heads, tails and trimmings, add 2 doz raw shrimp, a minced onion, salt, 2 bayleaves, a stalk of celery and half cover with water. Cover tightly and simmer slowly until shrimp are done. Shell shrimp tails, remove the top-side dark vein. Pound heads, put in sieve and drain stock through several times; then reduce this enriched fluid gently by half. About ½ cup of strong stock is needed. . . . Mix 2 cups dry white wine, 2 tbsp Jamaica rum, and 1 pinch each: basil, savoury, thyme, crushed bayleaf, 1 tsp chopped green mint. Put lightly salted trout in bowl and cover with wine-herb marinade for 2 hrs. . . . Use big pan to cook fish without bending, poach in the wine marinade about 2 minutes. Mince shrimp tails, toss them in butter. Put poached fish on platter carefully, rub sauce through sieve, add shrimp and 1 tbsp fine chopped parsley for garnish, and pass in gravy boat. If sauce is too thick, reduce slightly before adding shrimp. A very delicate and lovely dish.

AND NOW a COMPANIONATE LIST of THIRTEEN ADDITIONAL EXOTIC FISH SAUCES with which the AMATEUR CHEF MAY BECOME HONOURED among MEN, & without MAY BE HOIST by the TRITE PETARD of SALT & PEPPER UNADORNED

1. *Babcock Sauce,* a tested classic, and mainly for boiled fish: 1 cup strained clam broth, ½ tsp hand-ground *black* pepper, ¼ tsp salt—no more! Then ½ tsp hot mustard, 3 tbsp butter, 1 tbsp flour. . . . Do not use white pepper, or finely ground black. If no hand pepper mill, crush up whole peppercorns in bowl, as visible pepper is part of the tradition. . . . Melt butter and make roux with flour and mustard. Season, stir in clam juice slowly, heating very gradually. . . . When it boils note chronometer. Draw off in precisely 2 minutes, no more!
2. *Four Savoury Butter Sauces:* Very finely chopped mixed pickle, a little fine-chopped watercress, butter to suit. . . . Anchovy paste, dash tabasco, butter to suit. . . . Finely chopped parsley, little lemon or lime juice *strained,* butter to suit. . . . Anchovy paste, finely minced capers, butter to suit. . . . Mix all of these well until butter is creamed and light. If sweet butter is used, add salt to taste.
3. *A Piquant Fish Sauce from Dijon, which is in France:* This is very admirable with baked fish, as it is derived from such bastings founded on butter-in-pan. . . . Put fish bastings through coarse sieve, add a trifle of fine-chopped chives, shallot, or spring onion top, a pinch of basil. Add a little water and reduce slowly until very thick. Then donate 2 tsp mild French mustard, 2 cups white cream sauce, 1 doz finely chopped capers. Simmer up once more and it is ready.
4. *Old Key West Lime Sour:* This is a native classic from the Florida Keys, from the Bahamas. It is good in fish sauces, on fish itself in small quantities; good for salad dressings for fish and green salads. . . . To 2 cups strained lime juice add level tsp salt. Stand in warm kitchen 2 wks; cork then and keep in cool place, as it is ready to use. Queer scent, exotic taste!
5. *A Sauce for Broiled Fish, from Nantes, also in France:* Rub 6 sardines through a sieve, cream with 4 tbsp butter, juice 3 limes or 2 lemons, tsp fine-chopped parsley, ½ tsp scraped onion pulp. Brush over fish when it comes out sizzling.
6. *A Shrimp Sauce Suitable for Boiled Fish:* Much in favour abroad, and varies the usual caper sauces found everywhere. . . . Take enough white sauce to fill boat; stir in 1½ tsp anchovy paste, juice ½ lemon

or 1 lime, strained; 6 shrimp tails broken small; Cayenne to taste. Small cubes of lobster will also do well, small chopped oysters, sliced hard eggs. Let sauce simmer up once, then serve. White sauce for fish should be made on base of ½ milk and half fish stock or court bouillon.

7. *A Viennese Sauce for Boiled or Grilled Fish of Size:* Make roux of 1½ tbsp each butter and flour; don't brown. Add 2/3 cup hot sour cream. When worked smooth add 1½ tbsp tarragon vinegar, salt to taste. Now add 2 tbsp or slightly more *freshly* grated horseradish. Now ½ tbsp chopped capers. Simmer all together once, and serve very hot.

8. *Pepper Sauce for Boiled Fish, Mainly:* Here's one we found at a fine seafood restaurant in Nice, in 1931. . . . Pound 1 tsp whole peppercorns finely, simmer in ½ cup tart white wine. Reduce until nearly dry, then turn in 2 cups cream sauce based on half cream and half court bouillon. Boil up once; strain.

9. *Dr. Kitchiner's Piquante Sauce for Fish, & all other Flesh:* This classic dates back to 1817, and the immortal Doctor. . . . Pound yolks 2 hardboiled eggs with 1 tsp French mustard; pepper and salt, and 2 tbsp olive oil. Mix well and add 3 tbsp tarragon vinegar. Now add your preference of these: 1 tbsp mushroom ketchup, walnut ketchup; or walnut pickle, or a few fine-chopped capers. Rub through a fine sieve. . . . To our private thought a little cayenne and onion pulp would aid.

10. *A Cubaño Green Sauce from a Favourite Haunt of Ours in Matanzas, and Utterly Delicious on all sorts of Delicate Fish, Lobsters and the Like:* To ½ cup of thick sour cream add 1 cup good mayonnaise. Now comes 1 tbsp watercress or spinach for colour, fine-chopped of course. Next a speck of garlic pulp, enough green lime to suit tartness of taste; tabasco, a dash. Whip thoroughly and rub through sieve, or toss in Blender. Should be very cold for cold fish. Rub through fine sieve in all cases. . . . A tsp green tarragon, chervil or basil is also wonderful. Dry herbs are permissible but not so delicate or attractive to the eye in this receipt.

EXPLODED OLD WIVES' TALES No. I, on the BETRAYAL in USING RED WINES either in FISH COOKERY, or in FISH SAUCES

Now and then we have stumbled—especially in rather ancient foreign books on fish cookery and modern American efforts neither based upon authority, nor personal culinary experience—upon dishes commanding the use of red wine in fish cookery. Eschew such snares like the plague. Except for infrequent French *Matelotes* of fish where red wine is traditional, use unfortified white wines, tart preferred, in fish cookery. . . . Where sherry and Madeira are indicated for flavour, *add immediately before serving, never before,* for reasons explained.

"Health, Beauty, Strength, & Spirits—& I might say the Faculties of the Mind, depend upon the Organs of the Body—*one of the most Important of which is the Stomach*. . . . When these are in Good Order, the Thinking Part is Most Alert & Active; the Contrary when they are Disturbed. . . ."

Dr. Cadogan, England, 1757

CHAPTER V

SHELLFISH, CRUSTACEA, FROGS & TURTLES

Not Forgetting Smothered Conch, *Ernest Hemingway,* the true Norfolk Oyster Roast, Peppery Stuffed Crabs from Pointe à Pître which is in Guadeloupe, Devilled West Indian Crawfish, *Cat Cay,* Old Scottish Spiced Lobster, Shrimps dealt with on the Kona Coast of Hawaii, and a Duet of Turtles.

THIS IS another favourite chapter, not alone because we are so fond of seafood ourselves but due to the amazingly varied flavours the amateur chef can effect through slight changes in seasoning, through broiling *au naturelle* and without that perennial American habit of boiling in plain water first, through cooking certain crustacea in oil *with the shells on,* through roasting oysters in their own succulent juices and not merely frying or stewing these sweet bivalves.

Possibly the most important thought to hold with regard to these strange seagoing bedfellows is to remember that, with a few rare exceptions, their charm is in the delicacy of their flavours—so let none of the native virtue be subdued by over-seasoning; but where there is high seasoning—like certain stuffed crabs—make the seasoning truly high and peppery. And the second grain of counsel is that when cooking seafoods American chefs tend to use too much water and too little hot fat, as will be explained anon.

Here again we purposely concentrate on Caribbean or Latin-American exotics, since the French school especially is billed on menus in any metropolitan restaurant; but particularly so due to the constantly growing fleet of American yachtsmen and winter visitors now visiting those sunny tropical shores where we too have spent so many happy months during the last ten years—on ships great and small. Each one set down here is featured for mighty good reasons. Each guarantees its own unique and exotic taste experience. Some are old classics. If we have been able to discover something here and there which is new, or little known, we take joy in the fact.

IT IS of INTEREST to NOTE that FIVE EXOTIC COLD SEAFOOD COCKTAIL SAUCES, VARYING the TRITE THEME of KETCHUPS and CHILI SAUCES, MAY BE FOUND OUTLINED at some LENGTH under *HORS d'OEUVRE* on PAGE 29.

A NASSAU CURRY of CONCHS, that LOVELY & FLAVOURFUL SHELLFISH COMMON to the FLORIDA KEYS, the BAHAMAS & WEST INDIES, & already TOUCHED upon as an EXOTIC CHOWDER

Pound the white meat of 8 conchs until tender; cut into pieces 1" x 1½". Fry out 1 big mild minced onion in 2 tbsp fat, until tender and clear. Work 2 tsp curry powder into ½ cup rich milk, fresh or evapo rated. Add to onions, and also toss in bayleaf, pinch thyme, 4 cut up tomatoes. Everything goes into a big covered skillet or iron kettle and simmers in its own pleasant juices until conch tenders. Add a trifle of coconut milk or water from time to time, to keep fluid enough. Serve with freshly grated coconut kernel, slivers of smoked sailfish, smoked haddock or salmon—first flaked small and oven-dried. . . . After personal experience with this receipt we recommend cucumbers peeled and cut in ¾" cross-sections rather than the tomato, which spoils the typical curry appearance, and adds nothing typical of curries, either old or new. This dish nourishes six to eight.

SMOTHERED CONCH, *ERNEST HEMINGWAY,* as PREPARED by CARLOS then HEAD GAFFER on GOOD SHIP *PILAR,* while SAILFISHING off SOMBRERO LIGHT in the GULF STREAM; and WHICH FED SIX

This delicious Key West–Florida Keys favourite can easily be prepared in any deep heavy frying pan, dutch oven or kettle. Prepare 8 conchs as above, this time parboiling in a little water to tender, while preparing other ingredients. Fry out 6 slices fat salt pork with 2 medium sized sliced onions, 4 or 5 medium tomatoes cut in eighths, juice 1 small lime, 3 bayleaves and a dash or so of worcestershire. Drain off conch broth, reserving for future stiffeners; add 2 tbsp butter before covering tightly and smother slowly until tender. Add 2 tbsp sherry just before serving, and have oven-crisped pilot biscuit in quantity. One red pencil pod or red bird pepper is optional, but nice.

EULOGY to STONE CRABS, which ARE without DOUBT the REGAL EMPEROR of the WHOLE CRAB TRIBE, before DISCUSSING THEIR COOKERY

The Florida or West Indian Stone Crab is a big fellow growing rarer every hour due to merciless pursuit by market fishermen everywhere from Daytona southward to Cuba. In the old days market men kept only the larger claw, releasing the crab; now both claws are wanted, and the crab—instead of growing another mandible and meantime feeding himself one-handed, is a sacrifice to the nut-like delicacy of his own tender flesh. These stone crab claws are huge, a glorious colour scheme of pale cream yellow, scarlet touched as to pincers, and finally tipped in shiny jet black. The epicure's traditional way of eating stone crab is with drawn butter; cold with Hollandaise or with a simple French dressing made of salt, hand-ground black pepper, olive oil, a dash or 2 of Key West Old Lime Sour, and lime juice. We list an assorted array of drawn butters for this and other marine citizens which we've collected during our wanderings about the world—to vary the rather trite plain drawn butter we see everywhere.

TEN VARIATIONS of the ETERNAL DRAWN BUTTER THEME for CRABS, STEAMED CLAMS, CRAWFISH, LOBSTERS, PRAWNS, *LANGOSTAS* & *LANGOUSTES,* SHRIMPS & SUCH VARIED CITIZENS

To each One-Half Cup of Drawn Butter Add:

1 tbsp lime or lemon juice; 1 tbsp lime or lemon juice plus 1 tsp chili sauce; 1 tsp each lemon juice and scraped onion pulp; 10 capers

chopped very fine and 1 tsp caper vinegar; 1 tsp lemon or lime juice and same of freshly grated horseradish. . . . Add speck garlic to butter before melting, then discard the lily and add 2 tbsp walnut pickle liquor; work 1 tsp anchovy paste to cream with same amount of lime or lemon juice, adding cayenne; snip 1 tsp chives very fine with scissors and add same of lime or lemon juice; speck fresh garlic pulp and ½ tsp Key West Old Lime Sour, see Page 169; 1 tsp lime or lemon juice, oil twisted from curl of lime peel and dash tabasco. . . . These were culled from seven different countries.

In all cases whip up flavourings thoroughly with melted butter.

DEVILLED STONE—or MORRO—CRABS, *á ZARAGOZANA,* sometimes CALLED *CANGREJOS de MORRO, RELLEÑOS*

Now and again in travelling about we find that all fine native restaurants need not be in the basilicas of ancient churches nor in buildings once occupied by irregular royalty or Mme. Sarah Bernhardt. Now and again they are bright, new, frighteningly moderne as to chromium plate; but when there is a fine chef they are invariably crowded. Such is Zaragozana in the old city of Habana, where we were taken by a friend fourteen years in Cuba—and, *amigos,* what sea food! What red snappers; what *langostinos* and *langostas,* those slender graceful clawless lobsters of Cuba's rocky coast! . . . Although we eat only the claw meat of Stone or Morro Crab, in this case the shell—which affords so little meat in usual cases as to be unprofitable—is retained as a vessel for the fragrant receipt.

First rub empty shells of crabs boiled in sea, or salted, water, with cut garlic clove and olive oil; and set aside.

Next pick meat from claws and that easily salvaged from shells, but do not chop up fine; leave in reasonably large bits. To each cupful of meat allow: 2 tbsp lime juice, 1 tbsp chopped capers, 1 tsp onion pulp, plenty of tabasco or hand-ground black pepper to make hot; salt—then stand on ice.

Now for the extra stuffing. For each cupful meat allow: ¼ cup fine diced avocado pear pulp, *not too soft and ripe;* ¼ cup fine chopped mushrooms; ⅛ tsp dry mustard; 1 pinch each of mace and basil, well rubbed between palms; 1 tsp melted butter; ½ beaten egg yolk; 1 tbsp *Carta de Ora* Bacardi Rum; enough fine crumbs to mask, and a little olive oil.

Mix marinated crab meat thoroughly with this stuffing. Pack into shells. Cover with crumbs, moisten with olive oil and brown in medium oven around 350°. The avocado is the typical *Cubaño* touch. Heat breaks down pulp and rich nut-like flavour permeates the whole business. . . . Also wonderful for all other kinds of crabs, lobsters and crawfish. Should be seasoned highly, please remember.

PEPPERY STUFFED CRAB, *à la HOTEL des BAINS,* Guadeloupe, French West Indies, which Confound Their More Conservative American Cousins

Here on this volcanic double French Island we journeyed up into the high mountains where we found a charmingly seedy little French Hotel maintained by one M. Dole, who then—and we hope now—for bedroom, sitting room and verandah took tariff at one dollar twenty-five per day with red wine and meals. There was a ravishing view of green ex-volcanoes cooling their toes in blue sea; ancient casked rum was ten cents a noggin, and to top it off there were a trio of big square pools in varying depths and delicately framed between feathery bamboos and mahogany trees just above the place, where warm mineral spring water flowed perpetually. We had this crab with a slim waistless bottle of *Berncasteler Doktor* Moselle.

6 to 8 empty hard crab shells
1 small clove garlic, crushed
1 tbsp chives or shallots, chopped
2 tbsp butter, melted
½ cup fine dry crumbs
1½ tbsp lean bacon, minced fine
1 cup milk, fresh or evaporated
1 hot pepper; or 4 dashes tabasco
Salt, to taste
2 tbsp strained lime juice
Soft bread, several slices
3 dashes Angostura bitters
Meat from shells and claws

Figure two parts crab meat to one of soft bread. Moisten latter with milk and bitters mixed. Fry out garlic, shallots and pepper, with bacon. Mix everything thoroughly, stuff shells previously painted with olive oil. Cover with fine crumbs, dot with butter or olive oil, brown around 375° Fahrenheit. Seasoning is always to taste, of course; but should be very peppery.

A WORD on the VIRTUES, HABITS & CULINARY SUCCULENCE of the FLORIDA, or WEST INDIAN, CRAWFISH; also CUBAN *LANGOSTINOS,* & HAITIAN *LANGOUSTES*

The former is known also as "spiny lobster." It has no claws and frequents rocky holes along the coral reefs, and tidewater creeks under shelving banks or mangrove roots. They are plentiful from Bermuda southward through the whole vast sweep of the islands; while the smaller, tenderer, slenderer *langouste* tribe is found the world over. Both species are guiltless of claws, but are otherwise comparable to any usual lobster. Muscular tensile strength is determined by age, so choose smaller specimens, especially for broiling. Crawfish are much tenderer when broiled, grilled, or deep-fat fried as-is, and *not* boiled first.

EXPLODED OLD WIVES' TALE No. II, on the FALLACY of PLUNGING LOBSTERS, or for that MATTER *any* CRUSTACEAN, into BOILING WATER

We are glad to announce that what we, in our modest and fumbling way, found to be true twenty-five years ago when doing our own cooking on a canoe trip down the east coast of Florida, is now confirmed by none other than the incomparable Henri Charpentier—probably our greatest living chef, and luckily for America, long domiciled on these shores.

Never plunge, toss, slide or push lobsters or crawfish into boiling water. Sudden contact of fleshly tissue with this scalding bath sets up an aggravated and permanent case of rigour-mortis. Once-tender muscles toughen; tough muscles become adamant. . . . Rather take kettle filled with sea, or salted water—preferably with slight acidulation of vinegar or lemon juice—and gently lower the victim into it.

Lobsters, crawfish, crabs, *can not feel.* It is not cruel. The slowly mounting heat lulls them to rest, and they emerge rosily tender as they went in.

It's the same as making a stew. Hot or boiling water toughens meat fibres instantly.

WORDS to the WISE No. X, NOMINATING SEA WATER as PROPER FLUID for BOILING LOBSTERS & CRAWFISH, if THEY MUST BE BOILED

Lobster meat boiled in fresh water is relatively tasteless flesh; in plain salted water it is better, as salt permeates every fibre; but boiled from a start in *cold* sea water is best. Just enough salt, plus an impressive list of blessed chemicals such as iodine, which physicians, chirurgeons and such professional leeches assure us is beneficial to the human machine. . . . Most important of all is that salting is correct.

DEVILLED CRAWFISH or LOBSTER, *CAT CAY,* being an Excerpt from *MARMION'S* Log

This is another dish created by our Afro-Portuguese pilot, chef, and big fish gaffer, Jim Arañha—mentioned elsewhere in this volume. We weren't fishing tuna or marlin that day because Hemingway had gone to meet Grant Mason's very decorative wife on the Pan-American Airways Plane. We'd gone ashore to visit with Charlie Cook—or "Cookie"—Lou Wasey's major domo on that tiny island paradise on the west Bahama reef. Then we picked up a basket of crawfish by the sunken concrete ship, landed on Piicquet's Rocks to hunt sea bird nests while Jim concocted this chef d'oeuvre which would make Prunier's head chef blanch with envy!

Boil 4 medium crawfish; split shells and mince to ½" cubes, reserving shells. Scald 2 ripe tomatoes and skin. Take heavy iron pan or saucepan, melt 4 tbsp butter, add 1½ tbsp mild mustard, 1 tsp worcestershire, 2 bayleaves, juice 2 small limes, 4 tbsp chopped up mango chutney—Ah there's the touch, shipmates!—a scant handful of chopped peanuts. Add cut up tomatoes, crawfish; saute *very* slowly covered. Add a few bits soft bread, 2 tbsp sherry. Stuff the half shells, previously rubbed with garlic, with this savoury blend, and either brown under broiler as-is, or dust with Parma cheese, freshly grated, before doing so. We've never tasted anything better anywhere.

WORDS to the WISE No. XI, EMPHASIZING the CARDINAL SIN of MINCING LOBSTER or CRAWFISH too FINELY, & on the MERITS of BROILING UNBOILED, and DEEP-FAT FRYING UNBOILED

The delicate flavour of this sort of meat becomes dissipated and invaded with foreign tastes further than is good, when chopped very small. Cubes ½" thick and up to ¾" long—possibly longer—are best. . . . This applies to newburgs and all allied dish as well as Lobster *Thermidor, l'Americaine,* and as above.

If truly native taste is to be retained don't forget when broiling such specimens to broil raw, not after boiling away half the taste first in water! . . . This goes for all but the largest and toughest specimens. Split, brush with lime juice, rub with garlic, paint with olive oil, salt and put to coals. That's all.

When deep-fat frying, either crawfish or lobster retains its characteristic delicious flavour much better when not boiled first, and much flavour thus dissipated—see the duet of Batters, listed later in this Chapter.

Any Broiled Lobster is especially worthy when garnished with Dr. Kitchener's Piquante Sauce or *Cubaño* Green Sauce, listed under *Fishes* on Page 63; or the Devilling Spread, below.

CRAWFISH or LOBSTER, BROILED or GRILLED *en BROCHETTE,* a TASTY ROUTINE from the CHEF at CAFE de PARIS, across the little PLAZA from the CASINO, in MONTE CARLO, 1932

Cut lobster into ½" thick cross-sections if small; into cubes ½" x 1" x 1¼" if large. Marinate well moistened in liquid: ½ white wine, ½ olive oil, for an hour. Rub brochette with a trace of olive oil, with a garlic clove and arrange things in sequence: 1 small mushroom top, bit of lobster, bit of lean-fat smoked bacon or Virginia ham, and so on again—ending with a final mushroom. Brush with olive oil, grill over coals, dust with salt and cayenne. Put in platter, moisten with savoury butter. Fetch to table flaming from 1 tbsp pre-heated brandy, set alight.

ONE DUET of THOUGHT on the FRYING of CRUSTACEANS & FISH. CRAWFISH, or LOBSTER or SHRIMP or FISH, Is DELICIOUS FRIED in BATTER—RAW—of which THESE ARE TWO EXOTIC EXAMPLES: ONE from NAGASAKI, JAPAN, 1931; ONE from PORT ANTONIO, JAMAICA, 1933

The Japanese have always been magicians with frying delicate sea foods that adapt typical Japanese genius to suit western palates. They fry in peanut oil, sesame oil, or lard. We find olive oil best, due to its added flavour, with lard a close second. . . . To 1 cup good mayonnaise add 1 tsp very finely chopped chives or spring onion tops and a speck of crushed garlic, and mix well. To 2 cups crumbs, dry and fine, add 2 tbsp finely chopped roasted and blanched almonds or pistachio nuts. Dip lobster first in mayonnaise, then crumbs, then brown in deep fat at 370°.

The Port Antonio Batter: Having friends possessed of a plantation in the rainbow-garlanded, lush windward mountains, we came to know Port Antonio first in 1929, when yacht made harbour. . . . Sift 1 cup flour and 1 tsp salt in bowl. Now mix in 2 tbsp *finely* grated fresh coconut kernel, *not* the shredded dry kind which has all the flavour of cork life preserver filling. Make depression in top; work in slowly 4 egg yolks, well beaten, and 3 to 4 tbsp olive oil. Mix well; add a little warm milk until like thick cream. Stir in 1½ egg whites, *not* beaten. Dry seafood well, dip in batter, fry in deep fat at 370° also.

A PROPER DEVILLING SPREAD from the BRITISH ISLAND of JAMAICA, & which Is EXCELLENT on CRAWFISH, LOBSTER & ALL VARIETIES of SEAFOOD; both as a CONDIMENT & a SPREAD PAINTED on before the FINAL FEW MOMENTS of BROILING or GRILLING

To 1 tsp dry mustard and the same of worcestershire, add 1 tbsp drawn butter, 2 tbsp ketchup or chili sauce, 1 tsp scraped onion pulp, a speck of crushed garlic, the juice of 1 small lime and salt to taste. The final touch is 1 dash angostura. . . . Wonderful on big fish steaks like kingfish, swordfish and the like.

FROGS' LEGS, *à la PALAIS de la MÉDITERRANÉE,* which Is on the *PROMENADE des ANGLAIS,* in NICE

Contrary to many friends we have discovered a surprising number of delightful dishes in large well-lighted places as well as in musty 16th Century buildings all stuffed with history and mystery. Gould's incredible Palace-Casino is typical. We found a small friendly *bar-maitre* who knew Mood Indigo Cocktails; there was a girl with us who was very eager, very young, very near-sighted and very pretty. Her ankles were very pretty. The champagne was very cold; the frogs' legs—*Jambes des Grenouille*—were also very pretty. This should nourish eight guests to perfection.

2 lbs of frogs' legs, jointed;
2 doz legs, 1 doz pairs
6 finely chopped spring onions
¼ clove of crushed garlic
1 cup chopped button mushrooms
Salt and cayenne, to taste
4 oz butter
3 tbsp tart white wine
2 cups of good cream sauce
1 tbsp chopped parsley
2 bayleaves
2 tbsp sherry or Marsala wine

Dip frogs' legs in milk, dust with salt and cayenne, dip in a little flour. Heat butter, turn in onion, garlic and bayleaves, chopped mushrooms, and then brown frogs' legs to a delicate gold colour. Take them out and reserve on a hot plate. Add wine to saucepan, simmer up, poach frogs' legs 5 minutes longer. Put this cooking sauce through a sieve, after taking out the mushrooms. Stir into hot cream sauce and put mushrooms back again. Stir in the sherry or Marsala. Serve with sauce poured over frogs' legs, and dusted with chopped parsley for garnish.

OLD SCOTTISH SPICED LOBSTER, which Is an HONOURABLE & ANCIENT CLEIKUM CLUB RECEIPT from the TIME of MEG DODS

Meat of 2 boiled lobsters or crawfish, cut into slices, should be put into saucepan and browned lightly in 1 tbsp butter. Then put into 3 cups rich chicken broth or stock. Season with 3 tbsp walnut ketchup, or same amount pickled walnuts crushed with liquor to equal amount; 1/4 tsp worcestershire, 1/2 tsp each powdered clove, nutmeg and mace; salt and cayenne to taste. Now donate 2 tbsp tart red wine—an unusual thought—and simmer it all very slowly for 10 minutes. Serve on toasted and buttered trenchers of bread. . . . Personally we prefer white wine in seafood cookery, but when a Scotsman does anything there's probably a sound reason for it!

RAW OYSTERS after the BORDEAUX FASHION, or CHILLED OYSTERS with SIZZLING SMALL SAUSAGES

Just why this enticing and contradictory oyster feature hasn't become better known in the States is baffling. Not only is it a superb midnight snack, but makes a fine first course at dinner. Instead of cocktail sauce have a small very hot garlic-rubbed dish put in center of oysters on half shell, containing four sizzling hot tiny spiced sausages such as we call "cocktail" sausage. Garnish only with salt, cayenne, lemon. . . . *Voila!* Oysters cold as the poles, sausage hot as hades—and just watch the guests exclaim with favour!

EXPLODED OLD WIVES' TALES No. III, on the MAJOR SIN of WASHING ANY SORT of OYSTER out of SHELL

Next to scouring out a well-seasoned, fragrant salad bowl with hot water and soap, what could be worse than washing a fine raw oyster? Regardless of what dear old Aunt Besorah Fittich may say about germs and cleanliness—either eschew oysters entirely or else please let's not dissipate most of their delicate flavour down the drain!

WORDS to the WISE of DUAL IMPORT, BEING No. XII of the SERIES, on EATING ALL OYSTERS SUDDENLY from TIME of SHELLING, and NEVER FRAMING THEM on the FLAT SIDE of SHELL

Oysters shelled hours ago become anemic caricatures of themselves. If at all possible get them unopened in shell; serve either right from shell into pot—or on shell, chilled and fresh.

The man with soul so dead that he will bed down a neat self-respecting raw oyster on its convex, flat shell—thus permitting all the native liquor to waste itself in a welter of cracked ice, is an improperly adjusted citizen who might well be watched that he does not buy a red headed bride big purple hats, or put ice in vintage still champagne!

THE NORFOLK, VIRGINIA, OYSTER ROAST, *MARMION*, from a Stormbound Week Spent aboard Ketch in Norfolk, while a Sixty Mile Gale Walked Past outside the Capes

With downcast lash and delicately tinging cheek we submit this original dish as an exotic, generated from what to do with a bushel of unshucked oysters, five hungry shipmates and a good yacht stove! . . . Also half a dozen Smithfield Virginia hams swinging from the galley carlins, as we rocked at anchor in the tide-set, suggested trimmings. . . . First open oysters and save liquor, and, unless an adept, better leave this to the oysterman to save wrists and temper. Wash deep halves of shells, rub each with a touch of cut garlic clove, and center up with ¼ tsp scraped onion pulp. Put strained liquor—to avoid sand, gravel and other littoral addenda—in saucepan. To each cup add juice 2 limes or small lemon, double dash tabasco, and reduce by 1/3. Stir in 1 tbsp Virginia Dare Scuppernong Wine—made not too far away from where we were by our grand friend Paul Garrett—adding a little salt to taste. Thicken with a little flour and butter. Sauce should be thick, piquant. . . . Put oysters in half shells; mask with sauce, center with 2—¼" cubes of rosy Virginia ham. Pop under broiler until edges barely curl. Serve with Virginia Dare dry white wine, or Chablis.

WORDS to the WISE No. XIII, on the HARMONIOUS WEDDING of OYSTERS & Chablis

We can't say why, with all the fine dry white wines on earth,—and perhaps no one can say why—but really well chilled Chablis was simply intended for oysters in any form. It is limpid, delicately amber, suave, dry. But watch the year; '19, '21, '23, '26, or '28 are good. A poor Chablis is nothing, being both tartly sharp and of small rank or discretion.

OYSTER PAN-ROAST, *DIABLESSE,* from the Log of Fritz Abildgaard (Alone in the Caribbean) Fenger, Sailor, Author, Explorer, Raconteur, Naval Architect & Gourmet

Fritz, whom thousands of Eastern yachtsmen know, not only sailed his tiny rudderless canoe *Yakaboo* right spang from Trinidad to the Virgins, alone and across wide and dusty tide channels, but along with mate—wife—and boatswain—son—spent some years on schooner *Diablesse*—both these voyages being set down in a pair of books *Alone in the Caribbean* and *The Cruise of the Diablesse,* which appear constantly in reprint. Fritz and ourselves have swapped lies, drinks, swizzles and food receipts for some years. His oyster pan-roast is a classic which has been copied but never equalled.

Shell oysters and put in bowl, saving deep halves of shell. Wipe these dry and rub with cut garlic clove. Take a tin pie plate, or other shallow oven dish; fill level with ice cream salt or other coarse salt. Press shells down in this bed. Put oyster in each. Melt out plenty butter, add a little worcestershire and lots of Harvey's sauce, to taste; salt and paprika for added colour. . . . Pour this basting over oysters, mask with fine buttered crumbs, and brown in hot oven until edges curl—around 400°. . . . Fenger's final advice is: "That rock salt does all sorts of good things coming through the garlic and all the rest, and just why God only knows. So don't skip it. Besides it keeps the oyster shells from capsizing in a seaway. Eat as fast as they come out of oven. Good chow!"

TORCH-BEARER OYSTERS, being a Prize Receipt of Certain Distinction which May not Idly Be Ignored, Here or Anywhere

Three years or so ago Dorothea Duncan, Food Editor of the Washington *POST,* won herself a trip to Bermuda through invention of this thought, donated by the Oyster Institute of America through unanimous decision of its judges. . . . Now we do not know precisely just what the Oyster Institute of America is, or what interest they may have had—singularly or collectively—in the certainly brilliant lady Duncan. But we do know that her oyster conception is exotic enough to take position with all comers, far and near. We have noted it as a smart modern course for an amiably questing bachelor to serve, *à deux* and *chez lui,* with the electrics darkened and only the candles and the blue-blazing oysters borne to the table with ceremony and dignity befitting the occasion.

Allow 6 large or 8 small oysters to each person, and dry between towels. Oysters should be freshly opened. Next put in cocktail glasses set in cracked ice. Chill very cold. Next add a small amount of rum barely to cover: Bacardi 4 parts, Jamaica 1 part is good proportion. Set afire and bring in flaming. Garnish with quartered limes or lemons, not thinly sliced; salt, pepper, tabasco, or other flavours to taste. Too much doctoring, however, destroys the rum taste and aroma.

AN AL FRESCO DISH of UNSHELLED SHRIMPS, Browned in Brazilian Style from Rio de Janeiro

We have discovered that upon arrival in Brazil every North American is politely confronted with five circumstances by the native patriots: Brazil is larger than the continental United States, Rio has the loveliest harbour in the world, Brazil grows more coffee than any country in the world, the Amazon is the biggest river in the world, and the Brazilian ladies are the handsomest in the world. Much as we would like to discuss these matters we find that all—with possible exception of the gallant last—are strictly true.

Oddly enough, whereas the rest of South America claims to stem from Spanish discovery and settlement, Brazil is Portuguese. This shrimp dish too is Portuguese. Right today we can find the very same cooked shrimp in big baskets for sale in the streets of Lisbon or Oporto; to be eaten like popcorn on the spot, or while strolling down the avenue. It makes a rather hilarious dish to serve on a cruising yacht, on beach picnics, or when camping in shrimp territory. And, as with all crustaceans cooked in shell, we get a peculiarly delicate and satisfying native flavour retention which is lacking when they are boiled first. Rules for this dish: lots of room, plenty of paper napkins, a dish for discarded shells.

Serve heaped in a big wooden drugget, or basket; eat with fingers, discarding heads and tail shells; and of course the dark vein as well. Cook as follows: get as many shrimp as we estimate guests can eat, then 1/3 more. Have enough olive oil to fill our biggest frying pan, or deep fat kettle—and this once please don't use *any* other fat except olive oil. Heat oil to 370° Fahrenheit; chop 3 or 4 cloves of garlic and throw in with first batch of shrimp. Discard when dark brown, and renew with fresh garlic as needed to disburse flavour. When shrimp are redly done drain on paper towels, dust with salt and pepper; and there we have it.

CHINESE FRIED SHRIMP from Happily Renamed TAIWAN, in Formosa; Noted During Voyages there in 1931 & 1932

Shrimp dishes, especially deep-fried or in curries, are delicious all through the Far East—from Japan to Bombay. This dish is very simple, requires a touch of the garlic lily again which Henri Charpentier, the incomparable, lists as one of the cornerstones of fine cookery—but with no deleterious aftereffect we can assure you.

Soak 2 lbs of shelled *raw* shrimp tails in enough water to cover, to which has been added the juice of 2 limes or 1 lemon, and a sprinkling of salt. Make furrow with thumb-nail, and remove the dark sand-filled vein—*which should be done in cooking any larger shrimp: not needful with small ones.* Contrary to popular superstition this vein bears no harmful substance; merely samples of terra firma consumed with the little beastie's food. Marinate 1 hour. Drain and fry in a little very hot lard with ½ clove of garlic for 2 minutes. Add 1 cup tart white wine—like Chinese rice wine or *saki*—1 scant tbsp brown sugar, 1 tsp salt. When tender drain; and serve with a sauce made from this pan gravy diluted with equal amount of soya sauce. The sugar may be cut down slightly so as not to shock the American palate too much; also soya content may be reduced by half if guests do not admire its potent taste.

SHRIMPS DONE in KONA COAST of HAWAII STYLE

Here we offer a native dish from Kona Inn, near Kailua on the

"Big Island" of Hawaii, where big marlin swordfish, huge Pacific sailfish, and other large and violent fishes are sought after by American anglers with rods and reels. If there is a lovelier, more peacefully drowsy spot in all the world than the Kona Coast of Hawaii we have yet to find it. Made to order South Seas transplanted north of the Equator—blue water, wide beaches, rustling palms, delightful population.

Fry raw shrimp tails until very light golden red in a pan with butter, a speck of crushed garlic and a big onion sliced; salt and pepper to taste. . . . Now the sauce of coconuts. Grate kernel of 1 fresh coconut in its milk; simmer up 5 minutes gently, put whole business through cloth and squeeze out the rich cream at last. Add to pan along with 1 tbsp soya sauce per pan. . . . Drain shrimp, strain sauce and thicken with flour worked smooth. Put shrimp in buttered earthenware—or other—oven dish; mask with sauce and finally with grated white kernel of a second coconut. Brown delicately under broiler or in a very hot oven.

WORDS to the WISE No. XIV, a CREOLE CHEF'S THOUGHT on the SAVOURY BOILING of SHRIMPS

New Orleans, France and the Far East; and possibly Charleston—there we find shrimps vital and important items of food, deliciously prepared not just fried, or boiled and dumped into a cocktail glass with a dab of warm ketchup. . . . Creole chefs contend seasoning must go in first *while cooking,* not applied to the surface of flesh afterwards when it is too late to penetrate the fibres. . . . Salt water stoutly and to 1 qt add: 2 bayleaves, 6 whole cloves, 1/4 tsp tabasco or small hot pod pepper, 2 coarse chopped celery stalks, 1 pinch each thyme and basil; 1/4 to 1/2 clove garlic—optional and to taste. . . . Note the changed expression of guests when this routine produces a shrimp cocktail, or boiled shrimp for any purpose.

A *PULAO* of SHRIMPS, or PIECES of TENDER FISH, which WE FOUND JOURNEYING from the GULF of MANAAR, on the NORTH COAST of CEYLON in 1926

The cookery of southern India, Ceylon, and the Malay Peninsula, sometimes is much milder than the torrid eye-watering curries of Bengal and the Punjab country. This receipt asks for several ingredients but all of them are easily found, so try not to skip any!

To 4 cups raw shrimp allow a boiling medium consisting of milk from 2 coconuts, in which grated kernel has been simmered 10 minutes then strained through a cloth; finally squeezing rich milk out from kernel. Add juice 1 green lime, a little salt, 1/4 clove garlic. Simmer shrimp until red, drain; break off tails and shell, and remove the dark vein in the tail. Crush heads and shells and put in a sieve; pour shrimp water through several times to collect richness.

Now melt 1 cup of butter in a saucepan and fry out 3 big mild onions until golden and tender. Add 1/4 cup chopped blanched almonds, 1/2 tsp ground cinnamon, same of mace, 1/4 tsp powdered ginger, 1/2 cup raisins, 1 tsp curry powder, 1 1/2 tsp whole peppercorns and salt to taste, and the cooked shrimp. While this is cooking slowly, covered, put 1 cup thoroughly washed rice—Patna type preferred due to its solid blunter grain—into the shrimp stock. When almost tender add 1/4 to 1/2 tsp saffron, purchasable at all good grocery or drug stores. . . . Turn shrimp and trimmings onto a hot platter. Cover with rice, which has meantime absorbed all the delicious coconut-shrimp stock. Serve grated fresh coconut, grated dry smoked fish or Bombay duck, and chutney for side dishes to be passed to each guest.

CONSIDER SHRIMPS HAPPILY MARRIED with CHOPPED HAZEL NUTS, & OUR OWN PRIVATE TASTE DISCOVERY in COOKERY: FRENCH VERMOUTH of the DRY TYPE

This receipt may be varied by using chopped almonds, pistachios, piñons, or pecans. It is quick and easy, and very flavourful. . . . Fry 1 lb fresh shrimp tails that have been marinated 2 hours in 1/2 cup of blended lemon juice and olive oil, in 3 tbsp butter, along with 1/2 clove garlic. Reserve this marinade. When done, discard garlic. Put shrimps on a hot dish. Add 1/2 cup finely chopped nuts to hot butter in the pan; add lemon-oil marinade, perhaps adding more lemon juice to tart taste. Now 2 dashes tabasco and 1 1/2 to 2 tbsp dry French vermouth.

Simmer 5 minutes and turn over shrimp. We've added 2 tbsp tomato paste with good results, on occasion.

BROILED TURTLE STEAKS, *á ISLA de PIÑOS,* BEING a RECEIPT from an AMERICAN PINEAPPLE PLANTER in ESTATES there before OUR GOVERNMENT RETURNED the ISLAND to CUBA

Steaks may be from green, hawkbill or loggerhead turtles, but not too thick or too aged—½″ to ¾″ thickness is correct. Rub with cut lime vigorously so as to get oil from peel into steak, rub with a cut clove of garlic, sprinkle with salt and let stand in squeezed juice of lime for 1 hour. Brush with lots of olive oil and broil like any steak over coals or under broiler, seasoning to taste.

SMOTHERED TURTLE in the MISSISSIPPI *CAJUN* STYLE, a LUSCIOUS, EASY CLASSIC from the VAST DELTA COUNTRY

The Cajuns are strange people, a blend of Portuguese, Indian, and heaven only knows what else. They fish, shrimp, trap fur in the maze of bayous and marshes of the big Delta. Priests wade into the water and bless their shrimp boats at start of season. They know how to cook turtles. Our only recommended addition is a small can of chopped button mushrooms.

Trim 2 lbs steaks into 1½″ squares, season well with salt and hand-ground black pepper, squeeze on some lemon or sour orange juice and stand a while. Add plenty of chopped onion, a sweet pepper chopped well, 3 or 4 tomatoes cut into eighths, 3 bayleaves, a crushed garlic clove, and mushrooms. . . . Moisten well with stock made by boiling salted turtle trimmings, and smother very slowly in tightly covered skillet until turtle is tender. Serve with big mounds of rice. This will nourish 4 hungry folk.

A NATIVE TURTLE SOUP from MEXICO, GULF of CAMPECHE STYLE; and a KINDRED DISH, which IS ACTUALLY a STEW of FRESH WATER TURTLES DONE IN their own SHELLS, & KNOWN as *CALIPASH* by Our Afro-American Plantations, Will Be Found on Page 45, under *SOUPS*

ARCHBISHOP ALFRIC: "And what, Good Cook, is thy Profession worth to the Community?"
COOK: "Holiness, without me all People would have to Eat both Greens & Flesh Raw."
ARCHBISHOP ALFRIC: "But might not they Readily Dress such Viands Themselves?"
COOK: "Ah yes, Holiness, but in Such Case all Men would be Reduced to the Role of Servant."

Literal Version from *Archbishop Alfric's COLLOQUY,*
England, 10th Century

CHAPTER VI

POULTRY & *THE* INNER DRESSINGS *OF* FOWLS

Dealing Briefly with Ducks, Geese and Turkeys, but Being Concerned mainly with Chickens; Remembering *Rijstafel,* which Is in Reality a Lordly Curry Ceremony from Lovely Java, *Arroz con Pollo* from Panama, the *Small Water Angels of Soochow;* Tortola Chicken Baked in Coconuts, a Louisiana Jambalaya, not Forgetting a Guadeloupe Dish Called *Poulet aux Pistaches de Terre et Bananes, à la Morne sans Toucher.*

During all our collection of poultry receipts we long ago decided not to enter into the technique of frying, roasting and the like, but try, rather, to offer a totally new list of dishes; each notable for this special reason or that, and all possible anywhere within reach of a decent grocery store.

Ducks, geese and turkeys are touched upon very lightly and that part of the text is devoted mainly to a few pertinent words of cooking technique, on bastings or sauces that have delighted us in times past. Guineas and pigeons we feel, have always felt in fact, are more correctly game than tame barnyard fowl, and for that reason are treated in the GAME Chapter following.

Those receipts immediately following this paragraph all possess some marked nuance of flavour, a touch of herb, of fruit, a certain basting, this or that seasoning, completely elevating them above an everyday question of cooking in frying pan, on grill, or in oven. Seasoning, as always, may be varied from mild into the very torrid classification, to suit individual taste and digestive apparatus; therefore we suggest that the amateur approach each dish still fired with a spirit of adventure and vary the overtones to harmonize with mood and larder. Our one bit of advice in poultry cookery of the usual sort is to remind readers that the usual fault is dryness. Therefore in roasting or grilling, brush well with fat, baste diligently. All items about to be fried should be blotted or wiped dry in order to avoid those miniature and painful volcanic eruptions of hot fat caused by water drops exploding into steam.

All items to be boiled should be started in cold water, simmered gently; and bear in mind that if they are boiled *beyond* the point of being tender they will be stringy, sodden and lack flavour.

If broilers have passed the adolescent and tender birthday usually associated with such cookery, a few moments of gentle steaming will work wonders, before putting into the fat.

ARROZ con POLLO, the OLD TRADITIONAL "RICE with CHICKEN," NOTED in the UNION CLUB, PANAMA CITY, during ONE of OUR DOZEN or so TRIPS to the ISTHMUS

Cristobal on the Atlantic and Balboa on the Pacific—those are the model towns under Uncle Sam's jurisdiction in the "Zone," and they lie like neat, prim, starched maidens, cheek-by-jowl with the modern evolution of the civilization left by the Conquistadores for better or for worse in Colon and Panama City. There in Old Panama the ruined cathedral tower points up an accusing finger denouncing its sack and burning by Morgan's men. Culture and lotteries, courtly Spanish girls with big gazelle eyes whisk by in shiny motor cars and guarded closely by their duennas; while a block away is the so-called Coconut Grove section with ladies of all nations behind their grilled windows. . . . In the Union Club, perched high on stilts above the huge Pacific tides is where the cream of Panamanian society gathers. They have a good chef there. His *Arroz con Pollo,* although basically still the old favourite from Spain, has local and tropical touches. It will nourish from four to six guests.

2 plump chickens of tender years
6 thin slices dead ripe pineapple
2 tbsp lime or lemon juice
½ cup fine bread crumbs
1 tsp, scant, of tabasco sauce
Salt and pepper, to taste
2 pinches saffron
4 to 5 cups of Spanish rice
½ cup raisins or currants
4 tbsp tomato paste
1 orange, sliced quite thin
1 cup butter
½ cup sherry wine
½ cup guava jelly for garnish

Cut chicken into pieces, brush with lime juice, season with salt and pepper; let marinate in this lime juice and seasoning both for 2 hrs to seal in flavours. Now fry gently in butter, and when tender add tomato paste, raisins, wine and other seasonings. Stir once, cover tightly and keep warm but do *not* cook again. . . . On a large hot platter make a ring of Spanish Saffron Rice, and in the center of this pleasant atoll pile the chicken. Turn sauce over chicken also. Meanwhile cut up ripe fresh pineapple slices into 1″ square bits and fry out for 5 minutes with the crumbs—using canned fruit if no really ripe fresh ones at hand; but discard the juice entirely. Turn this over the chicken, garnish with thin slices of orange, mounting a crimson jewel of guava jelly on each slice. . . . Scarlet pimento also garnishes well.

TO MAKE SPANISH SAFFRON RICE

Take 1 cup rice; pick out any dark grains or foreign substances, but do not wash. Put 2 tbsp olive oil in the top of a double boiler, place directly on a slow fire and gently fry out 1 finely minced onion with half a bisected garlic clove. When tender, discard garlic, turn in the cup of rice, ¼ tsp saffron, ½ tsp salt. Stir well and add just enough beef or chicken broth to cover. Cook uncovered in a double boiler until tender, adding more broth as needed. Stir gently with a *wooden* fork to keep from breaking grains. When tender, turn into a shallow pan and dry in a *warm*—not hot—oven. Rice should be quite dry.

CHICKEN BAKED with PLUMPED RAISINS, VARYING NUTS, WINE & LIMES, *á GUATEMALTECAN*

We collected this one in hauntingly beautiful *Antigua Vieja,* set like a neglected white gem 7000 feet up in the Guatemalan mountains, when we and our then recent bride were making pilgrimage down the west coast of Mexico and Central America. There in Antigua we found an amazing half deserted city of broken marble and stone and stucco, cracked and rent palaces and churches, huge crumbling dwellings of long-dead Spanish aristocrats, all stricken by the earthquake of 1773. The whole place was like a city under a spell, most buildings being inhabited by Indian families; sometimes with several packed in a wing, in a single room, of a house; and cooking fires blackening wonderful frescoes, or a carved white marble frieze! Once the richest city in the New World, in all this strange contrast we found a hushed and tragic charm brooding over the place, with the volcanic peaks of *Agua* and *Fuego* soaring a mile higher still, back of the place, from whence the fire and boiling water came to smother Antigua over a century and a half ago. But a few good Spanish names still carry on gallantly. We have a German acquaintance who operates a small inn, in what was once the cloister of a nunnery. He knows these people well. This dish came from his place; a memory of a luxurious and by-gone era.

2 plump young chickens
1/3 cup chopped blanched almonds
1 sweet pepper chopped fine
1 cup butter
3" piece cinnamon bark; 2 bay-leaves
1 dash Angostura bitters
2 limes sliced very thin
3 large onions, sliced thin
1 doz large stuffed olives, sliced
½ cup raisins or currants
Enough bread crumbs to stuff
Salt and pepper to taste
½ cup sherry or Madeira wine

Wipe chickens inside and out, then stuff with the mixed raisins, onions and chopped pepper—this last peeled by scalding, and seeds removed. Season highly and add enough bread crumbs to fill the cavities. Sew up neatly, brush the birds with a little lime juice, dust with salt and pepper, and brown lightly in a pan of hot butter. . . . The next step is to cover the bottom of a buttered oven dish with sliced limes, add two dashes or so of Angostura; then come the successive layers of almonds, coarsely sliced almond-stuffed olives—or ripe olives—then the stick of cinnamon broken into bits, 2 bayleaves, and finally the chickens. Put in all the frying butter. . . . Cover tightly and roast these comely twins in this fragrant atmosphere very slowly until tender, at around 275°. A few minutes before taking out remove the cover, sprinkle on the wine. Peanuts, Brazil or cashew nuts, all lend distinctive variations to this dish. Chop them up coarsely.

SIZEABLE OLIVES STUFFED with CHOPPED BREASTS of CHICKEN, a TRIFLE of HAM, NUTMEGS, PARMA or ROMAN CHEESE, a TOUCH of SWEET WINE, then FRIED in BATTER in DEEP FAT

Whenever we get to Naples we always look up Pat Marighliano about sundown, when his job as head guide for American Express finds him weary and ready for food and rest. Then Pat searches out odd spots unknown to outlanders, where red mullets are cooked in mysterious ways, and shrimps, and succulent bits of cuttlefish deep-fried in boiling oil—all washed down with white dry Pomino wine from Tuscany, and then when we are full and tobacco comes out, there is always an old Italian with what was once a glorious tenor, perhaps in La Scala, and a guitar for him to sing by. And Pat orders tiny glasses for both of us and we take green Certoza in the hawk's-foot-and-ball pottery bottle, and he always gets blood red Alchermes, which is a cordial compounded for objects problematical but charming to our naive mind, and which embraces—among other things—spices like cinnamon, clove, and coriander, and perfumed with jasmine, or rose essence, or iris. And alcohol too, of course, in strength enough.

Then sometimes before we eat, the Madonna of the house fetches in a small basket to keep us busy while the kitchen affairs progress, and once in a basket we found these fried stuffed olives, which would make a delicious relief from the eternal pigs-in-blankets our hostesses seem to have lurking on every hors d'oeuvre tray these days! Better allow 6 olives for each guest present.

Cooked chicken white meat & ham to fill, both minced very finely
12 huge stoned Spanish olives
3 pinches grated nutmeg
2 tsp butter
1½ tsp freshly grated Parma cheese
1 beaten yolk to bind stuffing
Salt and pepper, to taste
Enough simple frying batter to cover

Take cooked chicken and lean smoked ham in these proportions: 2 parts chicken to 1 of ham. Mix well, season, and brown lightly in butter; add the nutmeg. Draw off fire and let cool. Now mix in beaten yolk, pack tightly in olive jackets, cap with grated cheese, dip in batter and brown in deep fat at 370°—olive oil being traditional, of course. Drain on paper or cloth. Serve sizzling hot.

THE LOUISIANA *CALALOU,* which Is Strictly a Catch-All Dish Inherited from West Africa through the Plantation Cooks of the Great Delta Country, Has Been Listed in a Succeeding Chapter under *MEAT DISHES both TEMPERATE & TROPICAL,* Page 143.

A GUADELOUPE DISH of JUVENILE FOWLS, Cooked *en CASSEROLE* with Bananas, Herbs, a Little Wine, Coconut Milk & Chopped Peanuts, & which Was Called: *POULET aux PISTACHES de TERRE et BANANES, à la MORNE sans TOUCHER*

Lovely Guadeloupe has been discussed elsewhere in this volume, also the place of the little Frenchman by the warm mineral springs far back in the hills out of Point à Pitre. In Guadeloupe as well as in Haiti, a *Morne* indicates a high mountain, for all high mountains in the tropics—especially with trade winds blowing—mean very prevalent fog or wind-cloud, hence the title "Gloomy."

This dish is very simple, and all ingredients are at the corner grocery in these days of enlightened cookery. . . . The basic requirement is for 2 fowls of discretionary and tender years, and plump as may be. Cut them into 4 major parts, each; brush with the juice of 2 limes, or 1 lemon, dust with salt and pepper, and brown delicately in

¼ lb butter. Now add 3 tbsp finely chopped smoked bacon or ham, 2 tbsp chopped spring onion, 1 tiny red podded hot pepper, or 3 dashes tabasco, 4 bayleaves and ¼ tsp each of thyme and basil. About ½ cup sweet white wine comes next, the pot is covered, and set on a slow fire.

Now take a ripe husked coconut, puncture 2 of the "eyes" and reserve the milk. Crack open the nut, grate the white part of the kernel, add to the milk and simmer 5 or 10 minutes. Drain through a cheesecloth, wringing at the last to extract the rich creamy juice. Add this to the cooking pot, and recover. Cut up 3 red bananas, or yellow, and along with ¼ cup of chopped roasted peanuts, impart their gifts to the steaming delight. Simmer very gently until chickens are tender, adding a bit of water, wine or chicken broth, if it seems to dry out too much. Serve steaming hot, garnish with snipped parsley, and offer barley as a companion dish, or boiled rice.

JAMBALAYA, Louisiana Bayou Style, & Done with Chicken

This famous creole dish comes down to us from mixed Spanish-French parentage, seasoned and tempered by the Afro-American Parish plantation cooks of the Delta, or among the bayous where they raised sugar cane, rich black Perique tobacco that comes from no other spot on earth, rice, or tabasco peppers. This particular formula is from the notebook of a friend now living and writing on Royal Street in a lovely ancient house down in the old French quarter.

Like a *Calalou, Jambalaya* may be varied with the meats and vegetables on shelf; veal or tender lamb may substitute for chicken; but rice must always be included, and piquant seasonings are traditional. This dish will serve six guests.

Take 2½ cups of minced chicken and 1½ cups of boiled rice which is not quite done. Mix together in saucepan and reserve. Fry out gently 1 big minced onion, a tiny speck of crushed garlic, 1 cup sliced okra—optional—2 cups of skin-free cooked tomato, 1 chopped green pepper, 1 small head of chopped celery, and 1 bunch of snipped parsley, in 2 tbsp lard or butter. When onion colours slightly, mix with chicken—rice; add 3 dashes tabasco and ¼ tsp ground mace.

Butter a pottery oven dish well, turn everything into it, cover with lots of bread crumbs fried a couple of minutes in 1 tbsp of butter, and brown in medium oven around 350°.

THE TRUE EAST INDIAN *MULLIGATAWNY,* which MORE OFTEN IS ACTUALLY a STEW & NOT a SOUP; which IS a CURRY, yet NOT STRICTLY a CURRY; & IS MADE of FOWLS, COCONUT MILK, HERBS, CURRY & LENTILS

We picked this up on our first trip out to India, and we guarantee it to produce the finest mid-afternoon siesta imaginable. Out at the bungalow at Juhu Beach, 14 miles above Bombay, where the Arabian Sea bathes tawny level sand wide enough for morning polo games, it was a great Sunday favourite. For 4:

Joint 1 chicken and cut into small pieces. Heat 1/8 lb butter and lightly brown 2 medium sized minced onions, and 1/2 clove crushed garlic, until they are golden brown—then discard the more potent lily, if so desired; your Indian cook always leaves it in! . . . Mix 1 tbsp curry powder with 1 tsp salt, then work smooth with a little of the hot butter, and add to onions. Brown chicken in butter drained off the onions, reserve edible meat, and put rack and all bones into a good sized kettle. Add onions to this, and the enriched milk of a coconut as described in second receipt before this one. Put on slow fire, add 2 bayleaves, the lentils previously soaked overnight in cold water, lots of black and cayenne pepper until quite hot, add 2 cups chicken broth or stock. Simmer for 1 hour, remove chicken racks, gristle and bits of skin, cook uncovered until soup-sauce is thick as heavy cream. Squeeze in the juice of 1 lime or 1/2 lemon, put the meat back. Simmer up once more and serve with a side dish of rice prepared in the true Oriental fashion noted on Page 96 under *Rijstafel.*

POLLO MOLÉ en PIPIÁN, à la RESTAURANT PAOLO, BEING an IMPORTANT MEXICAN DISH of DEBUTANTE FOWLS, PIÑON NUTS or BLANCHED ALMONDS, PEANUTS, SWEET PEPPERS & SOUR CREAM, to SAY NOTHING of GRATED ORANGE PEELS & SPICE

Here is another dish that beckons to the pleasant depravity of the siesta, after *almuerzo*—the heavy Mexican noon meal—during or, rather, after which our right-minded citizen down there avoids all outdoor exercises, sunlight, and extra-mural distraction of every species. It may come as a surprise to readers that in Mexico City the best Mexican cookery is not to be found in public restaurants, or hotels or night clubs, but right in the homes of local citizenry. After midnight, for instance, there isn't a decent bite to eat to be found. Gentlemen and ladies are supposed to get home at sane hours. Butch's—an enormous place, once a marble galleried bank and now a restaurant run by an American negro—offers good ordinary food; some of the hotels are good enough in the same way that average American hotels are good, but only Restaurant Paolo in that huge city of a million folk affords truly fine cookery—and that had to be produced by an Italian, as far as we could learn! Here we found lovely *Mexicano* food with European tendencies, beautifully prepared and beautifully expensive. This one was retained for your approval. It is very similar to the various legion of Mexican *Molé* dishes, but contains only the simple sweet bell pepper as we know it.

Pipián is actually a flour made of toasted squash seeds, and used for thickening sauces. Our secret is to say nothing and use cornstarch. Not even the oldest Mexican gourmet can tell the difference! . . . Start the chicken simmering in slightly salted water, with 2 bayleaves. Cover tightly. When tender cut into small joints, discarding rack; reserve stock. . . . Now mince a medium sized onion, 2 tomatoes, 4 sweet peppers and 2 cloves of garlic. Add 2 tbsp chile powder. Fry until tender in 2 tbsp olive oil, lard or butter.

We need 1½ pints of chicken stock, so if not enough on hand add a little canned broth. Add this stock to vegetables, put in ¼ cup sour cream, and also donate a speck of bitter chocolate the size of a thumbnail, 2 pinches each of clove and nutmeg, plenty of black pepper, 2 small red pod peppers, or equivalent tabasco; add 1/3 of the finely chopped nuts, and grated yellow peel of an orange. Simmer 20 minutes, mix 2 to 3 tbsp cornstarch with a little hot broth, work out lumps and stir in. Simmer until reduced by ¼, put in The Blender or rub through a coarse sieve, put chicken back; simmer up once more and serve. This *Molé* sauce must be rich and thick.

A *PILAFF* of CHICKEN LIVERS, *à la Turc,* BEING a SIMPLE *PILAFF* CHARACTERISTIC of the NEAR EAST, and FOUND in the KING DAVID HOTEL, in JERUSALEM, shortly after NEW YEARS in 1931

There are as many kinds of *Pilaff* or *Pilaw* in Turkey and Persia as there are *Pulaos* in India, or Spaghettis in Italy! This is typical. Make a ring of Saffron Rice, similar to that mentioned on Page 87 under *Arroz con Pollo,* and into the center heap a saute made out of chicken livers, a handful of chopped ripe olives, a similar amount of cubed eggplant, a pimento, chopped cooked mushrooms. A touch of curry is optional, but we find that even better still is to add 2 tbsp sherry wine—which Mohammed the Prophet doesn't approve of!

POLLO PIÑA, BEING a DISH of CHICKENS SMOTHERED with RIPE PINEAPPLE PULP, LIME PEEL, BROWN SUGAR, a SLIGHT GIFT of BACARDI RUM, & other AMIABILITIES

We have a schoolmate now "in sugar" with one of the big *centrales* in Camagüey Province, Cuba. He reports this dish may be made with 2 cups of canned pineapple pulp, but best results come from picking a fresh fruit as ripe as possible—standing in direct sunlight until quite soft. It will serve from 4 to 6 hungry guests. Bacardi flavour in cooking is mild, and any brown rum may be substituted.

Have 2 broilers cut into quarters, wipe dry, brush with lime juice, dust with salt and pepper, then flour; finally browning gently in 2 tbsp butter with cover tightly on pan. . . . When tender turn in 1 medium sized minced onion, 3 tbsp currants, peel of 2 limes grated, 1 tsp brown sugar, 2 average sized tomatoes rubbed through a coarse sieve, salt and pepper to taste. Crush up the pineapple in a mortar or bowl; or cut up, add enough juice to cover blades, and reduce to pulp and stir in. Simmer until reduced by 1/4, put in The Blender or rub then add 3 tbsp *Carta de Oro* Bacardi, or 2 tbsp brown rum. Saffron Rice is the best possible side dish.

NOW a TRUE BOMBAY *PULAO,* which Is a Stew Dish Made of Chickens, Spices, Herbs, Raisins, Rice & other Things—Being Similar to Many Spanish or Mexican Dishes, yet Subtly Different

This name is derived from the Persian *Pilaw,* and it is mother to the term "Purlo," or "Purloo," that to our southern darky cook means chicken cooked with rice-and-things. At first glance it may seem to parallel tropical Americana recently listed here, but in actual result it is not so hot in pepper content, but somewhat higher in spice. Raisins, as is the case in Spain and Latin America, are typical additions to meat throughout the Near East and East, and it more than likely was Spain's luck to inherit their use via the Moorish conquest of the Iberian Peninsula. . . . This dish was cooked for us by the Mohammedan Head Bearer of a friend living in Bombay, after return from a hunt away back in the Mahratti hill country.

Mature fowls may be used, but be sure they are plump and fat. First set chicken to simmer in lightly salted water, just enough to cover, and when tender cut into joints, discarding racks. Cut up giblets and add to chicken. Now heat ½ lb butter and lightly brown 3 big thinly sliced onions; add 2 tbsp raisins, 5 or 6 whole cloves, 3 tbsp chopped almonds, ⅛ tsp powdered ginger, ¼ tsp mace, 6 whole peppercorns, ½ tsp cinnamon, and 1 crushed clove of garlic. . . . Turn in ¾ cup dry rice, and the stock from cooking chicken. Cover tightly, do not stir or rice grains will break; and lastly be careful to keep at low heat so as not to burn. Just before rice is tender all through take a little broth and simmer it with 2 pinches saffron, and add to *Pulao* for typical colour. A trifling amount of curry is proper, but not imperative. Personally we prefer to ignore it in the dish.

WORDS to the WISE No. XV, Being a ÇANNY MOHAMMEDAN BIT of ADVICE from HEAD BEARER ALI SIDDIQ, *PULAO* CHEF *par EXCELLENCE,* on WHEN & HOW to CUT up CHICKEN for SUCH DISHES

If we cut up chicken before boiling down for stock and to tender, the flesh falls to shreds too quickly. If we attempt to cut up after the dish is done, the flesh gets torn to bits. Therefore cut chicken into as small bits as possible directly after being first tendered, and it is removed from the stock pot. Always use a keen knife for this operation.

NOW a FEW NOTES on that SUPER CURRY KNOWN as *RIJSTAFEL* in the DUTCH EAST INDIES, & MORE PARTICULARLY in JAVA where IT REACHES ITS MAJESTIC PINNACLE, in CLUBS like the FAMOUS *CONCORDIA* on *WATERLOOPLEIN*, the *HARMONIE;* in HOMES of DUTCH OFFICIALS and COMMERCIAL PRINCES, in HOTELS such as the *DES INDES* & the *NEDERLANDEN*

This dish is a classic everywhere throughout Holland's far-flung island empire of the East Indies. Literally translated it means "rice table," but that explanation is only half truth because a true *Rijstafel* is one of those inconceivable things which must be seen to be credited. These stout Hollanders are probably the only European nationals who can thus stuff themselves frequently in a climate like an orchid house, and live. Yet they do, and thrive on it.

Our first sight of this business was in 1932. We had chartered a plane for ourself, and with Ruth Elder, another charming young lady who was then our fiancée, her mother, and other adventurous souls, had set out to fly as near to Bali as we could get from Batavia by the Koninklijke Nederlandsche Indische Luchtvaart Maatschappij plane —ending up in Soerabaja after a look-see at the startling stupa of gigantic Boeroboedoer outside of Semarang. At the *Oranje* in Soerabaja we met up with a gray haired septuagenarian named Whitney, as we now recall it, who built bridges for profit and was then retired. His hobby was catching fish—anywhere and everywhere. He had just popped up from landing big rainbow trout in the mountain torrents of New Zealand, to dangle his baits before the suspicious snouts of some odd sort of fish or other he had recently heard tore tackle apart away up the Barito River in Borneo, and having caught them to heart's content, was now taking the "pig boat"—really an immaculate little KPM steamer—to Bali where there was a fantastic tale about fantastic fish lurking in the steel blue crater lake nestling at the foot of the sulphurously active lava cone of *Goenung Batoer* at *Kintimani.*

We saw him later and found those furious fish were a species of catfish—but that is another story! anyway, we happened to be looking at a table of a dozen Hollanders wondering how in heaven's name they could stand such tropical heat in their high tight military collars, when from the kitchen door came a winding queue of some fourteen or fifteen barefoot boys, in brown patterned batik sarongs and head kerchiefs, each bearing some sort of ceremonial dish. "Ah! A *Rijstafel!*" cried our fishing gentleman. "You should see one the Dutch Governor gave for the Sultan of Djokjakarta. There were fifty-five boys in line!"

We watched, fascinated. All twelve Hollanders sat up straight and serious. Hollanders are not a dour race, as so many writers have falsely written. They are a gay, jolly and even boisterous race—but, by thunder, eating proper *rijstafel* is a serious affair to be treated seriously and respectfully!

RIJSTAFEL ROUTINE for an AVERAGE SERVICE of DUTCH CURRY

First the Number One boy appears with a big platter or bowl heaped with more and whiter rice than we dream can be piled on any one platter. . . . Each guest heaps his plate with a bigger heap than we dream any mortal can consume at a sitting. This milestone reached, conversation resumes, and the gentlemen resume sipping de Kuyper *schnapps,* gin slings perhaps, but more likely they will consume endless big sweating brown quart bottles of Amstel beer to lay the dust and cool the pipes before its torrid attack so imminently present.

After the Number One comes the file of boys, looking like an American college snake dance, only come bearing gifts in platters; and at their head proudly stalks the Number Two, bearing as his appointed duty a big bowl holding vast tonnage of chicken curry still steaming in its own perfumed juices. Each guest makes a crater in his mountain of rice and heaps it brimming full of curry, spreading the sauce evenly over the rice.

Now the condiments, which vary from several kinds of chutney to small ground up forcemeat balls of deceased piscatorial citizens whose demise—judging from their scent—must have been sometime in the fairly remote past, and which the average westerner can't stare down—met eye to eye. For this reason we list only those condiments and trimmings easily had from the corner grocery, or at most through a letter to some large-town fine grocery in New York, Chicago or San Francisco.

1. Mango chutney of 2 kinds, hot and hotter. Both Indian types.
2. Bombay Duck, which is no duck at all, but a small dried fish peculiar to the Malabar Coast of India. This is usually broken up small and spread on the curry, or munched—as the guest wills.
3. Finely shredded smoked codfish, bought in fillets, toasted crisp in the oven, boned and broken fine.
4. Small bits of diced eggplant, fried in oil and highly seasoned, to taste.
5. Chopped hardboiled egg, both yolk and white together.
6. Plain freshly grated ripe coconut kernel—*not* the shredded, tasteless species Aunt Clutie-Belle uses on her birthday cakes.
7. Finely chopped orange peel, yellow part only.
8. Finely chopped pomelo, or grapefruit, peel; yellow part only.
9. Finely chopped mild onion.
10. Finely chopped sweet green pepper.
11. Shredded, sun-ripe pineapple. Buy one as ripe as possible, then put in full sun until soft as can be without inviting decayed or spoiled spots in outer shell. Slice lengthwise after peeling, cut into eighths, then remove all tough portions, using only ripe, softer pulp.
12. Chopped blanched nuts: cashews, almonds or peanuts; roasted almost black.
13. Small plumped raisins or currants. Scald to plump.
14. Fried ripe bananas, cut in cross slices, and dusted with brown sugar, clove and cinnamon.

This, now, will give us a fair sized *Rijstafel* curry. There is no East Indian Emily Post to worry about manners or technique with these trimmings. Most folk spread everything evenly over rice and curry on the plate, then mix the entire outlay with a sort of mortar-spading motion using fork, or knife, or both.

Guests may ignore certain condiments; others take all, and in varying amount. Some of these items may appear strange, if not out and out whimsical, but each one has been included for a purpose; each one has, through the test of lusty fork work and time, become accepted as correct; each one through its own small virtue seizes upon the basic curry-rice flavours, and points them up to hitherto unsuspected eminence much the way ambergris—itself a rather unprofitable odour—can, even in trifling amount, make a perfume essence into something miraculously impossible hitherto.

A SIMPLE CURRY ROUTINE for the AMERICAN HOUSEHOLD

Our Filipino Number One, Esteban Lueña, was once chef on a destroyer in the tropics. He has just whipped up a simple buffet supper party for a few kindred curry addicts. . . . At one end of the main table there were hot plates, silver. In front of these was a large wooden bowl of hot cooked Patna rice—buyable through any good store at a few days' notice, and having a plumper better grain shape for curry. . . . In the center of the table was a smaller bowl or platter of cooked curry; meat, sauce and all.

From this point onward, starting with mango chutney came small dishes of condiments with a spoon in each. Everyone mixed and blended to his, or her taste; and a vast amount of ale was on hand to put out the resulting inward conflagration. To make a curry party perfect, Roman couches really should be provided, if pertinent in risk, for every diner promptly begins to nod drowsily soon after.

TO COOK a PROPER DISH of RICE for CURRY, or any other PURPOSE, for that MATTER

Just as America has the handsomest ladies and the fanciest bath tubs in Christendom, she has won an all time low medal for rice cookery. Just why this relatively simple task should result in a sodden, compact, almost plastic mass of broken rice kernels is something no one has yet explained. For true cooked rice production, here is the easiest Oriental method. When cooked, rice should be a pleasant sight; each grain firm, yet done all through; each grain amiably separated from its neighbour; white, gleaming, enticing.

1. Use Patna rice, due to the better shape of grain. Wash thoroughly in several waters until all loose starch is gone and water is no longer cloudy.
2. To 1 cup uncooked rice allow 3 qts briskly boiling water to which has been added juice ½ lemon and 3 tsp of salt. Lemon juice keeps the rice white in hard water.
3. Put rice in a little at a time. Never stir with a spoon. Use wooden fork and "lift" the grains if they tend to stick. After 10 to 12 minutes, test grain between thumb and finger to see if it is soft all through. Job takes from about 12 to 20 minutes, depending on type of rice being used.
4. Check boiling instantly by adding 1 pint cold water.
5. Put into a collander or coarse sieve, and when drained turn into a shallow pan *very lightly* greased with butter and put into a *warm,* not hot, oven. In this way grains will dry nicely, swell, and keep separated.

AND NOW ANOTHER BRIEF LIST of Curry Requisites Involving Preparation of the Actual Curry Itself

1. Always stir curries with a wooden spoon. The strong natural chemicals of the sauce cause metal spoons to taste.
2. Never stand a curry powder bottle where light can strike it, for in this way flavour departs. . . . Without in any way being commercial we cannot but mention that Captain White's Curry Paste, which any good grocery may import from England through his agents, is the next best thing to a home-ground, freshly made curry powder—which last is too complicated to be possible in the average American household.
3. Never use all lean meat in curry. This applies mainly when using lamb, and four-footed flesh. Plan 2 parts lean to 1 of fat. This adds richness and character.
4. Meat should be cut around ½″ thick, and not over 1″ square, so that curry flavour may penetrate all through.
5. Eschew potatoes in any self-respecting curry. They blot up flavour from other things. Any proper British Colonial curry-master views potatoes in curry with the same mortification as he would if dear old Aunt Carbona should unlimber toothpicks at a Court garden party.

6. The vegetables in curry may be varied: cucumbers and eggplant are traditional; hardboiled eggs—duck eggs especially—added soon before service, are also good. Onions are imperative, and no curry worthy of the name was ever made without at least a touch of garlic. In fact, our Filipino boy puts ½ clove in the rice boiling water with no noticeable aftereffects of an ostracizing nature.
7. Besides chicken, which is favourite with western palates, excellent curries may be made of breast of veal, veal cutlets, lamb, mutton, sweetbreads; lobster, shrimp, any form of white fish, eels, oysters, prawns, crawfish or *langoustes;* rabbit or hare; leftover fowl such as goose, duck or guineafowl; even crabmeat and small tender clams.
8. Roughly these are the basic proportions: 1 to 1½ tablespoons of curry powder, with ¼ lb butter, with 2½ lbs or slightly more, of combined meat and vegetables to be curried.
9. Always melt out butter, then work in curry powder until it makes a smooth paste, in order to avoid lumpiness.

NOW a MADRAS CURRY of YOUNG CHICKENS, which MAY BE USED as BASIS for *RIJSTAFEL,* which WE PICKED up in SOUTH-EASTERN INDIA in 1926, during a TRIP from the GULF of MANAAR to CALCUTTA

An expert can tell a Bengali curry from one of Madras, from that of Malay type. We aren't clever enough to pick out varying Indian currys, but find that Malay curries usually are slightly milder, and naturally tend to involve seafood more often than inland dishes. Most Indian curries include enriched coconut milk, made by simmering grated kernel in the milk of a ripe nut, then squeezing through a cheesecloth to extract cream—this taking the place of the almond milk used here.

1 plump, tender fowl, meat only
3 average onions, minced
2 tsp sugar; salt to taste
2 tbsp chutney, chopped up
1 handful of small raisins
¼ cup blanched almonds
½ cup cream or milk
Flour, enough to dredge pieces
½ clove garlic, crushed well
8 whole peppercorns
½ tsp powdered ginger
1 cucumber in ½″ cubes; a big one
1½ cups chicken stock or broth
1¼ tbsp curry powder

Melt butter, roll boned bits of chicken in flour and brown lightly. Take out and put in saucepan, and meantime brown onion and garlic gently in the butter also. Work curry powder smooth with some hot butter, stir in chicken stock, chutney, raisins, peppercorns and salt to taste. Cover and simmer gently. . . . Meanwhile fry finely chopped almonds in a little additional butter, and when light brown turn into stout bowl and pound to paste. Heat the cream and add almonds, stirring constantly, for 5 minutes; being careful not to burn. After curry has simmered for ½ hr add the almond-milk combination, and the onions. Uncover curry pot and simmer that way until gravy is thick and rich, bearing in mind that East Indian curry does not depend on flour or other thickening for the major part of its density of sauce, but on thorough reduction by cooking heat. Finally squeeze in the juice of ½ lemon. If it dries out too much, add a little chicken or veal stock. . . . Curry strength may be raised or lowered to individual preference. It is wonderful in hot weather.

A ROYAL RUSSIAN DISH of SAUTE BREASTS of TINY CHICKENS, *à la SMITANE,* as SERVED at the BUNGALOW of ONE COSSACK NAMED BOYDYENKO in 1926, just BEFORE, for REASONS NEVER PUBLISHED, HE SUDDENLY RESIGNED from a POSITION on the ADVISORY STAFF of the YOUNG CHINESE ARMY

This dish is a delicate thing worthy of low lights, our best still white not-too-dry wine, and a charming companion *à deux*. . . . Only use small well-fed squab chickens, breasts only. Dust chicken lightly with salt. Poach delicately in plenty of hot butter and ¼ cup tart white wine, then when light brown place on hot silver platter and reserve. Meantime sauce should be under way. To make 1 cup:

Use just a trace of butter in a saucepan and gently cook 1 small sliced onion, 2 or 3 chopped spring onions, and a dash of salt and cayenne, until clear and tender. Add 1/3 cup dry white wine and 2/3 cup sour cream—or fresh cream warmed 15 minutes—with 1 tsp lemon juice. Simmer gently, uncovered; add salt and cayenne to final taste. When reduced to consistency of heavy cream, put through a sieve. Pour over chicken and garnish with crossed strips of scarlet pimento. May be served flaming by putting a little heated brandy in a ring around the silver platter, and setting alight.

CHICKEN *TORTOLA,* which Is as Good a Name as any for Chicken Baked in the Shells of Ripe Coconuts, Tropical Style

Just to the eastward of our own St. Thomas lies the British island of Tortola, with Road Town—which, by the way has no road!—its main town, and capital of the British Virgins. The outdoor and indoor sports of Tortola seem to be fishing, treasure hunting, begetting children—both black, white and khaki—and fishing. Their cuisine is slim. Finding this dish there was an accident and we report it in that location simply because a rambling yachting friend who pokes the bowsprit of his ketch in many strange spots had recently explored the rocky shores of Sir Francis Drake's Channel from Norman Island to Virgin Gorda—the "Fat One" mentioned by Christopher Columbus—and sent the formula back to us a scant week before it came in by mail from two spots in the South Seas!

Again basic indications point toward a fowl of tender years, although this is not essential. Cut into fairly small pieces and discard bones and skin. Fry out 4 rashers of diced bacon and brown chicken lightly; salting lightly, to taste. Take out chicken and reserve. . . . Now dice a big onion fine, do the same to a seeded green pepper, and along with a speck of garlic toss these items in the same hot grease until fairly tender—further adding 1 tsp brown sugar, 2 dashes tabasco, and salt to taste. Put this with the chicken.

TO OPEN the RIPE COCONUT SHELLS, a Tricky Proceeding, yet Simple if Instruction Is Honest

We've fixed this dish ourselves on several occasions when gourmets were impending as guests and can assure you that no man born of woman can take a saw and saw a cap off a batch of coconuts without hours of wasted time, blistered palms, slashed fingers, and discovery of additional vocabulary which, strictly, should be used only in prayer. . . . No, and even a vise won't hold them tightly without cracking, or popping them half way across the lot.

First puncture 2 "eyes" and drain milk into a bowl. Just hold coconut with end having the 3 "eyes" touching hard rock, concrete, or metal at a point ¼ of the way back. Strike smartly with a hammer on the top side, more or less vertically above the lower bearing point, and the nut will crack all the way around in a rough but clean circle.

Fill 2/3 full of the chicken-vegetable blend, introduce 1 bayleaf and 1 tbsp white wine into each nut. Season finally, to taste. Tie lids back on with a bight of string, and stand in a baking pan having 1" of water on the bottom. Put in a medium oven for 45 minutes, and serve one to each person. . . . Other vegetables also will do, such as okra, cut in slices, green corn off the cob, palm hearts, cucumber, egg plant, mushrooms, or what not. If sherry is used do not add until 10 minutes before service—removing the shell caps and allowing 1 tbsp to each coconut. This is one of the most attractive and delicious chicken dishes we know, for during roasting the coconut kernel donates a rich bouquet to the cooking chicken.

AND NOW WE PROGRESS to a Brief Discussion of Ducks & Ducklings, a Subject Treated further in Respect to the Wilder Varieties under the Chapter on *GAME & HOW LONG to HANG IT*

To our odd and unruly male mind there has been a great deal too much discussion on the subject of duck cookery, and especially when tossed off on the subject of wild ducks—taken up in our next Chapter—the orators have neither been hunters nor frequent consumers of waterfowl. They have read all the alleged etiquette about cooking ducks, both pressed and unpressed; have believed the romance, taken it up and shouted it from the housetops, just as they have read about the Orient and believe every Japanese a risky knave and all John Chinamen gentlemen of honesty and highest honour; just as they have read about the tropics and incorrectly believe the Southern Cross superior to the Big Dipper as a constellation; believe the tropic night falls "like a sudden black curtain," whereas there is a noticeable twilight in Singapore, Galápagos or Kenya Colony, right on the Line.

Except when dining possibly three, or at most five, guests, no amateur in his right mind will attempt duck *à la presse* if he is solvent enough to hire it done, or order it done in some spot like Tour d'Argent in Paris, where through the numbering ceremony of M. Frédéric Delair, alas for twenty years gone to his fathers, a Rouennaise duck is dedicated to the diner, numbered, cooked, pressed and eaten and paid for. To our mind this once charming thought is a form of alimentary exhibitionism. Besides all this, when done personally, this pressed duck is a gory process, a smelly process, and one already too well described in a host of cookery books to be covered here.

In other words, insofar as the amateur chef is concerned, fried duck isn't quite cricket except in haste in camp; boiled duck would hardly be profitable, therefore roast duck—in varying style—is the only usual answer. Barring the external application of condiments, wines and seasonings during the cooking process, it is our thought that in sauces, garnishes and stuffings, that most pleasure lies. A duck under any name is a duck; like a proper goose it is always fat and greasy in cooking; very rich to eat. The main problem is to divert the mind from these attributes, excellent though they be—through such sauces and dressings.

BUT FIRST LET US OFFER a Semi-Mad Chinese Receipt We Picked up during Our Next to Last Stay in Hongkong, Titled *ANGELS in MELON CRADLES*

This dish is just mad enough to be good, and although we have not gotten around to trying it yet we inscribe it here in hope that an adventurous soul here and there will try it out. . . . A young fat duck is first rubbed inside and out with salt and pepper, then stuffed with the following dressing: bread crumbs, enough to fill cavity, and moistened to a fairly stiff paste with Chinese rice wine—*saki* will do—or any semi-dry white cooking wine. Add 4 tablespoons of blanched almonds pounded to a paste with 1 tbsp of ice water, and sprinkle the whole with 2 pinches of anise seed, also pounded. Lacking this use 1 tbsp anisette, or *Anis del Mono,* the fine Spanish anise cordial. Then mix in ¼ tsp ginger powder. Blend this stuffing well, stuff and sew bird up.

Cut a small watermelon in half, hollow out a depression to receive the bird half way. Put duck breast in depression, dust the back with 1 tbsp brown sugar and 2 pinches of ginger, then roast in hot oven around 375° to 400° for 15 minutes; turn and roast for same time on other side, basting every 5 minutes with a sauce made from 1 cup white wine, 1 tbsp brown sugar, 1½ tbsp vinegar, ⅛ tsp powdered ginger and 2 tbsp grated orange rind—yellow part only. . . . After bird is well browned, lift out of melon cradle. Reduce pan juices with heat, thicken slightly with a little cornstarch worked smooth with gravy, add 1 tbsp tart jelly and serve in separate boat.

EXPLODED OLD WIVES' TALE No. IV, on the FALLACY of STUFFING CHILLED BIRDS IMMEDIATELY before POPPING in OVENS

Even if sweet old Aunt Beryl always stuffs her birds right off the ice and ten seconds before roasting, ignore this sinful act. Stuff all roasting birds at least a couple of hours beforehand, overnight is better still. This permits seasonings and savours to be absorbed by the bird even before being aided with oven heat. Each chilled bird should thaw at kitchen temperature for a good hour before roasting, or it may prove underdone within when almost burned without—especially in larger fowl.

A DANISH ORANGE SAUCE for DUCK, direct from the AMERICAN MINISTERIAL OFFICES in COPENHAGEN in 1933

After our duck is roasted pour off all except 2 tbsp of the fat floating on top of pan gravy. Reserve this fat. Next strain out 1 cup of the gravy itself—no fat—and keep hot in a saucepan. Work 1 tbsp or so of flour into a smooth paste with same amount of reserved hot fat, and stir in well. Season to taste with salt and cayenne. Grate the peel of an orange, yellow part only, add 1/3 cup orange juice. Work this orange business into gravy, then add 1 tsp orange Curaçao, along with 1 tbsp melted bitter orange marmalade. This is delicious!

A FRENCH BASTING-SAUCE, CONTAINING ORANGE also, together with CURRANT JELLY & PORT WINE

Use 1 cup orange juice, 1 tbsp brown sugar, 1½ tsp vinegar, a grated yellow rind of 1 orange, as a basting sauce. When duck is done pour off *all* floating surface fat from the gravy. Melt out 1½ tbsp flour with the same of butter, work smooth and thicken gravy in the hot pan. Add 1 tbsp black currant jelly, and reduce this sauce in pan until quite thick and gummy, then add ¼ cup port wine, stir once and pour over the bird.

GOOSE AFFAIRS, which ARE MUCH SIMILAR to DUCK, but LARGER

Geese are cooked the same as ducks, only longer—actually an hour or more. Sauces and stuffings are similar for tame birds. Apple sauce is so traditional with goose that we list one here; and not a usual one either, but made of roasted apples.

FRENCH CANADIAN ROAST APPLE SAUCE for ROAST GOOSE; QUEBEC, 1934

Peel, quarter and core enough tart apples to fill a baking dish. Impale each apple with 2 whole cloves. Boil up a syrup made of 1 cup brown sugar and ¾ cup of water. Stir in the juice of 1 lemon, add to apples, and bake ¾ hr at 350°. When apples are tender, sprinkle with 1 tbsp dark rum, dredge with plenty of added brown sugar, the grated yellow rind of 1 lemon, ¼ tsp ground clove and twice the same of cinnamon. Now—and here's the point!—pop under the broiler until the last sugar starts to caramel.

A RUSSIAN SAUCE for ROAST GOOSE, from a MEMORABLE CHRISTMAS in the YEAR A.D. 1926, DINING at SAMARKAND—a NEW YORK RUSSIAN RESTAURANT WE WEEP to THINK IS NO MORE

A feast day to a Russian is a time for joy and song; sad and minor songs it is true; but lovely, stirring songs. Samarkand used to be, like the Russian Eagle, a meeting place of wistful émigrés; and late at night someone would tune up the seven stringed Gypsy guitar, and the music would begin. Or Kousnetzov—we hope the spelling is right —would stand and sing the Volga Boat Song in his magnificent bass. Christmas was a feast night for us. It happened to be our birthday. We had a charming companion, and there was wine, and roast goose brought in flaming, and vodka and strong tea in glasses flavoured with a dash of orange flower water or jam. . . . The sauce for the goose, old time Russian style:

Add 2 tbsp freshly grated horseradish to ½ cup cooking gravy, strained, ¼ cup of very thick white cream sauce and ¼ cup sour cream. Add 1 tsp finely chopped chives, 1 pinch of tarragon, ¼ tsp dry mustard, 1 tsp sugar, juice ½ lemon, 1 tsp grated yellow lemon peel. Heat for a few minutes and mix very well, but do not boil. Serve in a gravy boat.

GUINEAS

Guineafowl or guineas, of any age, we always have held to be far more properly under Game classification, than classed as domestic poultry. Both in flavour and action in life they are allied to their wild cousins in shooting cover or forest. For this reason receipts touching on their culinary treatment will be found under *GAME, & How LONG to HANG IT.*

A FEW THOUGHTS on that NOBLEST of AMERICAN BIRDS, the TURKEY

American cooks actually get European credit, as they should, for methods of cooking this native fowl. Abroad it is a fallacious tendency to smother the bird in sad seas of messy vegetable dressings; in pot roasts and God alone knows what else—entirely ruining all possibility of the delicate flavour of the bird itself coming through in its original taste form. When exotic cookery rides our own doorstep in the eyes of the rest of the world we must record it here.

First a few technical warnings: be sure and lard the sharp edge of breast bone, and the ankle ends, with strips or rashers of salt pork or bacon, fastened on with string or skewers. This prevents burning before rest of bird is done. Greased brown paper will serve also. . . . Roast face down for all but the last ½ hr, then turn over. . . . A plump turkey cooked in an uncovered roaster needs occasional basting. But please don't spoil the delicate natural gravy by adding a lot of uncooked starchy flour, when a slight amount is all we need. Just brown the flour out after working smooth with an equal amount of melted butter, then add. . . . Above all don't always overload turkey dressing with quantities of sage, admirable though that herb may be; and, finally, avoid all beef extract "enricheners" like the plague. Vary the process through composing new thoughts on stuffings. A little adventurous originality is half the fun anyway, if for no other reason because of the surprise and delight it brings to the guest in our house.

WITH REFERENCE to Duck, Goose, Guineahen, Pigeon & Turkey Stuffings & Dressings of All Kinds

Since this poultry, or fowl, department fell under two classes of bird—wild and tame, and since our dressing collection for wildfowl is far more unusual than for tame, and because wildfowl dressings will enhance any dish made with a tame subject, all stuffings and such like matters are listed under *GAME, & HOW LONG to HANG IT*. . . . Ducks, Geese, Guineahens, Pigeons and Turkeys are treated in proper order, and in considerable detail.

> "We can not expect Tranquility of the Nervous System, whilst there is Disorder of the Digestive Organs. . . . *As we can perceive No Permanent Source of Strength but from the Digestion of FOOD,* it becomes Important that we should attend to its Quantity, Quality and Periods of Taking it, with a view to Ensure its Proper DIGESTION."
>
> *Abernathy's Sur.*
> *London, 1817*

CHAPTER VII

GAME *OF ALL* SORTS, & *HOW* LONG *TO* HANG IT

Companionate and Lively Dishes concerned with Furred & Feathered Game; such as Hungarian Partridges Cooked in Grape Leaves, *à la Budapesth,* the Way of a Scotsman with Grouse, Queen Elizabeth's Roasting Marinade for Saddle of Venison, & *Pigeons from the Temple of Heaven,* which is in Peking, in China.

FROM the start this became a favourite Chapter, partly through having been lucky enough to cook and eat a good bait of game in such widely scattered spots as the Florida Everglades and Maine, Idaho and India, British Columbia and Africa. We further must own to a definite stimulation in cooking a dish founded on items we ourself have hunted and taken. Added to this is the fact that almost all wild flesh, due to lawless matters of unbalanced diet and personal habit, has a more pronounced natural taste than tame; and for this additional reason game readily adapts itself to the lure of the unexpected in cookery.

But before a culinary shot is fired we must prick one romantic bubble which has bobbed about credulous tenderfoot ears since the serpent guided Adam—*there are no receipts of Famous Guides here.* We have no wish to dissipate any rosy Old Guide's Tale hovering about the north country moose caller or our soft footed Seminole turkey hunting guide, but we must simply rise and affirm that, by and large, in spite of all the mystery they love to conjure up about their art, they are the most abortive bunch of skillet wielders in or out of captivity. Oh yes, we know all about Moosehead Joe's famous braised moose meat and Kootenai Jake's roast Canada honker, and Okeechobee Tigertail's fillet of alligator tail. We've guided hunters and been guided. We've eaten guide cooking for going on thirty years. We say that such gentlemen may be mental giants when it comes to decoying fur or feather into ballistic proximity; but not half a dozen of the whole tribe we've met had time to care a hoot about game cookery, or had imagination to do much about it if they had.

No, it is our rigid opinion that the most imaginative game dishes today are worked up by amateur sportsmen-chefs; and actually it's about time someone put up a smoke screen of mystery about himself to match Moosehead Joe's mating call on the birchbark horn; high time we amateurs entered our guide infested camps with some assurance on our side; not as a disciple to his Guru, but with determination in eye and bearing. Let us look those fellows squarely in the eye and demand that the grouse or duck or venison haunch gets done—so, and so, and so!—thereby conjuring up a mite of overdue guide-respect heretofore only possible through a two hundred yard running head shot in timber, or an incoming double on pintail with a fifty mile gale under their sterns.

In game cookery America can hold her head high; can foot it on an even basis with England and France, and outstrip the rest of the world. In other kitchen practices Europe can level her cultured and palsied finger at our juvenile age as a nation; but inasmuch as there was no civilized cookery of any kind before the first third of the 18th Century, except in China, America has equal game cookery tradition. As a matter of fact our forefathers were at that time nourished largely by a sporting bill of fare in a new land teeming with game, while Europe was already in the midst of game depletion on all common lands, with stocking confined solely to titled landowners under stark prohibition to the rest.

Of course Italy had her spaghetti, France her fragrant meat stews and Russia her sturgeons' eggs, but despite all those reports about humming birds' tongues for the emperor there was scant culture in any of it. Henry VIII ate his stag bloody-broiled and half seasoned, and even his most elaborate state banquets were notable solely for their huge helpings and the coarseness of preparation. Even in Elizabeth's time any gentleman caught using a fork was viewed with the distrust we would grant a world's champion boxer in a Lord Fauntleroy suit. We have, in fact, a lovely formula of Louis XIV for burning the feathers off a live and kicking goose, later roasting it—undrawn—and setting it before guests half raw, unsalted, and basted with a fluid made of sugar syrup, then a viciously expensive luxury, and *violet perfume!*

No, Europe's game cookery is synchronized with our own. Their first great chefs came from Italy, as everyone knows, then the French school rose to its exalted estate. But after considerable travel and nourishment in Europe, after some two years spent living on European-owned ships, we found their game cookery intricate and amazing—when the old way was so nice. All right-minded folk will admit that the main charm in most game is its very own natural tastes, yet long-named foreign chefs dearly love to drown all sorts of game from roebuck to ortolans—buntings to us—in barbarous seas of boiled cabbage, onions, turnips, and even sauerkraut. Corned beef and cabbage is our friend, Bubble and Squeak our brother. Sauerkraut is a noble and healthy conception, but Odsblood! not smothering the finest game that flies. America was too busy fighting Indians or wolves or both, to have time for fancying up game in pot. That is our start, and we have kept on. In other words game, having its own unique and often delicate flavours—like quail, pheasant and partridge—should not be submerged in a tidal wave of other, commoner, flavours; not any more than a Frenchman should take a sound *Château Latour '04,* and trim it up with a lacing of six day old moonshine. We think sauerkraut is nice—with pigs knuckles and salt beef and things, but please not on quail, pheasant, partridge, snipe and guineas!

It springs from no desire to wave the stars and stripes when we promise that no American, with the taste buds of a mouse trap, would permit this sort of vandalism, any more than Henri Charpentier would cover a chafing dish of *Crêpes Suzettes* with a pint of black strap molasses.

Game cookery is a matter for reason and common sense, not a clutch of threadbare traditions founded on semi-barbarous quirks in the dim past. For this reason most Americans cook their game reasonably hung, not semi-putrefied and undrawn. We have always had plenty of healthy ice, now have healthy refrigerators; while Europe has never been that lucky. We have eaten English-hung woodcock with the trail left in. We found them perfectly edible but faintly tinged with the bitterness of the gall sac, and, through having their alimentary equipment in quiet decay for some days, they afforded scents and savours not one-tenth so delicate or vital or pleasant as the natural bird itself, drawn and undecayed.

This entire matter of game hanging is too variable to cling to any set of rules, sane or insane. The whole affair is dictated by humidity, climate, the type of diet, and the whole or mutilated condition of the kill itself.

Hanging at best is primarily done in civilized society to effect a certain breaking down of tougher fleshly tissues, not due to shame through lack of refrigeration causing us to nourish on a carcass high along the road to mortification. Personally we find that game plucked and drawn just as soon as possible and hung as quickly thereafter as convenient in a chamber under dry cold is best. We have now in our own refrigerator drawer six ducks that have been amiably awaiting there since the season's opening November 20th last—and this is July 1st.

Anyone who can eat a bird hung by the neck until it drops to the larder floor, like consumers of 6 minute roasted duck, and boasts he can carve up its long-hung, bloody torso with relish, either lies in his teeth, has cannibal ancestry, or needs an operation on his nose.

NOW a TIME-TABLE for the HANGING of GAME

1. Always remember this must be varied to suit warmish weather, and excessive humidity, or both.
2. Hang where it is cool and dry as possible, without freezing the game solid.
3. Even while in the field be sure to cover torn, shot-wounded areas to shut out the flies. Once the flies touch such game it spoils in an un-

believably short time. Same for eyes and beaks, which also provide ingress to fly attention.

4. Be sure game is perfectly dry before hanging. Inspect night and morning for dew or dampness forming. This means have in shade, yet in circulating air.
5. Our proven practice is to draw as soon as possible, plucking all birds at same time. Deliver to the butcher where he will hang indefinitely alongside his other meats, under dry and ideal conditions—yet not freezing or frozen.

TIME-TABLE, Based on Dry Average Cool Fall Weather, not Refrigerated

Wild Duck: 4 to 5 days. Mild weather, 1 to 3, depending.

Wild Goose: About 6 days. Mild weather, 1 to 3, depending.

Grouse: 8 to 10 days. Mild weather, 2 to 4 days, depending. Our British friends hang from 2 to 3 weeks, dry & cool.

Guineahen: 3 to 4 days. Mild weather, 1 to 2, depending. A delicate fine bird; don't spoil him!

Partridge: 4 to 6 days. Mild weather, 1 to 3, depending. Delicate too! Especially Hungarians.

Pheasant: 8 to 10 days. Mild weather, 2 to 4, depending.

Rabbit: 2 to 3 days. Mild weather, consume at once. Actually rabbit gains little from hanging.

Wild Turkey: 4 to 5 days. Mild weather, 1 to 3, depending. The grandest bird of them all, delicate flavour, so watch closely to avoid risk of "going by."

Woodcock: 8 to 10 days. Mild weather, 2 to 4, depending.

Venison: 10 days to 3 weeks. Mild weather, 1 to 4, depending.

A FEW MISCELLANEOUS & ADDITIONAL THOUGHTS on All Types of Game

By "mild weather," we mean warm weather. So watch game closely, for a sudden hot spell will ruin the finest brace of grouse ever shot.

Inspect edges of dissected abdominal areas. To average Americans the first sign of telltale blue-green discolouration is the danger signal. Personally we always trim these out, if and when cooking after that.

Remember that all game except fat duck, goose, raccoon or bear is "dry" meat. It requires lots of frequent basting, careful larding, or it will come from oven or grill tasteless as fibre—be it ever so prime when it goes in.

To our mind venison is a somewhat over-romanced meat. Unless we bag something so adolescent that game wardens begin doing forcible things, it is likely to be tough. It is particularly dry to cook—so be wary of trying to grill steaks as though that old buck were prize sirloin. Lard roasts; or wrap with bacon or pork; or better still marinate well for several hours, and baste religiously every few minutes when roasting. Don't overlook the value of lemon, lime or sour orange juice in tendering game, removing over-strong tastes and adding savour. Don't ignore the wild sour orange descended from the bitter-rinded fruit Columbus fetched to the New World and now gone wild in the bush all over Cuba and Florida. It adds great zest.

Strong birds, in addition to this marinating needed by strong meats, have most of their bad taste in skin, and in the bones. If we must eat coots or fish duck, and such like scabrous provender, skin and bone both; soak in salt water overnight. We ate pelican once because we had to, boned and skinned and soaked. There's nothing fishier than a pelican except fish.

When broiling or grilling game, brush with some good fat like lard, bacon grease, or olive oil. Sear fiercely hot, then cook at milder heats until done. Butter will not stand the fire.

WORDS to the WISE No. XVI, on the FALLACY of WASHING GAME

Beyond wiping with a damp cloth no game seems to gain from washing in water, although everyone does it everywhere, thus sending much flavour down the drain. Wet down, game can easily change to quickly spoiling meat. The earliest game receipt in our collection, dating to 1650, clearly states:

"Wipe jointe or game fulle welle, but do not in enny conscience washe the same in water."

PROPER GARNISHES for GAME, & the CONSTRUCTION of TRENCHERS

Fried Bread Crumbs: To a cup of bread crumbs allow 6 tbsp butter. Heat butter quite hot, brown crumbs, drain on brown paper or towel; serving either on main game platter or in a gravy boat.

Other Garnishes: Fried smaller rounds of bread make traditional garnish for small game. Also natural forest touches are in order: holly leaves and berries, leaves, other bright berries, sliced oranges.

Trenchers: Take a fairly short loaf of crusty French bread, slice lengthwise

1" thick or just under. Brush with butter and brown briefly under broiler or over coals; or fry in very hot butter. . . . Use it for a base for supporting game, and game cuts. The trencher should be as long as the game itself. There is nothing so wonderful for blotting up the fine gravies and juices which otherwise escape on plate. . . . *The last thing to devour is the trencher itself!*

SMALL BIRDS of MIXED BAG VARIETY, in the ITALIAN MANNER, & DISCOVERED during a VISIT in CAPRI not so LONG ago

While it has always given us a mild turn to think of fine Italian gentlemen dining off helpless migrating songbirds, and we have never seen the hair-raising thrill of shooting larks decoyed to a stuffed owl, there is no valid reason why we could not adapt what we learned to such small birds as snipe, plover, rails, pigeons, wild doves, quail, or what not, although a quail should be cooked more in a manner where his own delicate taste is undominated.

1 doz small game birds, 2 per guest	Enough olive oil to brown
¼ cup red wine vinegar; or cider type	½ cup veal or chicken broth
6 rolled & pounded anchovies	1½ cloves garlic, crushed
1 can Italian tomato paste	½ cup chopped ripe olives
Salt & cayenne, to taste	Trenchers of bread, see above
	Marsala or sherry wine, to taste

Heat oil quite hot and brown seasoned birds lightly. Make sauce by mixing tomato paste with the other materials, simmer up and pop the birds in; cover and cook slowly until tender—about ½ hr. Stir in ¼ cup of sherry or Marsala wine. . . . Have a pan lightly greased with hot olive oil, brown big 1" thick slabs of Italian bread on both sides. Place a pair birds side by side on each trencher, and pour the sauce over everything.

A *PILAU,* or *PURLO,* of SMALL DARK FLESHED GAME BIRDS DONE in the GULLA COUNTRY FASHION back of OLD CHARLESTON, from a PLANTATION OWNER'S NOTEBOOK

Blackbirds, dove, snipe, plover, pigeons, any or all will do, mixed or otherwise! Remember it is the piquant stuffing that sets off this dish dating away back into slavery time.

- 8 to 10 small birds
- 1 cup finely chopped celery
- 2½ cups rice, slightly underdone
- 1 medium sized minced onion
- 8 minced rashers home smoked bacon
- 6 beaten eggs, yolk & white
- 4 cups chicken broth, to cook rice
- ¼ cup vinegar & ¼ cup mild mustard
- Salt & hand-ground black pepper

Wash rice in lots of water, then boil in broth until not quite done. Drain and turn into a shallow pan to dry in *warm* oven, not hot. . . . Meantime fry out bacon, and reserve the latter. Use grease to brown both the celery and onion, lightly. Drain, mix with cooked bacon, seasoning lightly. Mix these with the rice, stir in the beaten egg binder. Stuff the birds and sew them up. . . . Meantime mix vinegar-mild mustard basting. Season birds well. Brush birds in olive oil and brown in a fairly hot oven, around 375°, for ½ hr, basting frequently with the piquant fluid. Serve on a platter inside a ring of cooked rice, and pour the basting juices over everything. . . . We have varied this by using wild rice mixed with plumped raisins instead of the onion. Very gratifying.

ROASTED WILD DUCK GENERALLY, & Roast Pressed Wild Duck in Particular—sometimes Called *CANARDS SAUVAGES, à la PRESSE*

Routine for a proper roast wild duck, for pressed duck, is simple but as inviolable as the late Queen Victoria's moral code. Probably it should be all the more rigid through the amateur having believed the foolish romance tossed around regarding 6 minute ducks. Now we've shot and eaten a good many hundred ducks, during the 2 years we've spent in tents or "sleeping out." We've cooked them over charcoal, in ovens, frying pans, over coconut husk fires on Andros Island; in metal containers over alcohol, wood, kerosene and distillate stoves. Our claim is that no raw 6 minute duck, hung or unhung, and regardless of age, sex, diet, social or geographical habitat, *ever* smells nice!

We've had to make 2 fairly well known and professed raw duck addicts back water before witnesses by cooking them prime wild-rice-fattened young hen mallards in oven exactly as they commanded—around 450° to 500°, *and giving them 8 not 6 minutes.* The unholy flesh tasted like slightly muddy raw meat. They had a scent that never came from any lotus petal. Just why America embraced this raw duck fallacy is unknown. It must be that folk have read this wonderful twaddle in English books, thought it smart, and wanting to make themselves out monstrous clever fellows both in field and with duck press—have retold the tale. This whole belief is on a par with our juvenile American faith in European diplomacy, and our erratic worship of sparkling Burgundy wine.

We can assure everyone that no big duck—mallard, redhead, black duck or canvasback—ever dull enough to fly within gunshot can ever be cooked in 6 minutes! A tiny greenwing teal can be done in 9 or 10 maybe—*maybe,* we said—but anything from sprig size and larger: impossible. Charles Nordhoff eats raw fish in salad sometimes, and so do we. Ernest Hemingway eats raw conchs now and then, and so do we. But no one except some wide-eyed citizen toting a 2000 dollar gun with a 14 karat trigger, and who believes everything he reads, can really say he likes duck flesh bloody-raw after actually having sampled the article himself, and not just through reading the printed page!

ROASTED & PRESSED WILD DUCK, Cookery Routine for the Purist

1. Pluck, draw, singe and rub clean with a damp cloth. Do not wash, either outside or in.
2. Hang for 4 or 5 days in a cool dry place; see above.
3. Thaw to kitchen temperature before cooking.
4. Brush with some good cooking fat like olive oil or bacon grease—*not butter,* rub inside and out with salt and pepper, perhaps insert 2 stalks of coarse celery into cavity. Butter burns too easily at 500°.
5. Be sure oven is hot—between 450° and 500°—*before* ducks go in.

Allow 10 to 12 minutes for teal, 12 to 15 minutes for widgeon, scaup, sprig, and all medium sized ducks; 15 to 20 minutes for mallards and other big ducks—this last varying with age and sex, a big man-about-town aged drake being a tensile package as anyone can verify who has tried to carve one. . . . These cooking times insure a prime duck, not a bloody one. Sear 5 minutes, then open oven door to reduce to 450° or so.

6. Slice off breast from wing toward breastbone, amputating legs and ignoring wings. Put on a hot platter and cover to keep from drying out any more than necessary.
7. Squeeze juices from carcass in duck press, and add to any casual juice extracted in carving. The purist seasons juices with a little salt and cayenne, and serves as-is. . . . Other gourmets prefer reserving some of the duck's blood and adding it a little at a time to juices simmering in a chafing dish—this slow addition being required in order not to curdle. This seasoned handmade gravy is poured over breast and legs out of a boat. . . . Other sauce additions start in with either of these two foundation sauces and: add a little grated yellow orange peel, melted currant jelly, butter, sherry, paprika, worcestershire—all or any of these. We personally favour the taste and scent of orange peel and apricot pulp with wild duck, after trying everything mind can conjure up. Soak apricots overnight, boil, and rub through sieve.
8. Serve the best still dry red wine the purse affords; decant it properly 2 or 3 hrs before serving. *Do not warm before a fire*—that is another old hunter's tale—merely decant and leave with stopper out in the dining room. Nature will do the rest. Nature always does.

WORDS to the WISE No. XVII, URGING FINAL DIVORCE of ALL WOMEN from ALL CONTACT with GAME COOKERY, VERBAL or MANUAL

May heaven shield us for setting this down in cold print, but employ no female aid or advice when cooking game. A curry, for instance, is also strictly a man's business. Male. And the same order applies to game. Women, by and large, seem to lack the proper psychology or respect for this serious business. Actually it probably isn't their fault, poor dears. They really haven't gotten much chance to cook game, for most men after coming to shaving age are bright enough not to take wives, sweethearts, or other feminine attachments, on camp-hunts or into duck blinds.

Thus far in our life we have known just 3 decorative women who, when in the field, didn't scream at many little things; and who, when they got any firearms in their pretty hands, could hit the proverbial bovine in the pelvic structure with a mop. And women who can't shoot shouldn't be taken hunting. And women who don't get taken hunting aren't sympathetic or interested in cooking game, except to confuse the male who is eagerly trying to whip up some amateur masterpiece. Naive and eagerly willing friends of either sex, incidentally, are the poorest form of risk in a kitchen. Give them easy indoor games and let them go away and play until the dish is ready to serve. This last bit of advice will save time, temper and friendships.

LET'S NOT SNEER too Quickly at all Thought of Stuffing Wild Ducks

There's a welter of accusation and rebuttal on this question also, mainly instigated by haughty addicts to bloody duck. Just why anyone pays attention to them we have never understood, for invariably they are men who don't get to eat many duck. For instance, in 1934 when British Columbia had a 20 duck limit, and 6 guns shot, the opening 3 days saw around 360 birds—ducks, brant and Canada honkers—hung in the meat safe under the buttonwood trees on the Kootenai River bank; all to be put in cold storage for future delectation, and with photographs to prove it. We ate duck on our houseboat camp; plenty of duck. We ate plenty more duck back home. We can swear you can get mighty sick of roast duck. You can get so tired of roast duck you welcome corned beef, only you don't—you think up different ways of cooking duck. . . . Some honest amateur chefs think that we of the occasional-duck-stuffing school use such stuffing to flavour the birds, or cover up their own natural flavour. That is incorrect. We think up duck stuffings because duck stuffings are damned tasty, and most ducks are strong enough in their own right not to be overwhelmed by a few condiments and bread crumbs; in fact we would like to make one additional duck statement before we get accused of conceit and undue authority on the subject:

Many ducks have quite strong gamey tastes. Diving ducks all tend toward this, especially salt water divers. The tippers who feed on grasses, wild celery, seeds and like vegetable and cereal produce are more delicate and sweetly flavoured. Divers that breed in the far north are sweet until they get to cavorting down south in tidewaters and sounds, then the fishy taste comes. A widgeon that has spent 4 weeks in Palm Beach may need stuffing to get our mind off himself, if you get what we mean. Any duck is usually better than no duck at all, even if it means eating only the skinned breast marinated overnight in salted water and lime juice. The whole business is comparative. There can be no hard and fast rules. There certainly should not be sneers and loud speech from gold-trigger gentlemen who eat a brace of duck every twelvemonth. Let's be reasonable, logical and happy about the thing!

MEDITATION on WILD GEESE, & on the SIN of OVERCOOKING

Wild geese are roasted much the same as tame, but a big 15 lb Canada gander can be tough. We've seen some with sinews that would make the village blacksmith look like a chorus boy. Most chefs we know make the mistake of extra long roasting, which is a boomerang in that instead of tendering the beast it merely adds temper to the metal of his deceased earthly shell, and after 2 or 3 hours carving may require 40% dynamite and a jackhammer quarry drill. He is totally different than his hand-fattened domestic brother. Cook him until he is well done all through. Beyond that man cannot go.

HOW to CHOOSE & USE a GOOSE, when THERE IS a CHOICE

1. Choose youngest and fattest, preferably a 6 months' old of the summer's hatching. His bill will be flexible at tip; his plumage lighter, his throat markings vague, his legs smooth and less horny than last year's bird.
2. Pluck, singe, draw, and wipe out thoroughly with damp cloth. Reserve liver—minus gall sac—heart, and in young birds the gizzard, for giblets.
3. After proper hanging for a period of 4 to 6 days, rub him inside and out with plenty of salt and pepper. Either stuff with some highly seasoned dressing, or be a goose purist and tuck 2 stalks of coarse celery —cut into 4 pieces—into the yawning cavity; or an unpeeled, quartered

orange; or a cored, quartered apple. In the first case sew him up; in the latter two, don't sew up.

4. Truss legs in place with piece of string tied around drumstick ends, and passed under his back.
5. Sear in very hot oven from 450° to 500°, for about 15 minutes, cut down heat by opening oven door slightly, then cook in slow oven around 300° until done all through; either basting frequently, or better still in a covered roaster to gain all steaming benefits from gravy. For basting merely add ½ cup water and ½ cup orange juice to the natural fats in pan after searing. Goose must be well done.
6. Pan gravy will be too rich so discard all but 2 tbsp of the fat, and tune up with seasonings to suit taste.

GROUSE DONE in the SCOTTISH MOORS FASHION

All grouse are delicious, and only our own western blue grouse is a bit strong, due to his diet among the conifers. Although very easy to cook there are a few points to remember. . . . Go slow in plucking so as not to tear skin, which is tender. Never wash in water after drawing. He should be moderately done—neither rare as duck, nor well done as goose. Young birds require around 20 minutes; mature birds nearer half an hour. The oven should be fairly hot—around 375° or 400°. Young birds may be known by their tender, downy feathers under wings; more pin feathers, and short, blunt, undeveloped spurs in the cock bird.

Your Scotsman would cover the whole body with rashers of smoked bacon, pinned on. Cover him with a discreet kimono of brown paper tied shut fore and aft, or in a paper bag. Roast 2/3 of his time thus, then remove paper, brush with butter, dredge with flour, mount on Scottish Trenchers, given below, or on plain buttered trencher of bread, and finish brown. The curse of most grouse is that they are cooked too dry, and lose flavour thereby.

SCOTTISH TRENCHERS for GROUSE, & TRADITIONAL GARNISHES

Take grouse livers and heart, cut out green gall sac. Grind up in fine blade of meat chopper, or pound smooth in a mortar. Add 1 pinch of salt to each liver-heart, a dusting of cayenne, a little melted butter. Mix well and spread on ¾" thick lengthwise slabs of bread cut long enough to bed down the whole bird.

Several tarts and sweets go well with grouse: cranberry jelly, currant jelly or jam, brandied peaches or apricots, or the plain gravy from the birds themselves, served separately in a sauce boat. In such event do not use trenchers to blot up these cooking juices when doing the final browning in oven, but supply them later.

A BRITISH EAST AFRICA BASTING SAUCE for GUINEA FOWLS

Guineas are splendid fast-flying game in Africa, and we have a friend who went out there recently on a shoot, and preferred eating them to any buck; kicked them up out of the cover, cut them down with a 20 gauge, while someone else backed him up with a .375 Winchester Model 70 magnum—just in case. The receipt given here is English.

In greased roasting pan add 1/3 cup Burgundy or claret, 2 tbsp chicken broth, 1 tbsp tomato paste, ¼ tsp nutmeg, salt and cayenne to taste. Rub bird all over with pepper and salt, paint with lime juice, place in pan and brown nicely, basting frequently. Thicken with a trifle of flour worked smooth with same amount of melted butter, and add. Then at the last stir in 1 tbsp port wine, and serve in a gravy boat.

PARTRIDGE with an HUNGARIAN TOUCH, & which also Would Serve as Well for Grouse, Prairie Chicken, Sage Hens or Valley Quail

This is a happy receipt from friends who shot in Hungary in the merry days before Swastikas and things. It came from Esztergom in the Danube valley below Budapesth, and almost within biscuit toss of what then was Czechoslovakia.

First rub 2 birds inside and out with salt, brush with olive oil and a trace of crushed juniper berries or leaves—lacking this a drop of essence in a little wine. Make a basting sauce from 1/3 cup dry red wine, 1½ tsp onion pulp, salt and cayenne, a handful of chopped almonds and the same of halved malaga or muscat grapes—or plumped raisins if no grapes on hand. . . . Sear birds to nice colour in hot oven around 400°, then reduce heat a little, add basting fluid to pan and cook until done. Reduce this basting at the last, thicken with a trace of flour, and pour over the birds.

A WILY GRECIAN METHOD with PARTRIDGES ROASTED in CHEMISES MADE of FRESH GRAPE LEAVES, and NOTED DOWN in ATHENS in 1931

The Grande Bretagne Hotel, mentioned elsewhere in these volumes, once afforded a chef named Jean Kriticos and while the routine cookery at this hostelry, like most others in the Near East, was nothing to weave sonnets about, this chef could on occasion produce surpassingly fine dishes. Actually the employment of grape leaf chemises in meat and game cookery is quite typical in that section of the world; Turks, Armenians, Syrians, all admire this touch. The dish is equally good with quail, snipe, woodcock, or any relatively small birds.

Brush birds with olive oil, rub lightly with garlic, and then dust with salt and cayenne. Inside the cavity of each put 1 pinch of rosemary. Brassiere them neatly with 2 or more large green grape leaves, pinning in place with skewers or toothpicks. . . . Remove gall sac from livers and chop them up with other giblets, chop an equal quantity of tender mushrooms, and saute them until half done in plenty of butter—also seasoning to taste. Then stir in enough tart white wine to do for basting. Now grease a casserole and seal cover on with a strip of pastry, baking in a medium oven at 350° for 45 minutes. The wine-giblet basting goes in with the birds. If uncovered, we were assured and later discovered for ourself, the leaves would turn dark brown at once and impart an unnecessary taste to the game. Reduce gravy at the last and pour over birds.

AND NOW A REGAL STUFFED PHEASANT, *MAXIMILIAN,* which Is also KNOWN as *à la BOHÉMIENNE,* & *à la CHASSEUR ROYALE,* SUFFICIENT in ITSELF for any REUNION in VIENNA

For generations fine chefs have named dishes after their royal patrons. It means nothing except confusion to the amateur, and whether the tragic Archduke who met death before the firing squad in Mexico ever knew the dish really does not matter now. It is the dish that matters, and there comes a time in the life of every man when a dinner gesture is in order—whether he has shot that brace of ringnecks himself, or bought them—they average little more than young chickens! —in New York's Washington Market from Joseph, or Tingaud's on rejuvenated upper Sixth Avenue. And also 4 or 5 snipe or plover, or 2 squabs—for reasons now disclosed. These are for the stuffing.

Broil the small birds for only 4 minutes, along with a slice of Virginia ham or a rasher of home smoked bacon. Mince the meat from the birds, dice ham or bacon, add ¼ cup of sliced truffles—or half-cooked mushrooms. Season highly with salt, pepper, add 1 pinch each of thyme, marjoram and sweet basil; also 1 tsp chopped parsley for each pheasant. Saute this stuffing for 5 minutes in hot butter, then draw aside. Bind with a little beaten egg, dredge with a tiny bit of flour, and stuff birds—being careful to sew up neatly. . . . Roast them in a buttered ovenware dish around 350° until tender, basting with plenty of melted butter mixed with a little white wine. A gravy may be made from the cooking juices, either reduced with a trifle of sherry added at the last, or with finely chopped giblets—already tendered in butter—stirred in just before serving. Heat 2 tbsp brandy, pour over pheasants and serve flaming. Garnish with sprigs of holly, grape leaves; anything decorative from the forest.

WORDS to the WISE No. XVIII, BEING TWO THOUGHTS on the TENDER SUBJECT of QUAILS

Never forget that quails are particularly "dry" birds; and relatively tasteless when thus dried out in cookery. Therefore lard with strips of bacon, or smother in lots of butter, when grilling or frying. . . . Also consider the strange and proven affinity of quails with raisins, and sometimes put a handful inside the cavity of each bird, plumping the raisins first in scalding water.

A PROPER ELIZABETHAN MARINADE for VENISON, & the More Tensile Large Game Meats

Venison, except when too young to be legal, is apt to be tough. Cooked in steaks it is certain to be dry, but may be bettered by handling like *Tom Davin's Steaks-in-Salt,* on Page 141. When roasted it is imperative that basting be unremitting, and this basting, together with cooking juices form basis for later sauces. This receipt dates back to the year 1592.

1 large mild chopped onion	2 large chopped carrots
2 tbsp chopped spring onions	½ tsp each of usual sweet herbs
3 or 4 whole cloves	5 tbsp olive oil or butter
1 cup tarragon vinegar	Lots of salt & pepper

Fry out vegetables in the oil, add herbs and seasonings, then put through a coarse sieve. Brush venison with oil, dust with lots of pepper and enough salt, and pour this marinade over the meat. Turn every 2 hrs of the 8 the venison is kept in soak. Sear in hot oven at first, then cook meat slowly until done—basting with the marinade every few minutes to keep moist and tasty.

A SELECT GROUP of GAME SAUCES

A FRIENDLY SAUCE of BRANDY & the Pulp of Apricots that Is Justly Famous in the Old World, & Equally Good on Wild Flesh or Tame; on Animals or Fowls

Put ½ cup of apricot pulp through a sieve. Add 1 cup water, ½ cup of sugar; then simmer. Thicken with a little cornstarch worked smooth with the syrup; simmer up again and add 1 tbsp cognac brandy or 1½ tbsp apricot brandy. Make tart with juice of ¼ lemon.

THE AUTHOR'S OWN DEEP SOUTH BARBECUE SAUCE, for all sorts of MISCELLANEOUS GAME such as 'COONS, 'POSSUMS, BIG FOX or CAT SQUIRRELS, MARSH RABBITS, WILD SHOTE & GOD KNOWS WHAT ELSE of DARK FLESH, or GAMEY FLAVOUR, or BOTH

We've been hungry plenty of times on camp hunts, and seem to have eaten just about everything that swims, flies or runs, through the Florida flatwoods, the pine islands in swamps and Everglades, or in the vast sawgrass marshes. We've nourished on alligator tail, sand hill crane, limpkin, crow, rattlesnake, 'possum, 'coon, wild razorback shote, pelican and—credit it or not!—whippoorwill. 'Coon, 'possum, and big brown marsh rabbits are good eating, but have to be smothered in a sauce hot and potent enough to disguise the gamey meat. This sauce is fine to add to the braising pot half an hour before meat is tendered, or to work up while game is being grilled, roasted, smothered, or what not. Make it plenty hot with peppers.

1 lb odd trimmings from the animal
1 big chopped onion
4 tbsp butter
1 to 1½ tbsp flour for thickening
Salt and lots of black pepper
1 big chopped carrot
½ tsp dry hot mustard
½ cup evaporated or fresh cream
2 to 3 tbsp lemon juice or vinegar
1 piece yellow lemon peel
1 tsp or more of worcestershire

Soak strong meats as long as possible, overnight is best, in strongly salted water, then use this sauce, made as follows: brown the chopped game trimmings, onion and carrot in 3 tbsp of the butter. Cream mustard with a little gravy, and add to trimmings pan. Take some roasting juices from the meat from time to time, and add—along with lemon juice and seasonings. Smother and simmer until rich; strain out bones and sinew, pound vegetables fine, thin out with more of the cooking gravy, reduce 1/3, and finally thicken with 1 tbsp flour and same of hot butter—worked smooth—adding the cream at the last.

MALAGA or MUSCAT GRAPE SAUCE for DUCK, PARTRIDGES, QUAILS, PHEASANTS, GUINEAS, and other GAME, from PARIS

1 lb grapes, malaga or muscat	¼ cup Malaga or Madeira wine
2 or 3 tsp dried mushrooms	4 tbsp butter
1 or 2 pinches ground clove	1 scant tbsp lemon juice

Stem grapes and scald in enough water to cover, simmering gently until nicely plumped. Drain and put in a saucepan with butter, wine and spice. Cover tightly and simmer for 6 minutes, no longer. Stir in dried and finely chopped mushrooms—truffle is even better—and after simmering a minute more, serve in a sauce boat. We find a handful of finely chopped hazel nuts add a good touch.

AN OLD ENGLISH JELLY-WINE SAUCE from the TIME of GEORGE III, WHO MAY HAVE BEEN FALLIBLE in BRAIN & STATESMANSHIP, but CARED for FINE FOOD. . . . EXCELLENT for DUCK, GROUSE, PARTRIDGE, RABBIT, SNIPE & DARK MEATED GAME GENERALLY, including VENISON

Slowly melt 1 cup of black or red currant jelly in a saucepan, add 1 cup red wine; mix up well and simmer gently while we add 1 pinch powdered ginger and the same of clove, 1 tbsp lemon juice. Thicken with equal parts game gravy—strained—and flour, worked smooth. Just before serving add 1 tbsp cognac brandy. Serve in a boat.

A MATCHLESS BITTERSWEET ORANGE SAUCE from SHEPHEARD'S in CAIRO, upon the OCCASION of a CONSUMMATED DUCK HUNT along the NILE with CERTAIN FRIENDS in the BLINDS of RUSSELL *PASHA,* BRITISH COMMISSIONER of EGYPTIAN POLICE

We needn't explain that Shepheard's, for all of its vast and gay nineties interior and equipment, is one of the world's greatest hotels. After we hung up sixteen ducks—mostly teal and mallards—the Swiss manager arranged with the fine chef to arrange a duck dinner intended, among other things, to impress our then fiancée into believing ourself to be not only a wing shot of parts, but a widely clever fellow through arranging such a repast—complete from gimlet cocktails to two precious bottles of *Romanée-Conti '19,* which we obtained through treason and stratagem, if not out-and-out bribery, from Shepheard's special reserved bins!

This platter of ducks was garnished with tiny Jaffa oranges cut into baskets, filled with pulp and honey, dusted with brown sugar and grilled alongside the 18 minute birds. The breasts were removed in two parts; bones and carcass were pressed and the juice brought to the buffet close by, and while the matchless array of duck breasts and candied grilled oranges sizzled under their gleaming silver dome, and we worked up our courage to proposing marriage as soon as we could inveigle the young lady into Shepheard's gardens, the master magician of the chafing dish wove his spell.

The whole secret of this sauce is the *bitter* tang which comes with equal gusto from Seville bitter oranges, the Cuban *bigarade,* the Florida wild sour orange, or the Florida bittersweet. Grapefruit peel is the next best substitute, and a good one too. Therefore to the gently simmering juices of 6 ducks the following is added.

4 tsp grated bitter orange or grapefruit peel; using yellow part only
3 tbsp sour juice of any kind, like limes
1 or 2 tiny dashes of worcestershire
1 tbsp Curaçao
6 big tbsp bitter orange marmalade
Salt and cayenne, to taste
2 tbsp brandy

Mix well, adding spirits at the last. Pour a little over duck breasts, put the rest in a gravy boat. The duck platter was swiftly bound with a ring of heated brandy, and served flambée. . . . There was a hush, exclamations of delight. Then later, much later, coffee on the terrace —sweet Turkish coffee in tiny cups; and thimbles of Drambuie. We found courage, we proposed, we were accepted. We have always had a warm spot in our hearts for bittersweet orange sauce with ducks—or with anything else, for that matter!

A DANISH ORANGE SAUCE for Duck Will Be Found under the Chapter Devoted to *POULTRY & the INNER DRESSINGS of FOWLS,* Page 106

A FINE OLD ENGLISH WALNUT SAUCE DATED 1761, but which Is Piquant & Tasty on Many other Meats & Game, being Founded on a Basis of Pickled Walnuts, & a Trifle of Bloater Paste

To 1 cup of the juice from pickled black walnuts add 2 of the nuts themselves, 6 chopped capers, 2 or 3 tsp of bloater or anchovy paste, 2 tsp finely chopped chives or shallots, 1 tsp of brandy. Simmer up just once and rub through a sieve. Wonderful for all sorts of game, and especially baked fish.

AN OLD ENGLISH STUFFING for Small Game of all Kinds, Dated 1829

Quite a few old stuffings ignore onions now and then in order to permit the flavour of the game in hand to permeate better. This receipt works well with almost any sort of stuffable game.

All the chopped tender giblets and 1/3 as much chopped lean smoked bacon
1 tsp chopped parsley per cup
1 pinch nutmeg per cup
Enough bread crumbs to bind, and moistened with lemon juice and beaten egg
1 pinch thyme per cup
Salt and cayenne, to taste

Shape into small forcemeat balls, which may either be placed inside the game, or ranged around it and browned at the same time. It is simple and quite delicate.

A STUFFING for GUINEAHEN, *à la KENSCOFF,* Brought back from a Trip to Haiti, in March 1933

Back in that incredible time when Toussaint Louverture, Dessalines and Cristophe, were conniving, each in his own way, to rule black Haiti, and the cane fields ran red with the blood of French men and women until there were no more, and even Napoleon's brother-in-law Le Clerc, and Pauline, and the French fleet were beaten off, there lived a monster in a marble villa high up in the cool hills a mile or so above the sea on the trail to dread Morne la Selle who hides her dark and fearful head in a perpetual scarf of tradewind cloud—Monsieur le Compte de Kenscoff. Only he didn't stop with murdering *blancs;* while the *vaudou* drums beat out the wicked heart-tempo of Africa, he would get his peasants inflamed on *clairine*—raw white sugar cane rum—and watch them in the courtyard below his terrace turn from caricatures of men to naked Africa herself. And then when this palled, he would send them home and put an amusing postscript on an evening's jollity by pretending to let one of his lovely yellow captured mistresses escape through a secret door, and when she had reached the open garden, Monsieur le Compte would lift a finger, and the bloodhounds would be released to tear her to pieces while he watched and delicately plied himself from a jeweled snuffbox of raw yellow gold, with its self-appointed crest done in diamonds and emeralds.

It is a far cry from this to guineahens, but near the site of this marble palace, long fallen to ruin, a canny, jolly little Frenchman has an inn, and through the wit of France, the produce of the lush tropics, and the half-wild cookery of African chefs he discovers things now and then. We speak of him again in this work.

Enough coarse bread crumbs browned in deep fat to fill ½ bird cavity
Enough red bananas to fill ½ bird
Salt and cayenne, to taste
½ lemon, juice and grated rind
1 tsp brown sugar; ¼ tsp nutmeg
1 tbsp brown rum

Mix everything into a coarse paste, stuff the guinea and sew up. Heat a little white rum, and serve the roasted fowl flaming, garnished with preserved guava hulls, or 1" quivering ruby cubes of guava jelly. The bananas are first sliced, then made into a pulp with a large fork.

A STUFFING of SMALL WHOLE OYSTERS, CHOPPED PECANS or other NUTS, together with WILD RICE, which will SERVE to DRESS WILD or TAME DUCKS, TURKEYS or GUINEAS, with EQUAL DILIGENCE & DELIGHT

This amazing dressing came from a sportsman friend named Samuel Galland, out in the Pacific northwest, who shoots a great many things and knows how to cook them—*has* cooked them, in fact around the world, and from British Columbia to *Baja* California, where, fairly recently he had his schooner burn from under him, his sole salvage being one locker drawer with which he returned to his home, containing underwear and socks. The small Olympia oysters of the west coast are indicated, but barring these tiny chaps, command the smallest oysters your source can supply. They will do as well.

Simply boil enough well-washed wild rice as the birds may require, in lots of salted water. Drain, then dry the rice well in a *warm* oven; and for each cup of rice allow ¼ cup tiny oysters, 2 tbsp chopped hazelnuts, 1 pinch of thyme and sweet marjoram—both of which harmonize with duck. Donate finally 1 tsp scraped onion pulp; salt and cayenne, to taste.

A NORFOLK PEANUT STUFFING, ESPECIALLY GOOD for DUCK, but MARCHING HANDILY with TURKEY, GROUSE, PARTRIDGES or PRAIRIE CHICKENS

We always ducked out at the Virginia Capes when going north in *MARMION* in the spring of the year, and on each visit to Norfolk we collected something interesting on game, Virginia hams, or southern oyster dishes. The mixture is in this proportion: to 4 cups of dry bread crumbs add 3 cups of *re-roasted,* quite dark brown, and crisp, peanuts—first put through fine blade of the food chopper—together with 1 medium sized onion, ½ cup crumbled cornbread, salt and black pepper to taste. Stir in 2½ tbsp melted butter. Moisten with a little veal broth and Virginia Dare white sweet wine—equal quantities; bind with 1 beaten egg. Stuff the bird. . . . This stuffing should not be too wet; merely a stiff paste.

ROY LAMMERS' PEPPER STUFFING for TURKEY, which Is a CLASSIC in the PACIFIC NORTHWEST, & ESPECIALLY AMONG those WHO MAKE YEARLY PILGRIMAGE to the BEAUTIFUL KOOTENAI VALLEY, when the NIGHTS GET CRISP and the BIG DUCKS & HONKERS START PITCHING in from the FAR NORTH.

Remember the tempo of this stuffing is very hot and high. Keep adding pepper and sage until we have reached our limit in pungency. Then stuff bird and roast him. . . . Take enough stale bread almost to fill the turkey, reject crusts and tear into small pieces. Work in 3 big chopped mild onions, 2 tsp baking powder mixed well with the salt; lots and lots of sage; lots and lots of black pepper—preferably ground with a hand mill. Moisten with just enough milk to make stuffing mesh together without too much compression, bearing in mind that the contented version in tin will harmonize just as well as dairy fresh. This is a masculine stuffing for those who want warmed innards and hot seasoning. Better taste as we mix in herbs and pepper, not forgetting that sage under cooking heat is far stronger than sage uncooked and dried, in packages.

NOW as a FINALE WE OFFER A RED RIVER PECAN—*PUCK-awns,* as THEY ARE CALLED THERE—& MUSHROOM STUFFING, further EMBRACING WINE & VARYING HERBS & other HELPERS, FROM NACHITOCHES—PRONOUNCED NACK-A-TISH—LOUISIANA

There is some mighty fine quail and turkey shooting in that old Red River country, and a gangling turkey shooter, recently enamoured of a Ph.D. degree at Columbia, entered this in our index of stuffings not-to-be-ignored. Pecans also are, and have been for long, a serious part of the cookery technique of that part of the south. Known in New Orleans as *pralines* they marry well with game in many ways. For a big bird allow the following comestibles.

2 cups chopped fresh pecan meats
4 to 5 hardboiled eggs, chopped
1 big onion, chopped fine
2 tsp celery salt
1 tsp nutmeg
3 or 4 tbsp chopped parsley
Heart and liver, chopped up
10 to 12 slices dried bread
1½ cups chopped mushrooms
¼ lb butter
Salt and black pepper, to taste
1 tsp powdered thyme
¼ tsp ground mace
2/3 cup, or so, sherry wine

Parboil giblets in enough salted water to cover, and while this is under way roll the dried bread to a powder, sifting larger bits out by using a coarse sieve. Blend all herbs and seasonings well with the crumbs, adding the pecans and hard eggs. Drain giblets, put through a coarse sieve and fry out with the coarsely chopped mushrooms, using half the butter. Tender the onions in the other half of the butter, then mix everything together, finally seasoning to taste with salt and hand-ground black pepper. Moisten stuffing with enough sherry so it will hang together, but under no circumstances should it be wet or pasty. We want the sherry flavour to point up the whole procedure, but when bird is taken from oven this stuffing should be fairly dry and crumbly.

Incidentally there is a Spanish turkey stuffing from the heart of ancient Castile which is identical with this one from Nachitoches. Substitute coarsely chopped almonds for the pecans, add 1 clove of crushed garlic, let chopped green olives pinch hit for the mushrooms, and finally add ½ cup of tiny dried apricots stewed gently until tender, and the transformation is done.

"We have some Good Families in England of the Name of *Cook*, or *Coke*, . . . but they may depend upon it, they All originally Sprang from Real and Professional Cooks; and They need not Be Ashamed of their Extraction, any more than the *Parkers, Butlers*, & c." (NOTE: Not to mention Smiths, Candlers, Wheelwrights, Hunters, Millers, Carpenters, Masons, Waggoners, Shipmans, Woolworths, Mercers, Boatwrights, Sadlers, Farmers—and Bakers! . . . *Author*)

Quotation from a British Volume on Cookery, not of this Generation.

CHAPTER VIII

MEAT DISHES *BOTH* TEMPERATE & TROPICAL

Concerning Beefs, Lambs, Porks & Veals, in such varied substance as Cuban Grilled Beefsteak *Bigarade,* a Costa Rican Affair of Ground Beef and Red or Yellow Bananas entitled *Empanadan de Plantano Maduro;* the Timely Matter of Russian Suckling Pigs, Lamb *Shashlik* and a North Indian *Sikh Kabab*—which are the Same but Different; to Say Nothing of a Russian *Piroshki* of Chopped Veal Kidneys and Other Goods Re-Stuffed and Browned in Rolls, and a Mexican Tongue of Veals *Taxcueño*—which means from Taxco.

UNFORTUNATELY or fortunately man is still a carnivorous animal. True, there are religious sects like the East Indian Jains who not only don't eat flesh but won't take the life of a serpent about to strike their own firstborn. There are thousands of more or less vegetarian folk who live and have their being in wide ignorance of meat, either for health's sake or one fanatical preference or another. But, by and large, they are all lean and tweaky pieces; prone to colds and random nervous tone, second rate in athletics, baffled by sudden problems, irascible, over-serious if not downright pessimistic, and of inferior reproduction.

No army, Olympic team or explorer can long keep energy fires alight without meat. The severe tendency of the Japanese soldier toward nose and throat fallibility is traceable to unbalanced rice diet over centuries, and insular lack of meat. Commander Byrd did not attempt to baffle Little America on a diet of prunes, canned corn, beets, beans and spinach. Inasmuch as the human alimentary routine seems to require flesh to fire our furnaces toward lively energy and companionate nerves, we have set out to collect proven—and sometimes strangely toothsome—methods of meat preparation, each noted in its own land and not unshot with cunning and imagination.

If any of these serve to elevate the flesh of some deceased quadruped into appetizing, odd and tasty nourishment, then our task in collection and presentation here has been most pleasant.

TOUCHING on the IMPORTANT SUBJECT of BEEFS

CUBAN BEEFSTEAK, *BIGARADE,* from OUR TWELFTH STAY in CUBA, which WAS in 1937

This pungent way of grilling steaks first came to us from a friend who has been some eighteen years on the Island, and was tried on our grill before tasting the native dish ourselves. It is easy, quick, and makes a nice surprise at a steak roast.

Bigarade is the name for the Seville bitter orange, the one they make all the good Scotch marmalade from!—which, as has already been cited, Columbus took to Cuba and which has gone wild in bush, both there and all over southern-central Florida, where it has turned into the mongrel "sour orange" with rough bitter rind. If these are not available use lemons, or limes, or better still small sour grapefruit.

Choose ½" thick steaks, not too large. Have the butcher pound quite thin, or do it in domestic privacy with one of those square small wood mauls with waffle-iron patterned face found in any household supply store. Next cut oranges in half and rub and squeeze well all over steaks to get maximum oil from the rind onto every part of the meat. Crush garlic cloves very fine and spread a trifle on steaks also. Salt lightly and place in bowl, squeezing juice on each layer. Let marinate 2 hours, brush lightly with olive oil and grill over fierce heat, or live coals; searing briefly first—one side then the other. Have salt and hand pepper mill at elbow, and season as served. A little butter helps now, and of course they should be served sizzling.

NOW a RATHER AMAZING AFFAIR of GROUND BEEF & *PLANTANOS,* or LARGE COUSINS of OUR FAMILIAR BANANA, which COSTA RICANS CALL *EMPANADAN de PLANTANO MADURO*

We once attended a boys' academy with a son of the current President of Costa Rica, and later on when on two occasions journeying down the Central American west coast from Acapulco, Mexico, to Panama we were able to gather many tropical and exotic dishes—Guatemala, Salvador, Costa Rica.

For those of us with no true plantains within plucking distance we recommend red bananas, or yellow; preferring those not too ripe, for once. In fact, their texture should be quite firm. Now much of the beef native to Costa Rica is well muscled from climbing the volcanic peaks of that region, and not always tender in original form, so a food chopper is everywhere necessary to save the teeth of the old ones!

To every ½ lb ground top round beef allow 1 average mild onion, red preferred, ¼ clove crushed garlic, 4 hard bananas; salt and black pepper to taste. Grind and regrind meat with onion, garlic and all seasonings. Parboil bananas, or steam *with skins on.* Crush to pulp, stiffen with a trifling amount of flour, and make a waffle shaped patty, put enough ground beef in center and fold over to seal in meat completely; pressing edges down with a fork. Fry in deep fat, olive oil preferred, at 370° Fahrenheit. A big deep skillet will do if no fat kettle and cage are at hand.

WORDS to the WISE No. XIX, on the NECESSITY of THAWING out ALL SORTS of MEATS, so that WE MAY NOT BE HOIST on the PETARD of RAW CENTERS

A great many folk, especially ladies, take meat directly from cold refrigerators and pop it into hot stoves. Under such a frigid barrier all time tables are off, as to how long to cook. A cut or joint will be well done on surface and raw within. Therefore let meat stand in kitchen for an hour at least before cooking.

BEEFSTEAK, *MOLOKAI,* which Last Is a Mighty Rugged Island in the Hawaiian Group, once Known for Father Damien's Leper Colony but Now for Its Cattle Ranches, Its Goat and Pheasant & Its Hospitality

Big thick juicy steaks come easily out there, and we have noted a trio of beefsteak dressings brought to us by the classmate of a big rancher gentleman; and which added zest and flavour to his outdoor grilling picnics set on stupendous cliffs pitching down a half mile or so into the sea, where waterfalls arc outward into pale white plumes, and die, and are whisked away by the urgent trade winds.

Sauce No. 1. Mix 4 tbsp roquefort cheese with 2 tbsp evaporated (or fresh) milk; add 1 tsp worcestershire, 1 tbsp scraped onion pulp, juice 1 lemon, a little salt and 1 dash tabasco. Spread on when steak is just done, top side only; pop back under broiler and count 10 slowly. Outdoors, spread both sides, put to fire for same time.

Sauce No. 2. Here is a fine background for a big 3" juicy steak! . . . Melt ¼ lb butter, add 1 tbsp onion pulp, ½ clove crushed garlic and 1 can button mushrooms, sliced thin. Simmer 5 minutes, season, add ½ cup red wine and 1 tbsp soya sauce. Add pepper and a very little salt, to taste. Thicken with a very little flour if necessary, first working smooth in liquid. Simmer up again, and pour over steak when done.

Sauce No. 3. Mixed deviled Virginia ham with prepared mild mustard, half and half. Just before steak is done, spread on lower side and then broil up; spread on other side, and repeat briefly. This is really more of a cooking adjunct than a sauce.

Sauce No. 4. Simmer 3 tbsp chopped yellow orange peel in same of water for 5 minutes; strain liquid and reserve. Melt out 3 tbsp guava jelly and to it add the orange-water, 2 tsp orange juice, same of lemon juice, ½ tsp ground ginger, 1 tsp prepared mustard and 2 tbsp port wine; pinch of salt and 1 tsp paprika. Spread this on sizzling steaks just before serving. Modify to suit taste at any point.

A TRUE BEEFSTEAK & KIDNEY PIE from the FILES of OUR FRIEND the LATE C. H. B. QUENNELL, ESQ., of CRAB TREE LANE, BERKHAMPSTEAD, HERTS: a GENTLEMAN, SCHOLAR, ARCHITECT, & the ONE MODERN AUTHOR WHO HAS BROUGHT the *EVERYDAY HISTORY of ENGLAND* CLEARLY & PLEASANTLY to Us in HIS BOOKS under such TITLE

One very pleasant summer we spent in Boxmoor, Hertfordshire, wandering about the countryside in a negligible motor car, visiting friends, meeting others. Quennell's intellect, his intimate knowledge of England's past, meant a great deal to us. This beefsteak & kidney pie dates back well into the 17th Century.

Cut 2 lbs ½″ thick rump steak into pieces 1″ x 1½″ square. Slice 1 lb veal kidneys thin, after trimming away useless addenda. Melt out 4 tbsp butter and toss in beef and kidneys, meantime seasoning with 2 tbsp minced chives or spring onions, ⅛ tsp powdered clove, 2 pinches each marjoram and summer savoury, rubbed fine, 1 broken bayleaf, pepper and salt. Saute 5 minutes, add ¼ cup sherry and a very little water. Simmer up and take off stove. . . . Beard ½ pint oysters; or leave as-is, depending on preference. Simmer these in their liquor, and simmer gently, while we count thirty, uncovered. Then take off. Pour off meat juices and reserve.

Take greased pie dish, put in layer beef and kidneys, then oysters. Repeat again, ending up with beef-kidney layer on top. Make roux of 2 tbsp each butter and flour, and thicken the reserved mixture juices and pour onto everything. Cover with ½″ layer of any good puff paste, to be noted in any good routine cookery book. Moisten edges and press down very firmly. Prick holes in center for vents, protect edges with circle of greased paper. Brown 10 minutes at around 400°, then reduce to 300° for around 1¾ hours. A little cold milk, powdered milk, powdered egg, or butter brushed on will glaze the crust.

TOM DAVIN'S STEAK-in-SALT, Broiled & Couched on Lengthwise-Cut Trenchers of Bread

Tom Davin, a quick-minded gentleman of Irish extraction, is also an eating man of most interesting and random career, varying from editing the *Natural History Magazine* up at the American Museum in New York, to marching with quaint and disordered fellows in May Day parades in Union Square. . . . We use his own words.

"Buy a decent steak, and a bag of salt for a dime. Either semi-coarse salt of ice cream generating variety, or the ordinary non-pouring table variety.

. . . Mix a bowl of salt and water until it is the identical mixture of your five year old youngster's sand pies, then spread it evenly on one side of the steak until about ½″ thick. Just to make it sound complicated, pat it with the hand to make firmly smooth on top. Pop under broiler not over 1″ from heat. And salt side up, naturally.

Broil as long as you usually do, no longer. A guide will be when the salt is a bit browned. Draw forth, turn over, repeating the salt paste process on the other side. Broil again. Take out and break the tile-like carapace with any handy hard object. Butter and pepper to taste. . . . There will be no gravy yet, it's all in the steak. Nor will there be cooking bouquet. That is in the steak too. There are no burned, dried out areas whatsoever, and you can cut it with a badminton racquet."

This routine may be varied ad infinitum by brushing with any series of marinades desired, and here again the salt chemise insures that all flavours be sealed in until the juicy finale when they are yielded up in all their unshared fragrance under knife. Our own routine is to turn steak, adding 2d salt layer, when 1st layer is barely hard.

BUBBLE-and-SQUEAK, Being Fried Salt Beef & Cabbage, which Is One of England's Classic Dishes

Our first introduction to this was through a London resident whom we met "under the clock at Charing Cross," and accompanied to a nearby many-storied restaurant corresponding in a gay nineties sort of way with our own Childs; only, if possible, noisier. Taken with a pint of bitter ale it makes an easy and fairly indigestible one-dish meal. The cooking sounds inspire the title. Even if we do not love this dish that title is worth a trial, certainly!

First brown slices of somewhat underdone boiled corned, or salted, beef in plenty of butter. Cook sliced young cabbage in lightly salted briskly boiling water for 10 minutes, no more. Drain and after removing cooked beef, put pan to fire again and toss cabbage in the butter. A minute or so is enough. Finally heap cabbage in center of serving dish, stack beef in a ring around it. Season with pepper, and don't skimp on the butter. A little hot or mild mustard is the traditional garnish.

THE ORIGINAL *CALALOU,* from which the GREAT MISSISSIPPI DELTA COUNTRY INHERITED HER MODERN VERSION often CALLED by the SAME NAME, WAS a RIB-TICKLING & MIGHTY DISH

This vast catch-all stew dates back to the dark heart of West Africa, back beyond the cruel slave ships. It was conceived within earshot of the drums of Damballa, the snake god, crying out their sinister message of *vaudou.* It came down, varying with tribes and seasonal larder, until it finally reaches us through Afro-American tutelage from slave cooks to modern kitchen boys or mammies. Palm oil was largely used in its original cooking; sometimes a sort of lard; and, later on, peanut oil. Olive oil is near enough for our palates, and easily had.

Simply cut up chunks ½" x 1" x 2" of any raw meat: beef, pork, chicken, lamb, mutton, game. To this add more chunks of West Indian or Florida crawfish, shrimp, northern lobster; a cut up rabbit, a jointed duck, pigeons, doves, coots, squirrels,—anything! Heat plenty of olive oil and brown everything slowly for 15 minutes. Save a little of the oil. This seals in flavour and parallels the jungle roasting over coals. Now put in a big heavy kettle with a little water, cover tightly.

Cut up an equal amount of mixed vegetables: okra, quartered tomatoes, cubes of cucumber, eggplant, onions, green corn off the cob, yams,—anything on hand. Although the Chief's wife didn't bother about herbs she knew salt, pepper substitutes, and an aromatic or two—therefore we urge addition of the following: bayleaf, 3 or 4 to each 2 quarts of solids, a small bunch of parsley, a handful of chopped peanuts, several pinches of marjoram, rosemary or savoury. Add enough beef broth or water to make a liquid stew-soup, simmering slowly until meat falls apart. There is literally no limit to the additional variations possible through using worcestershire, sherry or other wines, garlic, chopped up orange peel, chutney, capers, hard sliced bananas, in quantity and fineness to suit our mood of the moment. . . . It is like our own Brunswick Stew, the Spaniard's *Olla Podrida*—that dish of the oddly translatable name which further adds bacon, saffron, cinnamon, pork sausages, chick or black eyed peas, turnips, lean ham, corned beef, whole cloves and a pig's ear!

Calalou is the best big pot camp dish we know; serve with roasted potatoes and heaps of boiled rice—white or wild. A bottle of still Burgundy, Chianti or any not too tart red wine is companionate.

CORNED BEEF & CABBAGE FIT for an EMPEROR, from DINTY MOORE'S in SHANGHAI

Time before last, when we steamed slowly up the muddy Whangpoo River, past the ruined Chinese forts gaping from the high-explosives, past platoons of Japanese soldiers thumping out bursts of machine gun fire at indefinite targets for our American benefit, it was to find Chapei—the native Chinese business and residential quarter, a smoking shambles of crazy tottering walls, staring unglazed windows, and splintered trees. Under the scowling gaze of suspicious, stocky little Japanese sentries we went about with our f-2 Leica, then back to town again in the raw March wind, up a back street not far off Nanking Road, and there a sign *Dinty Moore's* cheered us mightily. . . . We'd give them back their oriental civilization and undeclared war, just becoming fashionable. There we'd find something we needed, something literally to sink our teeth into, something homely and lacking in evasions and racial arrogances; something to make us forget those limp dead Chinamen in faded denim lying unburied in the pools of water—and God knew if there is anything deader-looking than a denim-clad dead Chino boy, we'd yet to see it!

Then Dinty Moore's and the hearty sight of American gobs and marines, and corned beef and'! . . . The quality of the beef is what counts, and the brown sugar is the touch to point it up. *Kirin* beer washed it down in Shanghai; we suggest any good ale at home.

Command 5 lbs of good brisket, cut from butt end, and not overburdened with fat. Trim off ragged unsightly edges, for corned beef when properly done is a fine rose-petaled thing, not a drab frayed-out mass of fatty fibres! Put in plenty of cold water to cover, boil up *very* slowly and skim well. Let boil briskly for 5 minutes, skim again; add ½ cup brown sugar and then barely simmer for 3¼ hrs or so.

Draw off the fire and let cool somewhat in ½ the cooking water. Then put on platter, place plate on top with heavy weight on it to press firmly. Meanwhile have big pot of briskly boiling salted water containing ¼ tsp baking soda, and a chunk of smoked pork, or hambone. Cut cabbage in quarters. Cook uncovered for 15 to 18 minutes. Condiments needed: lots of butter, mild mustard; potatoes boiled in jackets, brushed with lard, and dried in oven.

A TONGUE of BEEF, Cooked with Butter-Fried Chopped Almonds, Herbs, Spices, and Swimming under a Delicious Mexican Sauce

Cuernavaca, summer colony out of Mexico City, lies in a raw red earth valley over the 12,000 foot range to the westward. Here in 1937, among other things, we found a civilized manner of living almost feudal in its self-sufficient exclusiveness. Each house has its own high-walled compound; its stout bolt-studded gates. Outside it is dry, almost barren; within we find green turf bordered with brilliant flowers. Purple bougainvillea flings its blazing fan across pale salmon pink walls, its vibration tone so high as almost to be physically felt through the eye. Birds in cages, running free; men and women in the smartest slack suits like Palm Beach or Juan les Pins. Conversation of merit; discreet flirtation, food, wine. It is a small jewel-perfect world sufficient unto itself. Then for the mid-day, the heavy, meal—this tongue *Mexicano.*

Take fresh beef tongue, soak an hour in salted water; drain, trim neatly, then set to boil in cold salted water skimming every 10 minutes or so. Simmer gently until tender. Meantime chop 1/3 cup blanched almonds, brown in 2 tbsp butter containing a 2″ piece of cinnamon bark and 6 whole cloves. Set aside. . . . Fry out ½ a large red onion, minced fine, and 1 clove garlic, in 1 tbsp lard. When gently tendered add 4 peeled, quartered tomatoes; then salt and pepper to taste. Add 1/3 cup sherry, 1 tbsp guava jelly, simmer up, rub through coarse sieve. Slice tongue, arrange on platter. Garnish with nasturtium blossoms and leaves. Pass sauce separately. . . . Chestnuts, piñon or pine nuts, and hazelnuts are also used at times.

A VARIED PARADE of LAMBS, & YOUNGER MUTTONS

LAMB BROCHETTE in the CAUCASIAN STYLE—or *KAVKASKI SHASHLIK*—which MAY NOT BE IGNORED

A *brochette* is French for a large skewer, of course; and that first time in Paris, in the spring, and living at little Hotel Daunou over Ciro's famous restaurant, our day began with the ordained pilgrimage across the narrow street to Harry's American Bar where we would meet the One Girl, and two New Orleans silver fizzes—treated elsewhere in this work—then a happy rambling about: to the Bois, to see Helen Wills at the Rolland Garros stadium; to Versaille, then like as not ending up at Kasbek, mentioned elsewhere, to hear the Tsar's guitarist, hear the superb chorus of big breasted Caucasian girls, the dagger dancers, and to consume *Shashlik* packed on bayonets, and brought into the small dark place flaming and spitting fire.

This receipt is not just the usual grilled lamb, but with things besides, such as Russian spiced vinegar for grilling.

Order 5 lbs of lamb with a little fat. Cut into 1½" squares about ½" or so thick, first pounding lightly to flatten well. Marinate 2 hrs in the Spiced Vinegar, noted below. Dry on a cloth, run onto skewers, alternating with squares of smoked bacon. First, brush with the spiced grilling vinegar, given below. Broil over coals or under broiler for about 10 minutes, turning now and then. Heat a little brandy, put on with spoon, serve flaming by candlelight—and there we have a smart bit of business.

RUSSIAN SPICED GRILLING VINEGAR

Take ½ cup red wine vinegar—tarragon-flavoured is best—and put in mixing bowl previously rubbed with a trifle of garlic and 1 tsp salt. To this add ¼ tsp black pepper, ¼ tsp clove, ¼ tsp nutmeg, ½ cup tart white wine and ¼ cup olive oil. Whip up well and pour over squares of lamb just before putting to fire.

WORDS to the WISE No. XX, how to DISPEL the TENDENCY of all LAMBS & MUTTONS toward STRONG TASTE

The answer is very simple: just remove all skin and the very tough fatty tissues, leaving the clear meat and pleasant fat.

A CHINESE METHOD of FRYING THINLY SLICED LAMB, together with PINEAPPLE, MUSHROOMS, SOYA SAUCE, & BAMBOO SHOOTS

In early spring of 1932 we were booked to see Mei Lan-Fang perform at the big Chinese theatre just off Chienmen Road, which fetched him in some five thousand dollars Mex each week, and our rickshaw boy Limo, a Manchu, took us to a native restaurant where, of all the typical Chinese dishes, this seemed easy enough to remember and record here. The Chinese cabbage looks like an overgrown stalk of celery and is in every decent market these days. Whereas sesame oil is correct for Chinese frying, in most cases, use butter or olive oil.

To 4 tbsp frying fat in a big pan, add 1 lb thinly sliced lamb in 2″ square pieces, brown very lightly. Then put in 1 cup thinly sliced bamboo shoots, 2 slices canned pineapple recut very thin into 1½″ squares; 1 cup thinly sliced fresh mushrooms, 4 cups sliced Chinese cabbage; 1 mild onion sliced thin also, 2 tbsp soya sauce, a speck of crushed garlic, a pinch or 2 of powdered ginger and 1 cup beef or veal stock. Season to taste. When meat is tender thicken with a little flour worked smooth with hot sauce, stir in 2 tbsp of any white wine, saki, or sherry. Serve on hot platter.

CURRIES & LIKE ADVENTURES, BEING MADE USUALLY out of CHICKENS, ARE DISCUSSED in the CHAPTER DEDICATED to *POULTRY & the INNER DRESSINGS of FOWLS*

Curries may also, and properly, be made out of lamb, sometimes of veal, but never of pork. Any right thinking Muslim would shudder at the very thought. Therefore, with curry in view and chickens scarce, our first suggestion would be curry of lamb—proceeding exactly as though curried chicken were in process, merely substituting one flesh for another. . . . Again let us emphasize that the usual error with western world curries is that we fail to cook the curry sauce into the meat over sufficient period of time, but tend to whip up a quick curry sauce or gravy, pouring this over meat that has been cooked with no curry powder in the pot. . . . For this reason the flavours do not really penetrate as they should, neither do they taste as they should, not having experienced enough, or continuous, cooking heat necessary to extract their best efforts.

LAMB, *HAWAII,* Being Something Very Different from a Ranch on the Northern Slope of Mauna Kea, on the "Big Island" of Hawaii

We have only seen the snow capped top of Mauna Kea, soaring nearly 14,000 feet into the blue Hawaiian sky, once. It was before the days of regular inter-island flying, and for reasons not so valid now we and another kindred soul chartered a small Sikorsky Amphibian, and took off from Honolulu to beat our steamer into Hilo, or to have more time that previous night in Honolulu, we forget now which. But there was a dusty head wind, and after quitting Maui, we weren't making 60 miles an hour over the water, and the gasoline gauges weren't too cheering, and finally our pilot said "There's Mauna Kea, you fellows, and somewhere in a nice sugar cane field on that slope is where we land."

Yes, he was right all right, and we saw Mauna Kea's dazzling white cone up there; only it wasn't a sugar cane field at all where he set that box kite down but a sort of pasture, and not nearly as smooth as it looked from upstairs, and the cactus plants were doing a Virginia reel under our landing gear as he pancaked her upwind. So there we were, nowhere in Hawaii, and when we looked up again—that quick—Mauna Kea snow peak was gone in a plateau of white cloud, and the mountain was so big the slope looked gentle on both sides of us, as though all the world were gently tilted—cactus and sugar cane and grazing cattle and all—toward some invisible top to everything. . . . Lamb, *Hawaii,* like many things to eat and drink in that charming fleet of islands, requires pineapple—either sun-ripe or canned.

Have the butcher bone a nice 6 lb leg of lamb; weighed after boning.

Crush ½ clove of garlic, mix it with 1 tbsp scraped onion pulp, turn into a pan with 2 tbsp melted butter, 2 tbsp finely chopped parsley, ½ tsp ginger, salt and pepper to taste, and finally 1 cup pineapple pulp. If canned add no sugar, if fresh add 1 tbsp brown sugar. Toss lightly for 5 minutes.

Meantime, or about 2 hrs before, brush outside of lamb with lemon juice, rubbing with cut rind. Stuff bone cavity with the spiced pineapple dressing after thoroughly mixing with 2 cups toasted bread crumbs. Sew up neatly. Dust outside with a pinch or so of ginger, salt, pepper, and flow on 2 more tbsp melted butter. Sear in hot oven, about 425°, then reduce oven to 350°, cover roast and baste with pineapple juice every ten minutes or so. When done make pan gravy by working a little flour smooth with hot basting juices; reduce to good thickness on top of stove, then put through coarse sieve and serve in sauce boat.

BOTH *JAMBALAYAS*—THOSE AFRO-AMERICAN ADAPTATIONS of FRENCH-SPANISH CREOLE DISHES, and the EAST INDIAN *PULAO,* SEEM to SUIT WESTERN PALATES BEST when CONSTRUCTED of CHICKENS, and ARE therefore LISTED under *POULTRY & the INNER DRESSINGS of FOWLS,* on PAGES 91 and 95

However, by substituting beef, veal, lamb, mutton, shrimp, lobster or any other miscellaneous flotsam and jetsam—and using the same receipt proportion given for chicken—will quickly readapt the dish to what is on the larder shelf, or in the amateur chef's cooking mind at the moment.

A SIKH *KABAB, KABOB* or *KEBOB,* a DISH from BRITISH INDIA'S NORTH COUNTRY BORDER not too FAR from KHYBER PASS, where THERE ARE MINGLED IDEAS & MINGLED PEOPLES from MANY OUTLANDS, such as AFGHANISTAN, THIBET, MONGOLIA & the RUSSIAS

Sheep used for food is traditional to Mohammedans, and through various conquests and interpenetrations this dish of the Sikhs is much like Russian *Shashlik* noted above. Oddly enough, too, it is quite similar to the way Cubans grill thin beefsteaks. As for the Sikhs themselves, we greatly admire them. They are the most loyal, most dependable soldiers Britain owns. Throughout the vast East—from the Church of the Nativity in Bethlehem where we met one with full side arms and pistol keeping watch to make sure the Armenian Christian priests and the Greek Orthodox priests didn't pull one another's hair due to the latter walking across a rug corner belonging to the former—they help police Britain's Empire. Being Muslim, Sikhs may eat lamb, mutton, veal or beef, but pork is forbidden—while neighbouring Hindus in India may eat pork, whereas consumption of veal or beef invites eternal damnation. This *Kabab* can be made of lamb, mutton, beef or veal; but lamb is best, and preferred out there.

Select 2 lbs of boned lamb with some fat, but have gristle and tough fibres removed. Pound lightly with back of a heavy chef's knife to firm, then cut into pieces 2" x 1½" x ½" or so thick, saving all juices. Make marinade either of vinegar base, or juice of 2 lemons—about ¼ cup total. Mix well with ¼ cup olive oil. To this add 2 pinches each of powdered mace, nutmeg and clove; ½ clove crushed garlic and 2 tbsp onion pulp. Heat is supplied with cayenne, dry mustard or black pepper—to taste. Salt fairly strongly. Brush pieces of lamb with this and let stand 1 hr. . . . Run on long skewers: a slice of lamb, a thin slice of onion, a slice of lamb—5 of latter total. Baste with marinade now and then. Grill over fierce fire and don't worry if meat is slightly burned on edges, as this is typical. . . . We recommend olive oil here as the semi-rancid fats so often used in the Orient will give an average westerner "a turn!"

Traditional accompaniment is a dish of *Chupattis,* which are unleavened cakes made of whole wheat flour mixed briskly with enough water to form a pancake batter consistency, lightly salted. Cook like pancakes, on a griddle. *Chupattis* are used with equal efficiency to blot up succulent juices on plate, and also to tidy up the face from eating our *Kabab* off skewers corn-on-the-cob fashion! . . . A trifle of curry powder is often added to the oil marinade.

A NOBLE QUINTET of PORKS, Ranging from a Wine Treatment for Our Own Immortal Virginia Hams to Spanish Haunch of Boar, to a Delightful Method by which Danish Gentlemen Deal with the Common—and too often Ignored—Item Known as the Spare Rib

VIRGINIA PEANUT FED HAM in a Fragrant Chemise of Brown Sugar, Honey & Spice, Garbed in a Pastry Jacket, and Baked in Native Scuppernong Wine, *à la JAVA HEAD*

We have spent some little time in Virginia, in school in Charlottesville where in one cellar there were still the oak pins for raising the slave beds during daytime hours; cruising the Chesapeake, and through the Sounds and Canals of the Inland Waterway. From our friend Pender, whose old-time grocery in Norfolk is a perfumed and aromatic cave of romance, we were taught what a peanut-fed Smithfield ham was, which other hams may not be. Taught how to boil and bake such hams; then from a friend in Keswick came news of the pastry jacket; from Paul Garrett—whose family has made Virginia Dare wines for a century, we learned about scuppernong wine. The rest was our own idea.

Scrub a 2 year old Virginia, or other plump country-smoked ham, and soak 3 or 4 days in cold water into which has been added ½ cup of vinegar. Change water twice daily. Simmer then, very slowly, in water to cover which also contains ¼ cup vinegar—or in ½ water and ½ cider. Change water after 3 hrs. Allow ½ hr per lb; when tender trim off skin neatly. . . . Now score lightly with sharp knife, cover with a not-too-moist brown sugar and honey paste to a good ¼″ thickness, into which has been worked 1 small handful of cloves; then cover further with a ¼″ chemise of good pastry dough—being sure to form a jug-like neck on top. Form a stopper, roll this in flour. Put in the neck lightly.

Put in slow oven around 325° Fahrenheit until dough sets hard. Take out again, remove stopper and *slowly* pour in all the Virginia Dare scuppernong wine that sugar-honey jacket will absorb. Cork up and brown in same slow oven for 1 to 1½ hrs, depending whether ham is medium or large. . . . Yes, men and women may come and go, revolutions wrack monarchies, wives and husbands deceive us, taxes mount, the mechanized age buffet our ringing heads, but one of these affairs will renew faith in the universe. Presidents, kings, premiers, dictators, head waiters, cinema stars and glamour maidens become merely animated organisms doing mad and aimless jigs, but such a ham is a gem pure, serene, comforting. To our wry and lawless mind such a ham is, during these chancey days, one of our few remaining importances.

ENGLISH BOILED HAM, from JOURDANS, BUCKINGHAMSHIRE, 1932, INVOLVING SUCH MATTERS as BLACK STRAP MOLASSES, DARK or LIGHT BEER, BROWN SUGAR, and OTHER AIDS to SUCCULENCE

Scuttling through the hedgerows we went to Jourdans to see the grave of William Penn, lying chaste and with nicely timed impartiality between his two wives, and to photograph the so-called "Mayflower Barn," framed throughout with oaken timbers taken from that worthy vessel after being broken up. Stopping for luncheon at the home of family friends we were delighted by thick cuts of boiled ham offering something entirely new in flavour. This is the answer, and if English hams are used, choose Buckinghamshire or Hampshire.

Scrub smoked ham and soak for 3 to 4 days in cold water; changed daily; the firmer the longer. Trim off dark portions, put in a kettle with 1 pint of beer, 2 cups black strap molasses, 1½ cups brown sugar, and 1 cup each of chopped onion, carrot and cabbage. Add just enough cold water to cover ham; simmer up slowly and cook well covered until tender. Then 20 minutes before taking off stir in a double cup of sherry. This is extra good served cold, with ale.

ROASTED FRESH RAZORBACK HAM, ADAPTED from the SPANIARD'S ROAST HAUNCH of WILD BOAR, or *PIERNA di JABALI*

In Spain, barring revolutions, roast boar's leg was a favourite delicacy. But to our mind boar of any nationality and diet is a bit strong fare. In fact, from our rather long experience in the Florida marshes, and, briefly, on India shoots, we really don't care for any part of boars, for several reasons not requisite to mention. While perhaps not so sporting, the rear end of a tender, discreetly wild and woods-ranging shote has far more stove-appeal, to our school of thought. Especially in the Fall when the acorns drop, are they succulent and worthy of turning this—or the other—cheek. And instead of putting them to fire in crude backwoods fashion let's treat them more kindly with the Spanish touch that their inherent gamey taste may be enhanced as much as possible.

After hanging in the refrigerator for 2 days, well rubbed with salt and lots of hand-ground black pepper, take out and put in a pan. Pour 2 bottles of tart white wine, ½ cup brandy—Bourbon whiskey here! —3 good pinches each of sage and thyme, 6 crushed bayleaves, into a vessel. Mix well. . . . Now rub ham with big cut clove of garlic, then cut several rough lemons, sour oranges of the wild southern variety, lemons or limes. First squeeze juice over ham, then rub hard with cut rinds to extract every drop of oil possible. Pour wine-brandy-herb marinade over the ham and hide in refrigerator for a day and a night.

Take out, save the marinade for basting. Let thaw for ½ hr. Paint *well* with olive oil, and first sear in hot oven at 450°, then open door to drop down to slow oven around 300° or just above. Roast thoroughly and slowly, figuring around ½ hr per lb. Baste every 15 minutes *without fail,* employing the Spaniard's marinade for this use.

WORDS to the WISE No. XXI, a WORD on the VIRTUES of BASTING PORK in any FRESH FORM, and of SLOW, THOROUGH COOKERY in EVERY CASE

The secret of pork cookery, that which is so marvellously understood by southern darky barbecue cooks, is cook *very slowly until well done,* and baste ceaselessly. Rare pork is a thing not to be served to any man; dry and juiceless pork is just as bad as dry and juiceless baked fish.

NOW in PASSING, in CASE YOU'VE EVER WONDERED, HERE'S ONE of the BEST TRADITIONAL OPEN-PIT BARBECUE BASTINGS from the REALLY DEEP SOUTH. . . . BASTE OFTEN, and THEN BASTE!

Heat 2 cups of vinegar, add 3 tbsp butter, 1½ tsp black pepper, 1 tsp cayenne, 2 tsp salt and the proceeds of 1 can tomatoes put through a coarse sieve to eliminate skin and seeds. Mix well.

POLISH PORK LOIN, POACHED *à la POTOCKA,* an EXOTIC from WARSAW, & OWNING a NOTABLE SAUCE MADE from a BLEND of MADEIRA WINE, HONEY, SPICES & TART FRUIT CONSERVES

In America boiled pork, like boiled turkey, is unknown and unbelievable. Sweet sauces also are ignored, the usual apple sauce being good enough. But here is a thought dating long before the day of Ignace Paderewski or the Polish Corridor.

Order a choice boned loin cut into 3" lengths. Boil slowly in salted water—starting cold and skimming well—with 3 or 4 bayleaves, the juice of a small lemon, 3 minced spring onions *and* their tops, a pinch of sage, and the same of rosemary if we have it on shelf. Done when tender. . . . The sauce amount depends on size of pork cut, but in any case it is made the same. Take a pint of veal or beef broth and when it boils add 2 tbsp bitter orange marmalade, the same of currant jelly or tart cherry jam, the same of quince or crabapple conserve. Stir well, add grated yellow rind of a lemon, ¼ tsp powdered clove, ½ tsp cinnamon, the juice of 1 lemon for tartness, ¼ cup sherry or Madeira. Mix well, stand aside.

Now blot the pork loin dry, cut into ½" thick slices, dip in egg yolk lightly beaten, fine crumbs, and brown lightly under broiler. Serve sauce in separate boat, or pour over on platter, as desired.

HOW OUR COPENHAGEN GOURMET WOULD TREAT the SERIOUS CHALLENGE of PORK SPARE RIBS

Outside of the deep south, pork spare ribs fetch steaming dreams of sauerkraut to most of our minds, but here's a variation from Denmark to try out on that outdoor grill with the sheet-iron roasting oven, we've just built!

Cut ribs into pairs, allowing 4 ribs per person. Brush with lemon juice, rub with salt and pepper, dust on a little ground mace. Let stand. . . . Soak large prunes overnight, allowing 1 per rib. Have 1 tart apple slice per rib; enough butter, melted, to brush well, and a little milk for basting. . . . Cut flesh between ribs, but not quite through. Put 2 stoned prunes and 2 apple slices in each slit between ribs. Skewer with toothpicks; put in buttered roasting pan and cook in hot oven around 400°. Sear uncovered for 5 minutes, then cover. Add milk to juices for basting. The cooking job takes around 40 minutes, or slightly less. . . . Just in case the name may be of use to us—and it probably won't—the official name for this dish is *Svinemorbrad*.

EXPLODED OLD WIVES' TALE No. V, on the FALLACY of AFFIXING a RED APPLE, or any other FRUIT for that MATTER, in the MOUTH of the SHY & TENDER PORKER, *before* ROASTING. ALSO ONE GARNISH ITEM

We had cooked our third suckling pig, under varied circumstances, before some wise ally informed us that the only possible method of serving him with a nice red apple in his open mouth was to introduce a small block of wood—apple size—between his teeth *before* roasting. When done, remove the wood block and substitute the shiny apple. . . . Red bird peppers of small size will replace the bleary eyes with a scarlet touch; likewise red maraschino cherries or fresh ripe cherries will do the job even better.

SUCKLING PIG DONE in the TRUE POLISH STYLE, and CONTRARY to USUAL AMERICAN CUSTOM, SERVED COLD & BOILED—not ROASTED & HOT

This dish was recommended to us by a random and unruly associate who distinguished himself by disembarking both himself and a motor car of parts at the northernmost tip of Norway and driving the blooming thing all over the Scandinavias, Finland, Poland and into Russia where, along with other more important things, it was impounded by some of Mr. Stalin's right bowers. His final instruction was to chill the meat *very* cold before serving.

Instead of cooking whole, have the animal jointed. Cover with cold water—no herbs or seasonings whatever, just water! Salt is added 10 minutes before taking off the fire,—just why, neither our friend nor his Polish informants could satisfactorily explain. This should be after from 1½ to 2 hrs, depending on size of piglet. . . . Chill cold as possible, serve sliced with chilled horseradish sauce made by grating *fresh* horseradish—under no condition employ the stale bottled type!—and mixing in the following proportion: ¼ cup horseradish, 1 tbsp tarragon vinegar and 1 cup sour cream. Cold tart white wine is in order, rather than the more conventional red. Receipt for sour cream is given elsewhere, Page 19.

THE LAND of FORMER PREMIER PADEREWSKI CONTRIBUTES, further, a DEVASTATING STUFFING for ROAST SUCKLING PIG, which WE COULD in NO CONDITION REFUSE ADMISSION

For an out-and-out man's party we have never found anything so satisfactory as a small porker weighing, say, 25 to 30 lbs, and roasted by an amateur; served brown and fragrantly sizzling with a bright red apple in his mouth; or perhaps covered with hot brandy and set alight. The usual stuffings of bread, onion, salt, pepper and sage, offer little variation; and as the stuffing is what men also admire almost as much as the piglet himself, we believe a bit more attention to the subject is likely to cause an amateur chef's name to be noted in the land.

Remove the green gall sac from 4 chicken livers and cut small. Chop 2 big mild onions quite fine. Put these in a wood mixing bowl and add 1 tbsp each of chopped fresh dill, marjoram, basil and tarragon, the last 3 rubbed between palms. Next add 2 tbsp chopped parsley, ½ lb melted butter, 3 or 4 cups of chopped mushrooms, 1 chopped tart apple, ½ cup coarsely chopped chestnuts, and 3 beaten eggs necessary to bind. . . . Now put in as many bread crumbs as may be needed to fill the cavity, first browning them lightly in a little very hot lard or olive oil. Mix thoroughly and add just enough rich brown gravy to moisten everything. Pack in well, and sew up with stout thread.

The distinction of this stuffing comes through lack of the eternal sage which in America always seems to walk hand in hand with any pork stuffing.

EXPLODED OLD WIVES' TALE No. VI, on the UNREASON of TRYING to CHOP FRESH PARSLEY in a BOWL after the MANNER of AUNT AMANITA

Ignore all antique advice toward bowl and vegetable choppers. Take parsley in left hand, or vice versa, and snip as fine as desired with a plain pair of scissors. It is vastly faster.

AND FINALLY WE INCLUDE a Brief but Intriguing List of Five Methods for Preparing Young Veals

FIRST of all ARE CUTLETS of VEAL, *á SEVILLANO;* Employing, as Is Now & Then the Case, a Small Amount of Bitter Chocolate in Connection with Meat Cookery

Brown 4 nice delicately salted cutlets, trimmed and lightly pounded, in 1/3 cup of quite hot olive oil. Brown ¼ cup chopped hazelnuts in a little hot oil also, while this is going on. . . . Take an oven dish, earthenware preferred, grease it and stack cutlets inside with several very thin slices of lightly grilled smoked ham in between each. Add 1½ cups of chopped fresh mushrooms, pour in ½ cup veal or chicken broth or stock, cover and start gently simmering. . . . Meanwhile gently tender 1 diced red onion in the oil used to cook the hazelnuts, add ½ cup tart white wine, 4 tbsp tomato paste, 2 pinches of saffron, and 1 pinch each of powdered mace, clove, and thyme. Heat in a saucepan, and into this put ½ square of bitter chocolate, cut into shavings. When thoroughly melted and mixed, put through a coarse sieve, reduce by about ¼; and along with the chopped nuts put into the cooking dish.

Simmer in a hot oven for 10 minutes longer; arrange meat on platter, surround with mushrooms in a ring, also the strips of ham; and cover with sauce.

VEAL CUTLETS or OLIVES, *alla ROSSINI,* Dedicated to a Composer Who not only Could Come out with Such Masterpieces as *WILLIAM TELL* & *STABAT MATER,* but also Was a Gourmet as well

From Pesaro Italy we bring this to you. It is very simple indeed and utterly delicious. . . . Have choice cutlets of veal trimmed and cut thin; pounded lightly. Spread each on one side with a slight coating of anchovy paste, and a sprinkling of finely chopped capers. Roll tightly, secure with a toothpick. Dip first in lemon juice, then in milk, then in beaten egg, then in flour. Fry in deep hot olive oil at 370°.

A RUSSIAN *PIROSHKI* COMPRISING ROLLS STUFFED with a Forcemeat of Veal Kidneys & other Desirable Things, then Browned in Oven

There probably weren't as many *Piroshki* variations in old Russia as there were *filets* of sole in Paris and curries in India, but the list certainly was limited only by the several imaginations of all the chefs in the land, and the food on the shelves. This one is especially attractive, and is easily done.

First poach or saute 2 veal kidneys in butter and a little white wine; then trim and chop fine. Next amputate the cap from one end of a hard French roll and set someone to work scooping out the soft interior, being sure they don't fracture the outer shell. . . . Now chop up 2 hardboiled eggs, mix with kidneys, and 1 cup of firmly cooked rice. Season with 3 tbsp finely chopped parsley, 2 tbsp chives or small spring onions, chopped fine, a finely broken bayleaf, ½ lb or less of melted butter, and a handful of sliced button mushrooms. Season delicately with salt and cayenne. Moisten with any saute juices and 1 tbsp sherry.

Stuff back into evacuated rolls, skewer lid in place with toothpicks, brush all over with plenty of melted butter and brown in hot oven around 400°. If kidneys are poached without using any butter, use a little sweet white wine rather than water. A lovely touch.

VEAL, *à la RUSSE,* BEING VIRTUALLY POACHED in COMMON WHITE WINE, CONCERNED with SWEET HERBS, SPICES, LEMON RIND, the WHOLE BEING SMOTHERED at the LAST in a DELICIOUS SAUCE of BLACK CAVIAR, the REDUCED COOKED JUICES of VEAL & a TOUCH of SOUR CREAM

This is the finest way of handling veal fillets that we have ever known. It is a *chef d'oeuvre* to keep secret until the dinner guest looms up who matters. Then, Ah then!

Have the butcher lard a fine 4 lb fillet with fat pork. Put in a large saucepan or average kettle. Put in a chopped pair of small spring onions, a pinch each of the usual sweet herbs: thyme, marjoram and savoury; 2 broken bayleaves, 12 whole cloves, 12 black peppercorns, the grated yellow rind of a lemon, and delicate seasoning of salt and cayenne. . . . Turn in 2 cups of dry white wine, and add enough veal stock or broth to cover the meat. Bring to a boil slowly and poach gently in this fragrant bath—skimming devotedly every 10 minutes, and 3 times during the first 5 minutes.

When veal is tender put it on a hot platter, slice it neatly, and keep hot. Reduce cooking sauce in saucepan by 1/3, strain through a coarse sieve, thicken with a little melted butter and flour, worked smooth, add 1 tbsp lemon or lime juice, additional salt or cayenne to taste, and finally 6 tbsp good black caviar. Simmer up once, serve hot, either out of a gravy boat or poured over the sliced veal. Garnish with green leaves, slices of hard egg, thin slices of lemon. A dry white wine, properly chilled, is complementary.

WORDS to the WISE No. XXII, concerning the RIGHT & PROPER MANNER in which to PREPARE SWEETBREADS before COOKERY

Many amateur chefs blush faintly when confronted with a veal sweetbread *au naturelle,* so to speak, hastily chop it up with averted gaze, assuming that in such dealing all the proprieties have been observed. Nothing could be farther from truth. . . . Face the sweetbread determinedly, eye to eye. Wash under the cold faucet and stand in slightly salted cold water for an hour or so. Blanch by dropping in a quart of boiling water containing 2 tbsp vinegar or 3 tbsp lemon juice—for from 10 to 15 minutes, depending upon age. Drain, pop in ice water, and put in refrigerator to keep attractively white. When needed for use, trim off any ragged portions, muscles or excess fat, split or cut into cubes. It only takes 5 minutes to broil or saute or poach, after this treatment. And remember, a sweetbread must never be rare; must be done *all* through. Therefore sample a small bit before serving.

SWEETBREADS, *alla BASILICA ULPIA,* as DISCOVERED by OURSELVES in ROME, in 1926, after a day SPENT at VILLA D'Este, at TIVOLI

Basilica Ulpia, that fascinating restaurant set in an ancient church cellar in Rome, is treated tenderly and at considerable length in the introduction or elsewhere in Volume II of this series, so through lack of space we must devote ourselves on this page solely to the dish in question.

Blanch, trim and firm as noted above in Words to the Wise, then poach gently in enough thin cream to cover, being very careful not to scorch, with lid tight on saucepan. When tender add 1 tbsp Marsala, Madeira or sherry wine for each cup of cream used. Season delicately with salt and cayenne. Thicken sauce slightly with a little white roux. . . . Now trim off bottoms of steamed artichokes, toss them gently in quite hot butter for 5 minutes or slightly less. Cut sweetbreads into fairly small pieces, mount on artichoke bottoms, and mask with sauce. Dust well with plenty of blanched almonds or pistachio nuts cut into thin slivers, surround with glazed halved apricots, well spiced. Pop in a very hot oven for just a moment. May be served flaming. Just pour a little heated brandy in a ring around the dish and set alight.

"As . . . Health & Spirits depend . . . upon Our Vivid Enjoyment of Our Meals, it seems to be a more Worthy Subject of Study than those . . . Occupations about which So Many busy Themselves in Vain."

The Art of Dining,
By the Honourable Thos. Walker,
England, 1825

CHAPTER IX

SALADS & SUPER-SALADS, *TOGETHER WITH* ODD VINEGARS & HERBINGS

Embracing an Elect Brotherhood from Famous & Humble Mixing Bowls around the World, such as Charles Nordhoff's *I'a Ota* from Faraway Tahiti; *Aguacate, Cubaño;* a Spine-Stiffening Matter of Bahama Conchs; a Vast Green Salad out of Damascus, & finally an Imperial Russian Affair of Crabmeats, Mushrooms, *Smetana,* & the Deity only Knows what Else, *à la Youssoupov.*

No ONE yet has satisfactorily explained why America, which makes the best fancy salad in the world, can produce the most horrific green affairs to be found on this confounded globe of ours. To our uncomplex and wry mind it can be due only to two causes: either we decline to learn the few conventional principles of the green salad, or when we do learn we don't give a tinker's dam.

With wide variation in native climate, more refrigeration than all the rest of the world combined, and with shops bulging with salad materials from Canada to the Argentine, we still slice our iceberg lettuce paper-thin with knives, and spill horrid, sweet, characterless liquids over the discouraged leaves, which labels laughingly inform us is "French Dressing." Inasmuch as our simple green salad came directly from France it, even in simple form, is an exotic. Salads made from vegetables or fruits having solid pulps are even worse here in the land of the free, for we naively douse sliced tomato, cooked artichoke, beets, and avocado, with the same ruddy fluid on moment of service—whereas one hour is minimum for marinating such victuals in dressing, and 3 to 4 hours is better. This last permits the oils, vinegars and seasonings to penetrate into the tissues of the basic ingredients, and changes them into a consummated salad, not merely cut up garden produce shedding dressing off like water from the proverbial duck, and in flavour finding itself flatter than a stepmother's kiss.

WORDS to the WISE No. XXIII, being a RIGID WARNING AGAINST the EVER-PRESENT SEPTIC-SALAD-MIXER, or S. S. M., and a PLEA for HIS IMMEDIATE SCOTCHING

This warning is no light matter we can assure you, for no matter what odd and unlikely spot we may find ourself in, just rig up salad bowl and condiments and, Presto! from some termite hole in the woodwork, out pops the S. S. M. . . . By septic we don't refer to the salad, poor innocent, but the self-anointed Mixer—that human microbe who for reasons known only to his progenitors and baby nurse, feels himself to be the sole elect person present at any gathering with grace or judgment enough to produce salad. His manner is condescending, his gesture, his tones, are mainly for the eye of the reasonably attractive female guests happening around.

His eye gleams with a baleful light, a fanatical light. The host is elbowed aside as an adolescent fallacy. We solemnly swear that if we don't scotch him then and there—be his name Percy J. K. L. Ponsonby-Foulckes, Bart., or Henri Etienne Vidal Compte de la Pharamonde, or Herr Doktor Wolff Chlodvig Putzi von Schnurrband, or just plain John Smith—that formerly emerald pile of crisp endive, brittle romaines, and curly chicorys, lively cresses, those fresh basils and chives for which we beat the markets, will all be weary, wilted and drowned; suffocated in a white hot brown highly seasoned liquid that tastes like a blend of the Boston Tea Party, chop suey, and muriatic acid.

For years we suffered in fulminating silence, while the addlepated women who had been as near France as "that cute restaurant on lower 5th Avenue," Oh'd and Ah'd; thinking such nice homey solutions as cyanide, arsenic gravy, slow strangulation over long periods of time with his own salad tongs, and an hors d'oeuvre of rat biskit and Stilton cheese causing him to die outside the house, seeking water.

No, valued friend, if we want a pleasant salad mix it as planned, ***with our own hand***. It is only too easy to divert the S. S. M. into verbal demonstrations about how he startled the chef at Foyot's, and that time he baffled the Frogs by drinking three bottles of claret after his coffee. Thus snow-blinded by the brilliance of his own self-mesmerism he is static for at least the 10 precious minutes we need to barricade ourself in the farthest pantry and see the thing through properly.

FIRST, then, the TRUE FRENCH GREEN SALAD, Rules for which Are Simple, & 9

1. Chill oil and vinegar until moment of use.
2. Chill greens. Discard old leaves. Trim brown stem ends.
3. If we are really a purist we'll store greens in the fragrant wood mixing bowl, in the refrigerator. Chilling both.
4. If really necessary for sand or sanitary reasons to wash, do so; if not, please do not. Blot off all trace of water or moisture with a cloth, or between cloths. As has been told, salad dressing simply will not cling to wet surfaces and the dressing does not stay put.
5. Break up the salad greens in the case of iceberg lettuce, with the fingers, don't cut into slices with a knife—just why we cannot explain. Neither can anyone explain why gentlemen should pay unpleasant ladies alimony. Just break up the greens willy-nilly.
6. Rub bowl with garlic clove, lightly or heavily as desired, *after* salt has been tossed into the wood. The abrasive action is perfect, and becoming attached to the solvent and soluble salt, the garlic promptly permeates the dressing.
7. Pour dressing over salad in the bowl. Toss briskly but never violently, *at once,* while leaves are crisp. Stop tossing when each individual leaf is coated. Soon we can proportion dressing so that when tossed the greens are coated and not one supernumerary drop remains in the bowl.
8. Serve on the instant, if crisp salad is desired.
9. If a moderately wilted salad is preferred, *fatiguer*—make tired—the lettuce by further tossing; or by letting stand for a few moments after the first tossing siege.

WORDS to the WISE No. XXIV, concerning the INEVITABILITY of GARLIC in GREEN SALADS

No salad mixer worthy of his bowl ever omits garlic from a green salad, and onion simply won't substitute. . . . The rules are simple, and 3.

1. Chopped garlic, *no matter how fine,* must never be used in an American salad.
2. Either toss salt in bowl before rubbing garlic around on the wood; or for more delicate palates, rub garlic on a bit of toast or hard stale bread called a *chapon,* for debatable reasons, and toss this instrument about and among the greens.
3. About ¼ clove of average size, rubbed off on the wood, will suit average tastes.

A FINAL FEW THOUGHTS on SALADS GENERALLY, Gleaned from all over the World during Our Various Wanderings

We have discovered that for the heavier Italian and Spanish salads it is wise to use olive oils from those countries, which are somewhat stouter in taste than the more delicate French oils—which last in their turn suit French salads to perfection.

Don't forget to get a couple of bottles of red wine vinegar for especial occasions, and that a cut up trio of garlic cloves kept perennially in the vinegar cruet will add a touch so delicate even dear Aunt Aspasia won't remark except how well the business tastes.

Any sweet herb goes well with salad, and in the case of chervil, basil, chives, tarragon and parsley, the fresh chopped herbs lend a more delicate and different taste than those dried. Salad is a chilled business, therefore use half again more herbs than in a like amount of food to be cooked. There are many sources for herbs among the bigger, more famous shops, but in all our experience there remains one source—a plant-wise Englishman come to these shores; an herb man and botanist of parts, who not only grows his own herbs, but picks them at dawn with the dew still fresh, and dries them as they should be dried —in shade, but in circulating air. There are no twigs or woody fibres, just tender leaves. He has a package of six: tarragon, summer savoury, basil, rosemary, and parsley in transparent celluloid jars with airtight screw caps that he will send with a booklet or leaflet on herbs for 1¾ dollars postage paid. Through no wish to employ commercialism, but for strict purity of product and merit we list his name: H. C. Pratt, Esq., Glen Tana Herb Gardens, Spokane, in the State of Washington. We have used his herbs for years. In cookery they will show more in a pinch than the usual in a teaspoonful.

When the salad requires onion pulp, simply cut the end off a large mild specimen, then scrape it with the concave side of a tablespoon. Pulp flavours evenly and inoffensively, which is not guaranteed with chopped onion, no matter how fine.

HERB VINEGARS to ADD that DELICATE TASTE & AROMA So DEAR to AMATEURS of the SALAD BOWL

Garlic vinegar has been described and tarragon vinegar is on the shelf of every grocery now, so we list 5 others worth knowing.

1. *Sweet Basil Vinegar:* Fill jar loosely with herb sprigs of dried basil. Fill with cider vinegar.
2. *Caper Vinegar:* Add 4 to 6 tbsp chopped capers to pint of cider vinegar.
3. *Elder Flower Vinegar:* Fill jar with washed flowers, no stems, leaves or entomological specimens. Fill with *boiling* cider vinegar.
4. *Sweet Herb Vinegar, Old English Style:* Take a wide mouth 1 qt jar and put in the following to the amount of 1½ oz each: summer savoury, shallots or chives, marjoram and tarragon; chopped fresh mint and balm, handful of each. Add cider vinegar enough to fill the jar.
5. *Dr. Kitchiner's Piquant Vinegar, probably the most Famous of All. Circa 1817, England:* Take 1 oz freshly ground or scraped horseradish, 1 tbsp salt, 1 tbsp hot made mustard, 1 tbsp minced shallots, ¼ tsp celery seed, ⅛ tsp cayenne (Or we suggest: to taste). Add 1 pt tarragon vinegar then handle as the others, noted below:

SALAD or HERB VINEGAR ROUTINE: Pound dried herbs fine, cover with vinegar, screw on top with a rubber ring, stand in the sun for 2 weeks. After this fermentation, strain, wring or press remaining juices from damp herbs. Let settle for 2 days, strain through cloth. It, or they, will add a delightful touch to any green salad, mayonnaise and so on.

EXPLODED OLD WIVES' TALE No. VII, on the FALLACY of USING MALT VINEGAR in SALADS

Forget the conventions of Aunt Mehitabelle, and keep malt vinegar for pickles, where it belongs! Also take guard from the storekeeper who will invariably thrust it at us when we ask for "vinegar." Use cider vinegar, and, if a purist, use red wine vinegar, which is far milder but Oh what a bouquet and taste!

NOW A DUTCH SALAD DRESSING from ANCIENT HAARLEM

Take 1 cup of thick sour cream, 2 tbsp tarragon vinegar, 1 tsp finely chopped chives, ½ tsp sugar, and salt and cayenne to taste. Mix just before using, and it is especially devoted to sliced cucumbers or mild onions. Be careful on the sugar.

A PROPER FRENCH DRESSING

There was only one Bernhardt, one Napoleon, one du Barry and there is only *ONE* basic French dressing which ethically may be varied by adding sweet herbs, and/or a trifle more vinegar. . . . 3 parts of the best French olive oil, 1 part wine vinegar (or a trifle less of cider), salt and hand-ground black pepper, to taste. Mix well; chill.

A SALAD DRESSING ITALIAN STYLE, from a VISIT to MILANO

This is especially valid with tomatoes alone, or tomatoes incorporated with mixed green salad. . . . ¼ cup Italian olive oil, 1½ tbsp red wine vinegar, ¼ tsp chopped fresh basil—or dried basil rubbed fine between palms; to this add ¼ tsp dry mustard, worked smooth with vinegar—or a trifle less, to taste. The final touch is 1 level tsp of anchovy paste, or a trifle less, to taste. Add no salt!

A SALAD DRESSING, *MEXICANO,* as PREPARED by the CHEF at the CASINO de la SILVA, which Is in CUERNAVACA, ANCIENT & MODERN SUMMER CAPITAL of MEXICO'S RULERS from CORTEZ to the PRESENT

This is a fairly torrid affair, and it has been toned down here to the tenderer *Americano* palate. Vary proportions of oil to vinegar, with vinegar strength.

3 tbsp red wine vinegar	9 tbsp Spanish olive oil
1 small round red bird pepper	1 medium sized onion, chopped
½ can scarlet pimentos	½ tsp sugar; brown is best
¾ tsp dry mustard, worked smooth	½ tsp worcestershire, to taste
Add enough salt to suit taste	½ clove crushed garlic

Pound up hot pepper, onion and garlic in a bowl, and rub it all through a coarse sieve—pouring vinegar through at the last to capture all the lily oils. Blend dry seasonings then work smooth with the olive oil. When well mixed turn into the rest. Stand 4 hours to marinate within itself, bearing in mind if no hot bird peppers use from ¼ to 1 tsp tabasco depending on the throat lining insulation against heat! Or 1 small red hot pod pepper will do.

WORDS to the WISE No. XXV, on LESS OIL INCORPORATION into DRESSINGS for AVOCADO, or ALLIGATOR, PEAR SALADS

From its first civilized use the avocado pear salad dressing has tended erroneously toward being dressed with liquids containing *more* olive oils than usual, when the *reverse* is required. Use at least 1 part vinegar to 2 or 2½ parts olive oil. Just remember these pears are the sort of rich stuff we pick nuts all day to get—oily beyond belief, so we must avoid over-richness in the dressing. Personally we prefer lime juice to vinegar in this case.

TO MAKE a PROPER AVOCADO SALAD

Please let's not slice up the pulp in every salad. Just pass a sharp knive lengthwise of fruit, continuing in to the seed along this line, all the way around. Lift off halves, lift out seed, and put dressing into the seed cavity; eat with a spoon. *Chill very cold always.*

ENSALADA de AGUACATE, FINCA el SITIO, a CONTRIBUTION from CUBA

As we mention elsewhere, there are dozens of small farms, or *fincas,* in and around Havana, which we can visit in order to see a little of Cuba's country life—can see enormous royal palms growing in forests, coffee, cacao, avocados, mangoes, papayas, pineapples, sugar-cane, bananas, and heaven only knows what else, growing in tropical profusion; there we can see cock fights, drink heady rum drinks, eat surprisingly lusty and excellent *Cubaño* dishes,—dishes with saffron rice, of pork and chicken, and seafood. The dressing we ran into in 1937, during our last stay in the Island:

Into the seed cavity pour the chilled blended total of: 1 tbsp strained lime juice to 2 of Spanish olive oil, 1 pinch raw brown sugar, salt and hand-ground black pepper, to taste, and about 1 tsp of rum—*Carta de Oro* Bacardi preferred. Chill *aguacates* also.

BAHAMA, & FLORIDA KEYS, RAW CONCH SALAD—sometimes CALLED "CONCH SOUSE"

This receipt for us dates back to a winter and summer spent in a tent on Upper Matecumbe Key, on the ocean side, precisely where the veteran's camp went out in the Labour Day hurricane of 1935, and which would have taken no lives at all due to risen waters if our father's advice had been heeded when he was engineer for the then-building railroad to Key West—he pleading for a viaduct, *not* a fill, at this point where the whole blooming Bay of Florida empties and floods with the tide every few hours.

We might tentatively mention in passing that throughout the West Indies the conch is endowed with certain mythical properties, and some not so mythical. Raw conchs are to clams what a diesel streamliner is to the de Witt Clinton. He is credited with the amazing birth rate of the Bahamas, with making confederate veterans behave like adagio troupes; he is guaranteed to insert a 1" structural steel reinforcing rod into the latex spine, and create sudden interest in the fair sex when such random inclinations had long thought to have joined outdated and betrayed considerations such as the League of Nations and the sanctity of national borders. Be all this as it may, we affirm to one thing, that a decent conch salad is the best picker-upper when withering on the vine from varying injudicious causes, than anything else on the face of the earth. We break out a dish whenever we start on a hard day's fishing, just as canny folk like Ernest Hemingway, Tommy Shevlin and Ray Guest employ its virtues in firing the energy furnace and sharpening the wits, when fishing big blue marlin or giant tuna.

6 conchs, pounded with mallet or knife
3 average sized tomatoes, in eighths
1 to 1½ tsp worcestershire
¼ cup lime juice; lemon will do
1 small bird pepper, or red hot pod type
3 large mild onions
2 green sweet peppers
¼ cup cider vinegar
4 to 6 tbsp olive oil
Salt, to taste; black pepper
Key West *Old Lime Sour,* 1 to 2 tsp

Cut conchs into small bits, and give same treatment to all the other ingredients. Mix everything well, marinate *on ice* for at least 3 hrs, and overnight is better. This allows the lime juice to "cook" the raw shellfish. If no hot pepper we can substitute hand-ground black pepper and tabasco. Vary with sweet herbs.

KEY WEST "OLD LIME SOUR," a RECEIPT which BEARS REPETITION

To 2 cups of strained fresh lime juice add 1 tsp salt, strain through a cloth and put in a pint bottle and let stand until it stops working—which will be in 1½ to 2 wks. Cork then, and it is ready to use any time. By adding 1/10 of 1% benzoate of soda to this fluid, it will keep indefinitely; otherwise it will tend to cloud after some days, especially in hot weather. It has an odd and weird flavour, used *sparingly* as-is, or mixed with other salad dressings and sauces it is a wonderful addition on seafoods, cold meats, green salads, avocado pears. Gourmet guests will exclaim with delight, wanting the secret!

A MAGNIFICENT DAMASCUS GREEN SALAD, in the STYLE EMPLOYED for a NEAR-EASTERN FEAST; a RECEIPT PICKED up from a FELLOW WAYFARER in TIBERIAS, as WE JOURNEYED to JERUSALEM around the CIRCLE by WAY of NAZARETH—NONE of which ARE in SYRIA

Personally we would not be caught dead eating this, or any other, green uncooked salad in Damascus; for in spite of all the Thousand and One Nights romance hanging about that French-administered city, we certainly would be caught dead if we did, which doubtless sounds involved, as typhus and cholera and certain unplayful amoebic disorders smite all white peoples haunch, paunch and jowl, who consume uncooked provender, icecreams, soft drinks, or unboiled milk and water, in those areas. However it is a salad among salads. Save it for a vast gathering, with appreciative guests invited. It is the finest we have ever known.

- 1 bunch each, romaine and dandelion; chicory and endive; 1 head lettuce
- 1 bunch small spring onions or leeks
- 2 tender centers of celery
- 1 bunch fresh green spearmint tips
- 2 sweet peppers; peeled; no seeds
- 4 average, and ripe, tomatoes
- ⅝ cup wine vinegar; or ½ cup of cider vinegar
- Salt and hand ground pepper, to taste
- Nasturtium blooms; marigold petals
- 2 cloves crushed garlic
- 1 average bunch fresh parsley
- 3 small cucumbers, sliced thin
- 2 bunches pink small radishes
- 1½ cups olive oil, any kind
- 1 tsp each, basil and thyme
- 2 cans scarlet pimentos
- 1 tsp cinnamon; ½ tsp ground mace

Routine from this point on resolves itself into 3 simple deeds: mixing the dressing, slicing and marination of the solids, tomato and the like, in a smaller wooden bowl for 3 hrs. Then finally the arrangement of the greens and garnish in the biggest wooden bowl in the township, in order to feast the guest's eye just before the *piece de resistance,* the sacred ceremony, of its mixing.

The Dressing: Toss salt and pepper into the small wooden bowl—about 1 tbsp of the former and not too much, at first, of the latter—then using these as abrasives, garlic cloves should be rubbed until nothing remains except discardable husks. Now mix in the vinegar and oil, the herbs and spice. Solids must be skinned, by scalding or with the knife, then cut very thin. Turn into dressing, and baste with a spoon; set to marinating, as above. . . . When fetching to table arrange greens as follows: with stems pointing inward and down, first the leaf greens, set in rings, each after its own kind. Have a partly opened head of iceberg lettuce in the center, this last garnished with chopped hard egg yolk to imitate flower pollen stamens, frame with a ring of white of egg slivers, and tiny dots of scarlet pimento. . . . The outer edge of greens can be ringed first with thin strips of pimento, then with nasturtium flowers, and all spaced with pairs of marigold petals—*all of which may be eaten with the greens, and each donating its own delicate tang to the whole!*

Now fetch both bowls to table with proper ceremony, and when guests have looked their fill, turn the marinated stuffs and the dressing into the bowl of greens; toss mightily but quickly, then serve.

TAHITI'S OWN FISH SALAD, called *I'A OTA,* which CAME to Us via CHARLES NORDHOFF, AUTHOR & GENTLEMAN, WHO DWELLS in PAPEETE, FRENCH OCEANIA

Nordhoff's co-authorship with his fellow Lafayette Escadrille flying mate of such volumes as *Mutiny on the Bounty, Pitcairn's Island, The Hurricane,* and so on, needs no mention here. When our sailing mate "Sherry" Fahnestock got there a while back headed for the Fijis in his old Maine pilot boat *DIRECTOR,* he set her much traveled and fan-tailed backside against the quay at Papeete for a couple of weeks, and she lay there 7 months! He visited Nordhoff now and again, and consumed his share of raw fish too. Let us use Nordhoff's own words:

"To make this you take a fish of not less than 5 lbs in weight and in the pink of condition, remove and bone the 2 fillets and cut them into pieces about 1" square and ½" thick. . . . You then put these pieces in a fairly deep dish and squeeze out enough fresh lime or lemon juice to cover, leaving the fish to "cook" in this citric acid for not less than 1 hour and ½. . . . At the end of that time you throw all the liquid away and serve the fish in 1 of 2 manners:

"With raw, very thinly sliced onions and a French dressing made of vinegar, olive oil, salt and hand-ground black pepper.

"In a sauce made by grating a coconut (kernel) into its milk, then squeezing through a cloth to extract the cream; adding salt, white pepper, thinly sliced raw onions, and a bit of garlic if you like it.

"The native name of the dish is 'I'a Ota.' The fish is anything but raw, for it is *completely cooked* in the acid of the lime juice. I think that you and your friends would pronounce this dish a most delicious variety of hors d'oeuvre; and it is widely known and appreciated in the South Seas as a specific for the man who has looked too long upon the flowing bowl the night before."

AUTHOR'S NOTE: We have tried this dish several times and find it everything Nordhoff has said. We used tarragon vinegar, and strained lime juice, not lemon. Enriched coconut milk is done as in *Chicken Tortola,* on Page 103, and the result is a bit more rich and satisfactory than by the usual manual squeeze.

NOW LET US INVESTIGATE, if WE WILL, a SALAD of PERSIAN ORIGIN, from TEHERAN, which, by the WAY, Is a THING of GAYETY just as TEHERAN Is a SMART & MODERN METROPOLIS SET upon ANCIENT FOUNDATIONS that ARE OLDER than TIME

Just slice plenty of ripe oranges and when we have enough for 4 people, halt. Stone 2 doz ripe olives, by this we mean peel in a spiral, then cut up, and add to 1 cup of mild onion cut thin-as-thin. Chop up 1 tbsp fresh green mint, the same of parsley, and sprinkle on as garnish after dressing oranges, onions and olives with a French dressing warmed well with cayenne, and containing ½ tsp basil leaves rubbed between the palms. Chill for 2 hrs before service. A very delicate event, to our way of thinking.

OFF ON OUR MAGIC CULINARY CARPET to OPORTO, which Is in PORTUGAL, & to a SPRIGHTLY AFFAIR CALLED *SALADA de PEPINO*—CONSISTING of SPANISH ONIONS, & VARIOUS IMPEDIMENTA, INCLUDING—of all THINGS!—CHESTNUTS

1 big red Spanish onion; ¼ clove garlic
2 big tart apples, not sweet
2 sweet green peppers
½ cup Spanish olive oil; or Italian
Salt and hand-ground pepper, to taste
2 average cucumbers
2 big ripe tomatoes
3 or 4 slices scarlet pimento
¼ cup lime or lemon juice
1 cup coarsely grated chestnuts

Take the sharpest knife possible and slice onions, cored pared apples, cucumbers and sweet peppers, as thin as can be. Take a chilled platter and arrange in a colourful design. Make the dressing by rubbing garlic on the bowl with salt; mix well and pour evenly over the salad. Marinate 1 hr. Boil chestnuts, the big kind, grate *while piping hot*—then when cold dust evenly over the salad. Garnish with hard chopped egg and strips of red pimento.

A SUPREME SPANISH SALAD of SALTED CODS, of ANCHOVIES, OLIVES & FINE RED ONIONS, not FORGETTING other NECESSARIES NEEDFUL to FABRICATE ENSALADA *á BILBAINITA*

We mentioned once before that it took a Spaniard and a Portuguese to show Boston what to do with their smoked or salted coat of arms! This is truly something different, *Messieurs*.

- 6 heaping tbsp, flaked (*not* shredded & dried!) smoked codfish
- 1/3 cup red wine vinegar
- 12 anchovies, rolled in oil
- 1 can red pimentos, sliced in strips
- 1 clove crushed garlic
- 2 doz olives *stuffed with almonds*
- 1 cup Spanish olive oil
- 3 chopped sweet peppers
- 6 hardboiled eggs, sliced
- Black pepper and cayenne
- 3 heads crisp lettuce
- 1 head endive, or chicory

Have greens cold, crisp, dry. Break heads apart and arrange in the bowl like a big green flower, with anchovies circling the heaped codfish in the center, the sliced egg stamens, the scarlet pimento pistils. Mix up the usual dressing and pour over everything, and serve. . . . Prepare codfish by soaking overnight in milk, draining, and simmering until tender—this last in ½ milk and ½ water. Bone carefully, then flake.

AND FINALLY, now, WE REFER OURSELF back to the SPANISH *GAZPACHO* which IS ACTUALLY CLASSED as a SORT of SALAD, & which IS LISTED under HORS d'OEUVRE, & other FIRST COURSE IMPORTANCES, on PAGE 22

The Spaniards really do consider this a salad. It is much similar to the Marseilles Frenchman's *aioli*. We earnestly suggest that either of these be exploded on the American scene as gently as may be. Just choose a nice rainy Sunday evening, with only our closest friends about; and no possibility of going anywhere! He who munches this salad-appetizer in the bosom of his, or her, family and then departeth abroad among the publicans and sinners—unless he equippeth himself, and them, or both, with gas masks enough for all citizens surrounding him—shall straightway find himself shunned like the Bubonic Plague. In truth there's nothing modest or retiring about a *Gazpacho!*

> "The greatest Care should be taken by the Man of Fashion, that his cook's Health be Preserved: one hundredth part of the attention usually bestowed on his dog, or his horse, will suffice to regulate her animal system. . . . should watch over her Health with Tenderest Care, and especially be Sure her *Taste* does not suffer from her Stomach being Deranged by Bilious Attacks. . . ."
>
> *The Cook's Oracle,*
> *Dr. William Kitchiner,*
> *London, 1817*

CHAPTER X

PARTICULAR VEGETABLES *FROM* DIVERS STRANGE KITCHENS

Conniving with Various Specimens of Tuber, Seed & Bud; but with Emphasis on such Odd Events as *Moros y Cristianos*—"Moors & Christians"—from Cuba; our own traditional Hopping John; Eggplants, *a Mallorquena;* Prickly Pear Leaves after Toreador Sidney Franklin; or Candied Yams, *Cap Hatien.*

It has always been a source of mingled pain and amazement how the average American cook could take all those nice pretty vegetables, set his jaw, and with the grim devotion of a knight praying beside his armour, reduce them to the watery, careless bogs of iniquity that he does. Then we lived in England for a while!

But the fact that we can level a superior finger at England's fantastic sins among the vegetables is no more excuse than a chap who cabbages a locket from a sleeping babe is pardoned the act just because his neighbour is a bad fellow and robs an orphanage trust fund.

The intelligent amateur on these shores already knows how to cook vegetables as well or better than the next—boiling, baking, or what not. Heaven knows it is not our mission to speak about boiling asparagus with the lid off—started fiercely hot; and boiling carrots with the lid on, started cold. Every passing cookery book cries this sort of lesson. We cling to the hope that these dishes, found in varying places and under varying, but always happy, circumstances may suggest certain points of departure for the amateur. So be of good cheer, and furthermore be surprised at nothing!

ASPARAGUS after the ROMAN MANNER, Advocated for the Sunday Morning Breakfast

One memorable year found us again in Rome, and happily in funds, and crisply nested at *Grande Hotel de Russie,* in whose rather impressive halls was a room boy, or *valet de chambre,* or whatever we should call a fellow who replaces broken shoelaces, cracks ice for varying heathenish American liquids, prays for the lost soul of a guest who visibly has no rosary by our bedside, bargains for us at not more than ten per cent backsheesh for himself, and generally advises ourself on all of the more intimate human relationships—both extra, and intra, mural—named Luigi. . . . Now one morning, with our mortal visibility somewhat withered on the vine from doing as the Romans do, we wondered what things interesting might be kitchened for breakfast. And this gem Luigi suggested asparagus, first verbally, then at our evident poor Italian, not too clearly through a rough pencil sketch—more starkly phallic than anything vegetable—leaving much to be desired. This is it.

Asparagus, enough to satisfy
1 tbsp, or so, of grated Parma cheese
1 shirred egg, as noted
¼ cup olive oil
Salt and cayenne, to taste

Trim off all tough portions of the asparagus, parboil in briskly boiling water containing salt and a trifle of soda. Drain and reserve. Take a shirred egg dish, put in 2 tbsp olive oil and tiny sliver of garlic, 2 pinches of rosemary. When garlic browns, discard it. Let dish cool somewhat, stir in 1 tbsp sour cream, season highly, and break in 2 eggs. With a small spoon cover eggs with plenty of the basting, and bake until they set just hard enough to be lifted out with a spatula without breaking—*not* until rubbery and tough! . . . While this baking goes on, heat rest of the olive oil in a pan—quite hot. Brown asparagus carefully, so as not to break stalks. Arrange platter with the eggs nested in a hexagonal ring of asparagus. Sprinkle the latter with the freshly grated Parmesan, pop for a brief instant under broiler, and serve.

MOROS y CRISTIANOS—or "MOORS & CHRISTIANS"—being BLACK BEANS & RICE in the TRUE CUBAN STYLE

We've always loved certain kinds of Cuban cookery, and this is a favourite *Cubaño* dish; simple and satisfying; easy to make. . . . First requirement is the "Christians," a nice mound of dry, boiled rice. Next come the "Moors," the black beans which must be soaked overnight. To 1½ cups of black beans, boiled in salted water until tender, add 4 chopped rashers of lean bacon fried out with ¼ clove of crushed garlic, 1 diced onion. Season with 1 tsp chili powder, salt and cayenne. Add enough meat stock to cover the beans, 2 tbsp of good mango chutney, and simmer until beans fall apart a little and make a thick, rich sauce for the pale, warm Christians. Seasoning is typically quite hot.

BARBECUED CORN NAWTH CA'LINA STYLE

This is one memorable dish we found during a summer of 1936 which we spent high up in the cloud-masked mountain ranges out of Asheville. The fillip of peanut butter with fresh green corn is a touch of genius discovered by an amateur sportsman chef we know up in those hills who has much to do with various forms of American tobacco.

Choose tender ears of golden bantam or country gentleman corn. Without necessarily removing more than the outer layers of husk, plunge 10 minutes into fiercely boiling, salted water. Husk now, trim off stems flush and wrap each ear with 3 thin rashers of home-smoked lean bacon skewered with toothpicks. Impale the ear on a long peeled rustic wand, paint well with a basting made from ½ butter and ½ peanut butter, lusciously melted together; then broil over the coals—turning to brown on all sides. . . . When at home use the oven broiler, omitting the wands entirely. If corn is not parboiled first it takes a long time to cook, burns cheeks, hands and bacon; tends to make the corn too tough.

A PENNSYLVANIA DUTCH CUCUMBER FRY, WHITEMARSH STYLE

Having Pennsylvania Dutch and Quaker branches on both sides of our family, we have always cherished memories of the brick Dutch oven one ancestor had built back of the main house down on a Florida plantation of all places!—which puzzled negroes would journey far to inspect—and of visits to Germantown and Whitemarsh where food was wonderfully ample and satisfying. The only cloud later to mar, materialistically and figuratively, all these pleasant Philadelphia recollections was later discovery that "Roxborough," our forebear's estate from a William Penn grant back in 1684 embraced some 1500 to 2000 acres, straddling the Wissahickon, and bordering the Schuylkill for a mile or more—and which went for one reason or another to outsiders. It would have been so nice to own Fairmount Park in this questionable year of Grace, with our very own bridle trails!

But back to our cucumber fry. . . . It is a simple dish, yet tasty; and it notifies us of one way of cooking a vegetable so often served raw, in salads. Just peel medium sized cucumbers and cut into ¼" thick slices. Marinate 1 hr in cold salt water, made slightly acid with vinegar. Dry in a cloth; dip first into milk then into beaten egg, then roll in fine crumbs and brown in deep fat at 370°.

A BLACK SEA CUCUMBER DISH, in the STYLE of ODESSA

All foreign races recognize the cucumber as food of importance. Turkish porters carry huge burdens, strengthened by a diet consisting of a fair proportion of this vegetable. The Hindu uses them in his curries often. Here our Russki stews them in sour cream and things.

Peel and slice 8 average cucumbers, and stand them in cold salted water 1 hr to firm them. Mince 1 big onion, donate ½ cup of chopped mushrooms, add a speck of crushed garlic, and brown lightly in 1 tbsp of butter. Now drain cucumbers and add them to the onion pan. Add 1½ cups of hot meat stock, thicken slightly with 1 tbsp each of butter and flour, worked into a smooth roux. Simmer until cucumbers are tender. Season with salt and cayenne, and finally add 1 cup of sour cream. Boil up gently once more and serve. A sprinkling of caraway seed is optional, but, to our experimenting palate, added nothing necessary.

A DISH of EGGPLANTS for the Lovely Little Seaside Town of Söller, which Is in Mallorca, where We Visited in 1932 and 1933

Spaniards, Italians, Turks, Greeks and Near-Easterners—all of them know things about an eggplant which we seem to ignore. This is a more or less peasant type of dish which will vary with larder and individual cooks; may be highly seasoned, or mild. Just peel and slice a couple of nice eggplants ½″ thick, stand in strongly salted water for 10 minutes to extract bitterness, then drain. . . . Heat lots of olive oil very hot indeed, and brown slices lightly on both sides. Reserve, and brown a big finely minced onion with a trace of garlic pulp—much garlic is typical—then fill a greased oven dish as follows: a floor of fried onion, then a layer of eggplant, then one of scalded, peeled, and sliced tomatoes. Season each layer to taste, and if possible squeeze out as many seeds as possible from the tomatoes. . . . Dust this last stratum with 2 tbsp of freshly grated Parma cheese; and repeat the process—finally ending up with a goodly cheese donation which has been well dotted with butter. Brown in a medium oven around 350°, which takes about 45 minutes.

OLD SOUTHERN HOPPING JOHN, Gulla Country Style, which Is Based on Rice, Smoked "Side Meat" and Cow Peas

We care for this name almost as much as England's Bubble and Squeak, for a dish title. For generations all true South Carolinians have been serving Hopping John. It is just as natural to the Gulla Country back of Charleston as balls of the sacred Boston codfish are to Beacon Hill, curry to India, chili pepper dishes to Mexico. Cow peas are the right and proper co-basis for this dish. Shelled fresh ones are by far the best, but dried are fine. Get in touch with any large grocery concern and fairly grant them a week to produce the dried items, and the most distant Maine Yankee can find them! Chick peas, pigeon peas and black eyed peas will do, but cow peas have a delicate and unusual taste all their own.

Cover 2 cups of the cow peas with 2 quarts of water, slightly salted, and toss in 4 rashers of smoked "side-meat," bacon—and home smoked country bacon is best—with rashers cut in half and ¼″ thick. Simmer slowly until peas are not quite done. Pour off all but 3 cups of this cooking water, add 1 cup of brown or white uncooked rice. Put everything in top of a double boiler and draw off when rice is well-steamed and tender. . . . Pepper seasoning varies with each southern cook. There may be none, or she may put in a small red pepper pod, a red bird pepper, or lots of ground pepper. . . . If dried cow peas are used—and fresh are not obtainable in the north, be sure and soak overnight. The bacon usually is laid about the rice-bean blend. If no double boiler on hand, use very slow fire so as not to have rice stick to the pot. Rice may be boiled separately, using cooking water from the cow peas, but the method given is the one Susan Rainey our old "Geechee" negro cook used for many years in our own family.

A ROYAL STUFFED MUSHROOM, *à la MADAME SACHER,* in VIENNA—when VIENNA WAS ONE LONG HAPPY WALTZ, & KINGS WERE KINGS

Sacher's place is too famous to describe here, and there after the opera royalty would gather, and food and wine served that grew famous 'round the world. Alas it is no more, but the memory clings, and this receipt came to us from an Under-Secretary to the American Legation during the gay years.

We need 1 lb of large mushrooms. Amputate the stems and after discarding all tough parts of the stems, put both tops and reserved stems into plenty of boiling salted water. Simmer until tops can easily be punctured with a fork tine—which requires some 8 to 10 minutes, depending upon adolescence of the mushrooms. . . . Drain and choose the biggest for stuffing, chopping other tops and stems very fine indeed. Melt 2½ tbsp of butter in a pan, turn in chopped mushrooms, ¼ cup finely diced celery, 4 minced pickled walnuts, ½ to 1 tsp of worcestershire, 2 tbsp finely minced onion, 2 tsp chopped almonds. Toss in the hot butter for 5 minutes, stir in 1 tbsp sherry wine, and pack this mixture onto under side of the mushroom tops; dust with dry breadcrumbs, dot with a little butter and brown under a hot broiler. Serve sizzling. This is a nice midnight snack, at times.

EXPLODING OLD WIVES' TALES No. VIII, BEING an EARNEST PLEA for MAINTAINING the DELICATE FLAVOUR of MOST MUSHROOM DISHES

There has always been a tendency, as far back as we can remember, to try and fancy up mushrooms a bit too steeply, as to added high seasonings, flavours and what not. The main thing to bear in mind would appear to be, not what Aunt Williemette has always done toward disguising the mushroom taste, but that the mushroom's own delicate taste and aroma is essentially valuable. Like fine chilled oysters, caviar, or wild duck, it shouldn't be completely overwhelmed with other—commoner—tastes.

MUSTARD or COLLARD GREENS, with Hog Jowl or "Side Meat"

Fresh green mustard has been totally ignored by the north all these years, and is much better than turnip tops and all that sort of thing. Collards are a sort of loose cabbage gone wild in the bush, so to speak. It has a much stronger taste, and we strongly recommend mustard—which any garden can grow in 5 or 6 weeks from seed. . . . Hog jowl, the smoked kind, is something to take up with a place like Pender's in Norfolk; otherwise stick to hambone, or home smoked bacon cut in ¼″ thick rashers. Boil the hog jowl or bacon in plenty of salted water until about tender, have pot really boiling when the greens go in—adding a pinch of soda. When the greens are tender, drain well to avoid the strong water; garnishing the sliced jowl or bacon rashers around the heap of green on the platter. Do not cut rashers less than ¼″ thick, please.

TAMAS DAVIN'S IRISH *COLCANNON,* which Is a Fine Lusty for an Outdoor or Camping Dish

Citizen Davin, referred to elsewhere, fetched this to us after a recent visit to his own home village in Ireland. The words are his own.

"I can't give you many original Irish receipts. There is no great variety of cooking in the island; mostly bacon, cabbage and potatoes, ad infinitum. They just never think of varying it. Occasionally a bit of lamb, veal or beef, but usually only when there has been an accident on the farm! City cuisine is, of course, like any other—more or less international and nothing in particular.

"The only dish I know that is truly Irish, and one seldom duplicated elsewhere, is *Colcannon*—an old Gaelic name. . . . Just imagine it, will you!—One immense mound of mashed potatoes seasoned with pepper, salt, and so mashed and whipped with butter and cream until it is a fine light consistency. Leaning around the sides of this mound are strips of fried Irish bacon, cut in edible sized pieces.

"Sunken in the top of the foot-high mound, hollowed out like the crater of Vesuvius, is a half pound chunk of butter, which is put in while the spuds are steaming hot and allowed to melt. . . . *Colcannon is devoured by the whole family from the same dish, each member armed with fork or spoon.*

"Each grabs his piece of bacon, and while munching this scoops a gob of potato, dips it into the melted butter, and allows this amalgam to glide down the esophagus. . . . Much merriment is caused by the scrambling for the bits of bacon, and a free-for-all usually ensues near the end of the meal when the last dwindling remnants are scooped for—spoons and forks flying like hurley sticks—and it is then the true *Colcannon* artists begin to show their true mettle. This consists of slithering a portion of the stuff from a competitor's spoon before it reaches his mouth. Facial expressions of the losers add much to the atmosphere, humour and excitement.

"This dish is the real 'McCoy.' Dietitians have fainted at the amount of starch—about 94%, but huge and lusty families have been reared on it for centuries. Once in a rare while the variation of some cabbage may be added to the potato-maché heap, to provide vitamins."

ROSIN POTATOES in the MANNER of J. MARQUETTE PHILLIPS & as DONE at BLACK CAESAR'S FORGE for VARIOUS FRIENDS & GUESTS, at VARIOUS TIMES

Marquette Phillips, sometimes called "America's Cellini in Iron," forges all sorts of things out of metals up to and including birdcages of bronze, aluminum and valuable hardwares costing the interest on 100,000 dollars for a year. He also has dug himself a cave in the solid coral rock south of this author's hearthstone, honeycombed it with wine bins, rigged up grills and what not, and here gourmets go to broil things of their own devising. Here we find many Americans hibernating with their trenchers. The last occasion we were there we took Coe Glade, Chicago Opera's luscious contralto, and there was Hervey Allen, with a poet named Robert Frost; there was Grantland Rice, and some Senators, and Don Dickerman of the *Pirate's Dens,* and Errol Flynn and his lovely wife Lili Damita.

Suddenly beside the sizzling 4″ steaks appear the Rosin Potatoes; and everyone laughs in superior fashion at them, and ignores them because they are wrapped in Walter Winchell's column, or pages from the *Commonweal,* or ancient *Atlantic Monthlies.* Then someone explains what in hell they are, and people cut them through with a sharp knife and plug them with gobs of butter and garlic salt or hickory salt, and Nepal pepper, then people start laughing and start asking pertinent questions on their later duplication back home. So here's the very simple secret.

Get enough common ordinary rosin to fill an iron cauldron or kettle ¾ full, and the bigger the better. Melt over a wood fire out in the open, and when that point is reached put in the potatoes. They immediately sink, and when done they demurely come bobbing to the surface. Take them out with a wrought iron fork or ladle but be careful and *do not puncture the skins.* Have 2 or 3 thicknesses of newspaper cut into squares big enough to roll potato in, and secure safely with a twist at both ends. The rosin sticks to the paper when it cools —which is at once. Cut straight across through the middle and break open—presto! there is the skin pulled away and a soft deliciously mealy affair that has literally been exploded in every inner cell from the high boiling point of the rosin, and which is better than any potato ever baked in mortal oven. . . . Besides all the virtue in the finished dish, the rosin pot makes a gesture of mystery about the thing. Also the aromatic yellow pine rosin smells so nice.

BOILED PRICKLY PEAR, or CACTUS, LEAVES, *à la SIDNEY FRANKLIN*

A while ago when Ernest Hemingway was headed back to Spain, he had Sidney Franklin, our American-bred bullfighter, stop off to see us. So as Pauline Hemingway had said once that we ought to get the matador to cook us some prickly pear leaves, we asked him to explain the dish between thimbles of Pellison Brandy, 1880, and Kirsch, and Drambuie, to Hervey Allen and ourself. Not believing much, either, beforehand.

You see we'd eaten prickly pear fruits of one shape or another, and cursed the whole cactus tribe hip and thigh when extracting their spines from our shins and the intimate rigging of Rip-Rap strain pointers we used to use on Florida quail shoots. We had seen dumb things like land turtles, asses and crabs, try to eat prickly pear leaves, but doubted their sense for human alimentation. But when Ernest said, "He fixed some down in Key West for Mommie and me, but watch out or they'll physic the hell out of you," we began to guess there might be truth in the thing—because both of them, and Mommie too, are gourmets, and like to think up new and eatable things.

Actually the business tastes like fine fresh okra; the supply is limitless throughout the far south and Gulf States. And cacti of the big, flat-leaved varieties grow the world around where nothing else *will* grow. Also we suddenly realized that lots of people in the tropics get fresh vegetables only about 6 months out of the year. And with cacti costing just nothing to grow why not see . . . ?

Choose the flat-leaved variety having leaf studded with little clumps of very fine spines, rather than the brutal single spine-to-a-spot type. Choose only the younger, tenderer leaves.

1. Trim off a strip 1" thick all around the flat leaf.
2. Place knife against the base of each spine tuft, and with a flip *toward the stem end of the leaf,* spines pop out roots and all.

3. Place leaf on flat surface and cut into lengthwise ¼″ strips; then crosswise, making ¼″ cubes.
4. Boil in three waters as follows: (1) Into briskly boiling salted water with a little soda, for 4 minutes. . . . (2) Repeat, only no soda. . . . (3) A brief stay in a third pot of boiling salted water will tender.

These three waters are needed to carry away excess mucilage. The native Mexicans have used cactus cooked in one water for centuries as a specific for indigent alimentary diligence, being a fine natural lubricant. Doctors consider it a specific of important rank, down there. For average table food three waters will cut it to normal. Serve with lots and lots of butter. The taste is like okra, the best okra, plus a strange exotic "something." It should make a wonderful basis for chicken gumbo, or crab gumbo soup. Arizona, New Mexico and Nevada, and of course inevitable California, actually have an inexhaustible free raw material supply.

CANDIED RED YAMS, *à la CAP-HAITIEN,* being a Delicious Affair from Haiti's Ancient Capital

Our ketch *MARMION* has dropped anchor in this port, surrounded with its wonderful mountains which pitch down to their eternal suicide in a sea bluer than man ever dreamed possible. Cap-Haitien it was that burned for 4 days when the blacks rose and put every Frenchman, woman and child to the machete, and took the richest island in the whole wide world for an African empire under Dessalines, then as kingdom under Black Cristophe, who built the fantastic Citadel on a mountaintop, and lovely Sans Souci at Milot —a ruined palace copied after part of Versailles which our friend Glenn Stewart almost acquired by certain devious yet legitimate tradings a few years back. . . . Yams are native to Haiti, and red yams are by far the best. These are obtainable in the States now, and don't buy the pale, rather tasteless sweet potatoes unless the others are impossible. . . . This particular receipt was fetched back to us by Christopher Clark on the Pan-American Clipper, after a six months' happy domicile on the island doing a series of paintings and immediately prior to a mural execution on our own dining room walls.

First parboil some well-scrubbed yams, and slice them. Take a casserole and butter it well, sprinkle the bottom with the grated yellow rind of 2 oranges, dust with 2 handfuls of brown sugar, flood with ¼ cup of dark rum and set alight. When the rum is half burned out, and the sugar well carameled, blow out the flame. . . . Now season this fragrant pediment with quite a bit more cinnamon than usually required, and plenty of powdered clove; then build up with alternate layers of yam and generous gifts of brown sugar. End up with a final layer of grated orange peel and the crown of sugar, also generously dusted with clove and cinnamon; and brown in a medium oven around 375°. Serve flaming, again using dark rum; and 2 tbsp are enough, heated first to insure good prompt combustion. Marshmallows and chopped peanuts are optional.

YAMS au MARRONS, FLAMBÉ à la FORT de FRANCE, which last Is Capital City of Lovely Martinique where We Visited

Many lovely things came from Martinique, including the Empress Josephine who was born on neighbouring Trois Isles. There the aristocratic French planters lived a life of luxury and ease seldom matched. There the school of creole cookery is toothsome, torrid and most original. The employment of candied chestnuts is a typically French gesture. . . . Choose round, fat yams. Scrub them and parboil until semi-tender. Slice lengthwise slices after peeling, and about ½" thick. Saute gently 5 minutes in hot butter, then arrange on a flat pottery or pyrex oven dish. Dust with sugar, the grated green peel of 3 limes; tee up 2 or 3 big candied marrons on each slice, ring each marron with raisins; and put under the broiler or into a hot oven around 400°. Arrange on a platter, garnish with small brilliant blossoms of any kind. Heat a ladle of cognac brandy and spill 1 tsp or so on each yam slice, serving with lights properly dimmed, *flambé*. . . . Personally we have found that any medium dark rum seems to marry with the tropical yam and the candied chestnuts, even better than the brandy. Martinique rum is procurable in all cities now. Incidentally this is one of the finest companion dishes to roast guineahen we have ever come upon; and it also suits wild duck, turkey, and all sorts of game. It is very rich and if served, cut the other vegetables down to perhaps a single partner such as broccoli *hollandaise,* wild rice, or artichokes.

WORDS to the WISE No. XXVI, DISCUSSING the EVIDENT COMPLEMENT of RAISINS & YAMS, ONE for ANOTHER

We have already mentioned how raisins and roasted quail were intended for each other, and we assure all gourmets that there is something in this mutual affection of raisins and red yams. Try them next time candied sweet potatoes are served. The result will be pleasant, especially if the orange peel isn't forgotten, and brown sugar is used instead of the entirely too usual white variety.

I pray & command you . . . *abstain from beans.*

Pythagorus, to his Disciples,
Athens, 541 B.C.

CHAPTER XI

DESSERTS, & FRUITS CONVERTED *FOR THE* FINAL COURSE

Encompassing Twenty-Nine or so Exotic Adventures such as Portuguese Pie of Crushed Almonds, Egg Whites, Spices & Wine; Bananas *en Casserole,* from Caracas, Venezuela; *Mousse au Miel,* or Honey Mousse, from Paris; Melons, *Glacé,* from Fabulous Rajputana in the Days of the Mughal Emperors; Stuffed Oranges, *à l'Indochine;* and Mrs. Joseph O'Dea's East Mayo Trifle.

ONE DELIGHT we have taken in assembling this book during all those years has been the splendid field, at long last, we had for turning our back on the miasma of bread puddings which through ministration of well-meaning female relatives constantly haunted our youth; to thumb a figurative proboscis at that whole septic tribe of tapiocas, floating islands, and sweet fancies generally.

Oddly enough when we resolved to collect a chapter of Desserts it never occurred to us that except for the French school of elaborate sweets, the finest possible desserts on earth were the countless fruits of tree, bush and vine, that so happily and generously bless mankind throughout the temperate and torrid zones. Another adequate and comforting discovery came with widening experience, and that was the inevitability of wines and liqueurs as being just about the only thing possible to take a ripe and perfect fruit, and elevate it to higher spheres—not merely confound its delicate natural flavours with lily gilding additions. In other words we discovered that heat benefits fruit in many cases, changing them entirely into new and adventurous taste poems, but treatment with delicately flavoured spirits carries the iambic pentameter of the oven to even more rarified heights.

So this, the final Chapter in this volume, we commend to you, and hope that from its files it may be possible to select some thing or other to leave a delicate and lingering fair taste in the mouth.

AND FIRST a FRAGILE and DELICATE ALMOND DESSERT MASTERPIECE KNOWN as ALMOND *SCHAUM TORTE*

Most Amateurs have been fearful of attempting this famous *Danska* delight. Chief cause of this fear and failure is that recommended cooking temperatures in receipts are far too high at start. Unless low first heat is used—actually it is a meringue-*drying* process as much as cooking—weird distortions follow. So here is a well-proven formula fetched to us by an American then high on the diplomatic staff in Copenhagen.

To well-beaten whites of 6 fresh eggs add 2 cups sugar; then beat stiff as stiff. Now donate 1 to 1½ tsps vanilla and 1 tbsp vinegar—Ah, there's a secret touch! Flavour with 6 or 8 drops (to taste) of almond essence. Turn into a buttered *and lightly floured* round baking tin. Start at no higher than 250° oven; then when *torte* has risen and set, turn up to 300° and lightly brown. . . . Serve with whipped cream between the two layers. It is especially delicious with your favourite ice cream on top. Cut into pie-shaped portions. The crisp fairy-light texture of this dessert literally defies description in cold print. Gourmets love it. . . . Also could be flavoured with spearmint or peppermint, or anything you especially admire. Will serve 6. Should be served with a nice and lightly-chilled sweet dessert wine.

BAKED ALASKA, *TROPICAL, et l'AUTEUR*

Our birthday, which occurs for better or worse on Christmas day, found us in Panama that winter of 1933. Theodore, matchless emperor of the Grill Room on *SS. RELIANCE*—recently and unhappily burned at her dock—was always a magician with cookery ideas. So this Baked Alaska was whipped up especially for us with enough tropical touches to make it worthy of notation; and here's a secret—we had it repeated in New York for our pre-wedding dinner!

One brick of rich tutti-frutti ice cream serves 4. . . . Now we need a plank or big cookie sheet. Next comes a sponge or angel's food cake layer 1″ thick and same size or better still at least ¾″ larger than the ice cream unit, in order to retain its subsequent jacket of meringue. . . . Beat 6 tbsp sugar, 4 to 5 egg whites, and 1 tsp of white rum, *kirschwasser,* or orange Curaçao, until very stiff. Mount sponge cake on plank, ice cream on cake, and spread on meringue in an even layer over everything. Now dust with 1 tbsp finely chopped cashew nuts mixed with the same of grated *fresh* coconut kernel. Have oven *already hot,* around 450°; brown meringue, and serve with utmost speed thereafter. . . . Please never attempt water ices in Baked Alaska; they simply won't stand the heat, and collapse with disastrous aquatic results!

CRÊPES SUZETTES, CUBAÑO, from the VEDADO CLUB, HAVANA, in the YEAR 1931

To Crêpes Suzettes addicts we submit the following variation: roll the French type pancake about a filling of guava paste, or jelly; dust with cinnamon and confectioner's sugar, moisten with hot, well-aged, brandy-like *Añejo* rum, and serve flaming.

VANILLA ICE CREAM, *PAULA,* BEING another FINE ORIGINATION of THEODORE on the *RELIANCE* ESPECIALLY for OUR (then) ONE YEAR BRIDE

We had just run into a dusty February no'theaster out of La Guayra, but it flattened out off the rocky coast of Dutch Curaçao, and to celebrate everyone's returned good humour there was a dinner given, with this fragrant dessert as a fitting period to it all. . . . Arrange 1 brick of vanilla or tutti frutti ice cream in a suitable dish with slightly over-capacity, and garnish the edges with glacé fruits. Brown 4 tbsp of finely chopped Brazil nuts in hot butter, and have these all drained and ready. Heap them on the ice cream in the form of a miniature volcano cone. First moisten this nut mountain with 1 tbsp orange Curaçao, then with 1 tbsp heated brandy; serve flaming.

MARRONS *PLOMBIÈRE,* another HIGH DISCOVERY from CAFE de PARIS in MONTE CARLO, in the YEAR 1932

We offer this as one of the finest desserts we have ever known. We don't know the name of the, then, chef at this fine restaurant in "Monte" because part of our original notes were destroyed; but he must have been a stark staring genius. . . . In few cases does a true French chef use what old coloured Susan Rainey called "store-bought" ice cream, but fabricates it himself very easily indeed.

Beat the yolks of 8 eggs with 1 cup of sugar. Stir this into 1 qt of rich milk flavoured with vanilla to taste. Heat slowly in a double boiler, stirring with a *wooden* spoon until it thickens. At this point step up the tempo with ½ cup finely chopped marrons lusciously soaked in a little dark rum, and 1 tbsp *kirschwasser.* Put into the ice cream freezer, freeze; then pack in individual moulds and press on a top layer of more rum-soaked marrons, broken into bits. Keep packed in ice and salt, or better still put into the freeze chamber of the refrigerator. Serve garnished with whipped cream, slightly sweetened, flavoured with vanilla and a tbsp more of *kirsch.* Dust a tiny bit of grated marron on top, and that's it! Incidentally a Gallic bit of wisdom: *kirschwasser,* pungently flavoured with an odd wild-cherry taste serves as a foil to amplify other flavours of a sweet dish such as this, and don't fear its evidently conflicting taste potency.

MOUSSE au MIEL, or HONEY MOUSSE, which Is a DELICATE and HAUNTING MEMORY—among OTHERS not PERTINENT to MENTION —of TIME-MELLOWED RESTAURANT LAPEROUSE

Laperouse has, easily for half a century, been considered one of Paris' fine restaurants; and for over a hundred years has been the old early 18th Century former domicile of Compte de Bruillevert. To romantically-minded patrons a slight emolument discreetly pressed into the hand of the proper gentleman will, unless already occupied, effect ingress to a tiny *cabinet particulier* off a minor stairway through a knobless door which when closed is totally unsuspected and invisible. With a charming companion at the time, we both were made to feel very stealthy, very wicked indeed—and imagined unannounced husbands, lovers or wives, storming in and vowing satisfaction of one species or another.

But regardless of the honeycomb of private dining rooms, Laperouse has a divine cuisine, an especially sound and sanely tariffed cellar. *Mousse au Miel* was our sweet, that day; and the amateur will find it easily created in his own kitchen. . . . Beat the yolks of 6 eggs so fresh they really should have been scheduled for laying tomorrow—for vintage eggs popping up in a honey mousse are just as bad as a vintage sweetheart popping up on a honeymoon!—together with 1½ cups of strained honey—the darker the more flavourful. . . . Put in a double boiler and stir diligently until it thickens. Chill well and fold in the whites of 3 eggs beaten stiff; then work in a pint of very heavy cream, also whipped. Now pack in mold, or molds, and store in the freezing chamber of the refrigerator exactly the same as *Plombière aux Marrons,* and do not agitate while freezing. Garnish with a dusting of finely chopped pistachio nuts, or better still do not garnish at all. There is something about the simplicity of this dessert so delicately perfumed and flavoured with the lovely gift of honey, that needs no additions whatsoever.

WORDS to the WISE No. XXVII, on the CHILLING of EGGS to be BEATEN STIFF

Please don't forget that if egg whites are easily to be beaten really stiff, eggs had better be well chilled first; especially in a naturally warm climate.

A SHERBET of VIOLETS, *alla FIESOLE*

There is no valid reason for dedicating this lovely ice to Fiesole, for it might have happened anywhere a chef drew breath with romance in his heart. But the fact is we were once, during a stay in Florence, impelled to call upon an American lady who for reasons of her own had taken up dilatory domicile in a jewel-like 17th Century villa near Fiesole. This sweet, served in a garden-close framed in century-old cedars, out of which peeped marble Daphnes and Satyrs and Fauns and what not, and the almond trees foamed with bloom, shall always remind us tenderly of Fiesole—and the lady. . . . To duplicate the dish is quite easy.

Put 2 cups of sugar in a saucepan and add just enough water to make a fairly heavy syrup; simmering gently for 10 minutes. Now add ¼ cup *Crème de Violette* out of the clever shaped *Bols* bottle, and simmer 5 minutes longer to dissipate some of the alcohol which otherwise would hinder freezing. Draw off fire and cool, meanwhile adding 2 cups of grape juice and the strained juice of 1 small lemon or 2 limes. Now put in the ice cream freezer and when almost frozen, add the white of 1 egg and 2 tbsp of confectioner's sugar whipped together. Freeze well. . . . Serve in crystal sherbet glasses with under plate garnished with a green violet leaf, and 3 violet flowers mounted on top of the sherbet in glass.

MRS. JOSEPH O'DEA'S *EAST MAYO TRIFLE,* a DELIGHTFUL LUSTY from the FIELD NOTEBOOK of ONE TAMAS DAVIN, MENTIONED before, & GATHERED from HIS AUNT in IRELAND in the YEAR 1935

This Gaelic-descended Editor, for reasons not entirely clear, decided to go to Ireland that year, by way of Jamaica and Haiti, and came back fairly bursting with Irish village lore. This Trifle is evidently a mighty serious business, like *Colcannon* which it follows shortly, in a big Irish family. We quote:

"Line the bottom of a large bowl with fine sponge cake made about 1" thick. Spread with strawberry jam or your own favourite jelly. Cover this merry business with another layer of identical cake. Spread this, again, with jam; and continue the process until a few inches below the bowl top. Now pour in enough sherry thoroughly to saturate the cake and make it almost a solid mass—and don't worry, me *spalpeen,* it will saturate the eater shortly.

"Now pour over it a good boiled custard. Put in the coldest spot of the refrigerator for ½ an hour. Serve on very large dinner plates surrounded by sliced-up fruits—fresh, canned or glacé: but preferably very ripe and lightly sugared flesh of peaches, pears, apricots; or sliced oranges and seedless grapes. Be sure and allow huge portions for every guest at the start. They all sigh about the waist line, but invariably come back for more, and decide they'll start that diet tomorrow!

"And here is my Aunt O'Dea's Boiled Custard:

"Beat 4 egg yolks until pale yellow, work in 3 tbsp of sugar, and beat well again. Bring 3¼ cups of milk to the boil and pour over the yolks; and when well mixed, put in a double boiler and cook until custard thickens, stirring constantly from the bottom—paradoxical though this last may sound. Finally 1 tbsp of vanilla flavours it, and you won't need any sherry wine here—it's all in the Trifle already!"

SABAILLON, or *ZABAGLIONE,* or Whatever the Dutch Do Call It in the East Indies, *à la MELCHIOR TREUB*

The *Melchior Treub* in 1931 was one of those spotless little KPM—*Koninklijke Paketvaart Maatschappij* to us—circling the Dutch East Indies: Batavia, Soerabaja, Bali, Makassar, Singapore and Sumatra. We had flown ahead of our globe encircling steamer, to Soerabaja to board the *Treub,* and at 5 that afternoon, with chronometer promptness we met our old French and Italian friend with new flavours—and we found it a truly delightful lift compared to British tea or American Martinis. It, literally, is a drink pick-me-up eaten with a spoon. And so we sat in the Captain's wardroom with the sun plunging into oblivion back of the volcanic peaks over Tosari way, and the dark green velvet mystery of Madoera Island slipped past our port elbow, already shadowed with the imminent dusk.

The receipt: Must be done in a double boiler; or in a round bottom bowl—better still—standing in a pan of boiling water, like hollandaise sauce. . . . Whip the yolks of 6 fresh eggs, put in the bowl, then add 4½ to 5 tbsp of sugar—stirring and beating constantly with a wooden fork or spoon. When it gradually thickens to a very heavy cream, work in 6 drops of vanilla, and add a little at a time as much ½ cognac —½ orange Curaçao blend as the mixture will absorb and still remain fairly thick. It may be served hot or cold, depending on host whim. . . . This Curaçao flavour is typically Dutch, using liqueurs made mainly in Holland from peculiar oranges from the Dutch West Indian Island of that name.

Our Frenchman would use cognac alone, B & B, Cointreau, Grand Marnier; the Italian, Marsala wine and Italian brandy, half and half; the Spaniard, Sherry and brandy, *Anis del Mono.* A little white of egg is sometimes added in France and Italy. In Martinique or Haiti rum would naturally be used—using half light and half dark.

WINE JELLY, *à la TSARINA,* which Is another DELICATE REMEMBRANCE from the GRANDLY ROYAL DAYS of OLD RUSSIA

We include this as suggestion for a wine jelly dish to be sent to the bedside of a favourite hospital patient, or invalid, as a taste-change from usual wabbly desserts dietitians seem to delight in inflicting on helpless souls. . . . Put jelly moulds on ice where they will get really chilled. Fill with any good usual wine jelly flavoured with the fruit which is favourite with the subject, and sherry, being careful not to pass the half-way mark in the mould—retaining an equal amount of the jelly. . . . While this last is still liquid, add 1 jigger of *Gilka kummel,* and whip with an egg beater so diligently that it grows white and thick. Put enough of this into moulds to fill, and chill very cold indeed.

AND NOW for the EXOTIC FRUIT DESSERTS, from ORIENT & OCCIDENT; and ARABIAN NIGHTS BAKED APPLES, a BIT of a CEREMONY from MERRIE ENGLAND that WE FOUND ESPECIALLY COMFORTING on a CHILL FALL NIGHT

Take big red, tart apples; core them, and remove peeling ¼ way down from the stem end. Stack them in a big kettle, but not touching each other. Add ¾ cup of hot water and after filling cavities with sugar, dust sugar on top, toss in the peel of an orange, and colouring each apple with a drop or 2 of red liquid, the lid goes on tight and they are cooked *very slowly* until tender. . . . Now remove them to a greased baking dish, stuff tightly with the following mixture: Chopped dried figs and stoned dates—equal amounts; and this seasoned highly with clove, cinnamon, and 1 tsp Jamaica rum added to soak into the stuffing. Dust heavily with brown sugar and spices, and brown in a fairly hot oven around 375°—taking out immediately when sugar caramels. We inquired as to the Arabian Nights title, drawing a vague answer about figs and dates and other Mesopotamian things, and about it being a very old receipt. After all the title doesn't aid digestion, noticeably.

OLD ENGLISH TOFFEE APPLES, a RECEIPT from BANBURY, in 1932

We have seen children eating candy covered small apples up in Kalgan, that railway junction town above the Great Wall of China, not too far from the Mongolian border; in Korea, in Nikko, Japan, in England, and at our own old style county fairs. Ripe crab apples simmered a few moments in sugar syrup first, dried, then chilled, are favourites. We, however, recommend small sweet ripe table apples.

1. Make small wooden skewers the size used on lollypops.
2. Dig out bud end of apple. Put in skewer, and put near the stove so apples can thoroughly dry—but don't heat.
3. Make caramel, see any routine cook book, cooked long enough for it to crack in cold water.
4. Dip the apples in this hot caramel. Dry in warm oven, or near the stove. Repeat until well covered with several layers of sweet. . . . Caramel may be tinted with scarlet colouring for a more intriguing effect.

BANANAS en CASSEROLE, à la KENSCOFF

Six years ago we, and our better half, in Haiti, thought it would be a good idea to wander out of Port au Prince and up into the back-country hills through Petionville, and Kenscoff, for a look-see from the road-head at mysterious Morne la Selle which towers dark and aloof over the weird shadowed valleys where ***vaudou*** drums still throb of nights in spite of probation period administered by the U.S.

Marines, in spite of the professed and Paris-educated culture of the Haitian aristocracy. Yes, the *bambosh* dance is still danced until the dancers, wildly drunk on *clairine* vanish into the surrounding blackness to capture the partner of their choice. Yes, there are *mamaloi* and *papaloi* in those mountains, and goats and white cocks to be sacrificed before crude altars carved with the figure of Damballa, the Snake God, alongside clay figurines of the Virgin Herself. We have told already of Compte de Kenscoff, in the text of another receipt; so here is another, found after we had gone back there and seen Morne la Selle, after hiking seven miles up the mountainside beyond where the road was washed out—a stark, mournful peak soaring almost 2 miles into its neckerchief of trade wind cloud.

We got back to Kenscoff alright, and in our car which had all the audible virtues of an International Harvester, the soul of a wasp and springs of granite, we almost succeeded in officiating at the debut of our first daughter and heir on that rockiest road this side of Ethiopia. It really wasn't the bananas' fault!

Take six red bananas preferably, peel them, and split lengthwise—then cut once across. Brush with lime juice and brown delicately in hot butter, salting lightly. Make a syrup out of 1 cup sweet red *unfortified* wine, not port; 1 cup brown sugar, ½ tsp each of cinnamon and nutmeg; ¼ tsp powdered clove, 1½ tsp grated yellow orange peel. Put bananas in a small buttered casserole, turn in this spice syrup, and cover with a layer about ¼" thick made of equal quantities of crushed macaroons and very finely chopped almonds. Brown in a medium oven around 350°, and just before serving heat 1½ tbsp Haitian, or other dark, rum; fetch to table flaming.

NOW a CONSERVE of DRIED BANANAS, which WE HAVE ASSUMED as a DESSERT, MADE of DRIED BANANAS SPRINKLED with RAW BROWN SUGAR, a TRIFLE of DARK RUM, then PACKED in BAYLEAVES for MELLOWING & which the PARIS-EDUCATED HOSTESSES of PORT au PRINCE CALL *CONFITES des BANANES, SECHÉS*

In the true West Indian manner these fruits are split lengthwise and then across, and dried in the sun; but in the States it is saner to put them on a lightly buttered cooky sheet, and slowly dry at around 250° in oven. When they are thoroughly dry moisten them all over with rum, roll in brown sugar. Put a layer of rum-moistened bayleaves in a wooden box, then a layer of the sugared fruit, then another of bayleaves—and so on until a final layer of bay finishes things off, this being well sprinkled with rum. . . . Cover tightly and put in a cool place to absorb virtue and discretion from the varied aromatics in rum, herb and sugar. Inspect from time to time, during damp weather. These Haitian bananas make a sweetmeat, chopped up they garnish ice cream; with whipped cream or hard sauce they would make a dessert in their own right; or with a fine Philadelphia cream cheese, for instance.

FRUITS with DRY WHITE WINE, *á CHILEÑO y MENDOZA*

To a lucky few North Americans the very mention of Chile's Mendoza province brings to mind a sunny, happy land which is as near to Paradise as anything can be in this troubled world of ours today; a climate like California in many ways, a soil as finely suited to grape culture as any anywhere. Here the proprietor of vast *estancias* reigns almost as a benign feudal baron. He actually owns whole towns and villages, supplies church and padre; endows doctors, hospitals; tends to his workers like a father, nurses them when sick, marries them, delivers them and buries them. In a way he *is* their father, almost their God.

Our *caballero Chileño* doesn't sit on cool verandahs sipping mint juleps, he quaffs a mild and delicate drink emigrated there from Old Spain, of mingled wine and sun-ripe fruits. . . . Apricots, peaches; purple, red or green plums; ripe pineapple, anything on this order will do—but be sure they are really ripe. Simply peel, core, stone, and cut into fairly coarse pieces with a sharp knife—enough to fill a tall 16 oz glass 1/3 full. Chill both fruit and glass, then fill to the brim with iced dry white wine, like Chile's lovely *Undurraga Rhin* that we discovered back in 1933 on the Grace Line's *Santa Elena* en route from Seattle to Panama and Havana.

When drunk with a meal this blend is delightful. Glasses are refilled with cold wine as needed, and finally the well saturated fruits themselves are captured—making dainty tidbits of married wine and fragrant ripe pulp. *Undurraga* always comes in squat brown saddle-bag type bottles, as much of Chile's wine goes into the Argentine where the *gauchos* pack them in saddlebags. We find a garnish of fresh green spearmint is a pleasant addition.

KILLARNEY CHERRIES

Next to negro mammies and levees and cotton fields, Killarney has probably had more songs dedicated to her lakes and dells than is credible, but, regardless of all this, her aristocracy was much quicker to appreciate fine Bordeaux claret than were their English step-brothers, if we are to believe the written histories of wines. This thoughtful dessert is original enough to satisfy the most critical gourmet.

Stem 1 lb of fine big black or red cheeked ox-heart cherries, being sure they are really ripe. Put them in a saucepan, cover with claret, and add sugar to make quite sweet; then toss in a stick of cinnamon bark, or 1 tsp of the ground spice; ¼ tsp ground cloves, or 12 whole cloves. When pot boils, reduce heat and simmer as gently as may be for 12 to 15 minutes, covered. Drain out the cherries carefully, reduce the sauce by about 1/3 through gentle simmering, add 2 tbsp of red currant jelly; let melt and let cool. . . . Put cherries in a deep silver serving dish. Chill everything very cold indeed. . . . Meantime make up some whipped cream, slightly sweetened, and flavoured with 1 scant tbsp *kirschwasser*—a cherry brandy—and serve as follows: first the cherries in silver, then wine sauce poured over, then whipped cream on top. Shaved or cracked ice in another silver dish, nesting the bowl into it for better chilling, is recommended. The taste fillip is the lovely cherry flavour pointed up with really chilled fruit and sauce. . . . These cherries served hot over any sort of ice cream except chocolate, are food for the gods—and this latter case, add hot cognac in chafing dish and serve in a sauce boat flaming.

RIPENED FRESH FIGS BAKED with VARIOUS LIQUEURS, *à la GRANDE CORNICHE*

Cooked ripe figs are almost totally ignored by Americans, although they grow well from the Carolinas southward and westward to California—both brown, purple and yellow varieties. . . . Now a whispered word of advice: *never* peel ripe figs to be cooked; merely wash them to remove travel stains and possible entomological companions. . . . In this receipt stand them in an oven casserole or baking dish, having a little water on the bottom; dust them well with brown sugar. Prick each fruit with a fork to permit egress of pent-up steam under heat, and bake very slowly at around 275° to 300°, basting frequently. When very tender, dust with cinnamon, a little powdered clove, and add ¼ cup of any fine liqueur like Curaçao, Cointreau, Chartreuse, Grande Marnier, *kirsch*. Chill them very cold indeed in the serving dish, being careful not to damage figs in removal from baking dish. Pour the sauce all over them. Make some whipped cream lightly flavoured with a little confectioner's sugar, and some of the cordial as is used in the sauce. This also is delicious as a crowning gesture to any delicately flavoured ice cream.

MUSKMELONS, *ORIENTALE*

Some years ago we were wandering alone across India, westward from Calcutta; Benares, Agra, Delhi and so on down to Bombay. In Jaipur in the State of Rajputana Agency, we were fortunate enough to meet the young Maharajah while inspecting his 300 or so polo ponies, a young gentleman of parts, who had awakened up one fine morning to find himself not only deprived of his august father, but wearer of the royal title and possesser of some 400 assorted wives and concubines of various ages, colours, dispositions and manners! We sat on a dais, or divan, under the General Electric *punkahs* in his lovely palace and compared notes on things western and things eastern—ethics, morals, liquors and foods. Some of his descriptions of the feasts and levees given for George V at the Durbar, beggared belief. He told us about Ambar, a few miles up toward Gulta Pass. We never think of the harem quarters of that deserted Ambar Palace outside of Jaipur—built in 1600 and abandoned in 1728—a lovely thing of fountains, cool water runnels, and marble fretwork jalousies, frescoed baths and cloistered gardens where they promenaded with attendant eunuchs—without thinking of those canny old bearded Rajput rascals taking their ease, as we might say, of a warm summer afternoon during the monsoon season, fanned with peacock feather fans, feasting the eye on their assorted ladies and feasting the lips on Muskmelons, *Orientale*. . . . Incidentally we might mention that when the young Maharajah's father, the Maharajah Madho Singh, went to England for Edward VII's coronation, he not only chartered his own steamship for the voyage but bunkered her up with enough wives, viziers, servants, food and water to last the trip there and back, and furthermore transported in addition to this modest equipment, a plot of Jaipur State soil whereupon to plant the royal *derrière,* when at meat or drink or what not, just so he would always feel at home. We challenge any adopted citizens of California to match that!

Choose only sun-ripened muskmelons or cantaloupes, and Persian or Spanish melons are the only type we recommend that are not entirely ripened on vine. First cut a slice off the bud end so melon will stand upright. Next, cut a 3″ trap door out with stem in the center. Remove seeds carefully, scoop out flesh with a melon ball scoop—making small balls of the best part. Put in a bowl and add ½ as much of really ripe fresh pineapple. Add to each melon 6 halved scarlet maraschino cherries, sweeten well with powdered sugar, and replace in melon. Before closing again pour in 4 tbsp of arrack, or lacking this either *kirsch,* Cointreau, or other good liqueur. Chill cold as possible without actually freezing for exactly 24 hrs. Garnish with green leaves on the platter, bright blossoms, or scarlet cherries.

MUSKMELONS in the SPANISH MANNER, a ROYAL DISH from CASTILE that WE COLLECTED in SPAIN, in the YEAR 1931

This, amazingly enough, parallels the *Orientale* dish very closely. The fact is that the Mughal Emperors brought their luxurious ideas from Persia, and in turn many of those thoughts filtered back into Spain through the Mohammedan Moors after their conquest of the Iberian Peninsula. . . . Cut off a flat spot from blossom end, make the same trap door, take out seeds—only now instead of cutting flesh into small balls, merely turning in 1/3 to ¼ cup of *Anis del Mono,* or Anis of the Monkey-Head Label—substituting French or Dutch anisette if this is not available. Chill for the same length of time. This is a favourite dish around Badalona where much of the Spanish *anis* was then made, and thereabouts is called "Stuffed Melon of the Monkey."

BAKED STUFFED SWEET ORANGES, PACKED with CERTAIN TROPICAL LOOT such as DATES, FIGS, and COCONUT, not to MENTION CHOPPED CASHEWS or ALMONDS, *à l'INDOCHINE*

This is a classic from Saigon, overnight stop before journeying by motor car supplied by *Le Bureau Central du Tourisme Indochinois,* up into the amazing jungle country via Pnom Penh and Siemreap to Angkor Wat, in Cambodia; and donated to our volume by the chef of the Continental Palace Hotel as we sat in Cabaret Le Perroquet, in Saigon, studying human relationships.

For 6 oranges allow 9 pitted dates, and 8 small dried figs; also 6 marshmallows, 2 tbsp finely chopped fresh white coconut kernel, and 2 tbsp of finely chopped roasted cashews or unsalted almonds. Cut cap off stem end, remove pulp, and mix this last with the chopped dates, figs, and nuts. Dust well with brown sugar, after stuffing the orange shells, and bake for ½ hr in medium oven around 350°. Add 1 tsp cointreau to each orange, arrange on a silver platter and splash a little heated cognac over them. Serve flaming, and garnished with something appropriately tropical.

PECHES à la GRANDE BRETAGNE, which CONCERNS ITSELF with PEACHES in ATHENS, & CUNNINGLY DEALT with by AGENTS like CURAÇAO, CHOPPED PISTACHES & HAZELNUTS, and ALL of IT SERVED COLD as COLD

Peaches must be dead ripe, of course, for acid fruit spells defeat. First make a quart of sugar syrup, but not too thick. Add 1 scant tbsp vanilla and when it boils well, drop the peaches into this bath for exactly 2½ minutes. Remove them, slip off their skins without breaking the pulp, then pop back in syrup for 5 more minutes' simmering. Now add sugar, and let syrup thicken until it is fairly heavy. Arrange the peaches in a silver or china bowl being sure to leave a depression in the center which is filled with peach or apricot jam, or conserve. Take enough of the vanilla syrup to drench the peaches well, add ¼ cup or so of peach or apricot liqueur, and pour over everything. Now whip enough thick cream to mask well, adding 1 tbsp of the same liqueur to this also, for the characteristic flavour. Chill everything well, mask when served with whipped cream, and dust all over with finely chopped pistachio and hazelnuts. This is another stroke of genius by Chef Jean Kritikos in Athens.

ANOTHER DELICATE DISH, this TIME of SUN-RIPE PEACHES STUFFED with POUNDED ALMONDS, CHOPPED CITRONS, PEELS, and LIQUEURS, in the MAJESTIC ROMAN MANNER

We have already touched lightly on one stay in *Grande Hotel de Russie,* in Rome; and suffice it to say that this dish was observed on a festive occasion when certain expatriate Americans rendered a dinner on the Eve of our departure for Pisa and Paris. And for no reason at all it suddenly came over us that except eaten *in situ* under the bough, as peaches and cream, or in ice cream, America shrugs the peach off into unnecessary and undeserved oblivion. Consider, then, the following.

Choose ripe specimens, for as is the case with our modern virgins, many a blushing cheek may camouflage a hard and durable heart. Allow 2 whole peaches per guest. . . . Scald in boiling water for a moment, and slip off their skins. Halve lengthwise and remove stones. To stuff 12 peaches, pound 1 cup of chopped, unsalted, blanched almonds in a bowl or mortar—adding a few drops of cold water to prevent oiling—along with 1 tbsp of sugar. Now mix in 1 tbsp of finely chopped candied orange peel, the same of finely chopped citron, the crushed pulp of 1 ripe peach for a binder, and finally 6 lady fingers cut small. . . . Pack the cavities with this toothsome stuffing, rejoin the divorced halves, skewer with toothpicks, then put in a baking dish. Now wet them with white wine, dust with sugar, and pop in a medium oven around 375° until sugar caramels a little. These are delicious hot, with half peach brandy—half cognac, heated and poured over them, and set alight; or, better still, served cold with or without whipped cream, flavoured with peach liqueur or apricot.

PEARS in PORT, *ARMENONVILLE,* which Are Sun Ripened Affairs Treated Fairly, and First Poached Modestly in a Bath of White Wine

Here at Armenonville in the Bois de Boulogne is a sort of chalet set beside a park lake, which at night changes itself to a fairyland. The glass enclosed lower part of the building makes it almost unreal—especially when viewed from the garden, where those both romantic and wise, choose to dine of a summer's evening. Perhaps the chef has forgotten that very especial dessert suggested to a certain two; perhaps not. Ah me—*tout casse, tout passe!*

Peel 2 big pears very carefully leaving the stem in, but do *not* core in this case. Poach, covered, in sweet white *unfortified* wine with a little sugar added, and when tender set in the refrigerator to cool. Now put 1 cup of ripe red raspberries or strawberries through a sieve, add 1 tbsp sugar and 2 tbsp of red port wine. Make a whipped cream using a little red port for flavouring. In service try and find a crystal bowl, or dessert dish, for the colours are pretty. First comes the pear, drowned in the port wine and berry sauce, then the rosy-hued whipped cream. Chill very very cold indeed.

PEARS, *à la CUILÈRE,* from MARVELOUS RESTAURANT JOSEPH, on RUE PIERRE CHARRON, in PARIS, RIGHT BANK

It hardly seems thirteen years ago since we were last in Joseph, and arranged our little dinner—calling at 10:30 in the morning to make sure of everything. And the pear was upon advice of the *maitre d'hotel,* and a wise one, that. . . . It is a mildly spectacular dessert, and one appreciated by those who know foods.

Take big ripe luscious pears, peel them with surgical nicety, and slice the bud end off ½" or so back, saving the slice. Remove core from this end, and pack the cavity with crimson bar le duc; or lacking this, with red or black currant jam—in either case mixed with 1 tsp *kirschwasser.* Now stand the pear stem end down in a big crystal goblet, chill as cold as possible without actually freezing, and serve with a liqueur glass filled with *kirsch,* this last to be added a drop per spoonful, as needed. In another place we found a little soft cream cheese put inside cavity in this manner: first 1 tbsp bar le duc, then 1 tsp cream cheese, ending with bar le duc at the last, *Magnifique!*

BAKED PINEAPPLE, *HAWAII*

Out Lanikai-way lived a friend of ours dating back to the first of our three voyages to that most charming fleet of islands, who considered this his pet dessert receipt. Much as we would like to shout the praises of our own ½ acre patch of Smooth Cayennes we really are forced to admit that Hawaii produces the finest "pines" on earth. . . . Choose a large sun-ripened pineapple, or one which has been stood in sun until beautifully coloured. With a keen blade, behead the top—cutting through 1½" down on the fruit; reserve this for future use. Now cut out the heart meat with a curved grapefruit knife, being careful not to dig through the shell. Discard pithy portions entirely, dice small, and toss with ½ cup or so of sugar until well coated. Now put diced meat back into shell, pour juices over, add 3 to 4 tbsp cognac, dust with 1 tsp cinnamon at the last. Put the cap back on, skewer in place with toothpicks, and bake in a medium oven around 350° until inner flesh is tender as can be. . . . Serve on silver platter, pour on 1 tbsp heated brandy and fetch to table blazing.

RIPE STRAWBERRIES, *à la TSARINA,* which ARE a FINAL THOUGHT on those INCREDIBLE DAYS in ST. PETERSBURG before the DEBACLE, when LIFE WAS LIVED, WOMEN WERE LOVELY, MEN GALLANT, and FIVE YEAR PLANS WERE NOT YET DREAMED of

Be sure berries are ripe. Stem 2 cups or so carefully an hour ahead of chilling time, tumble in a mound of powdered sugar, and put them in a crystal or silver bowl. Next we must blend 2 tbsp each of tawny port, orange Curaçao and cognac, and pour this over the sugared berries; or put immediately into the individual dessert dishes, portioning the sauce equitably. Make enough whipped cream flavoured with Curaçao to cover well. Serve with dishes in cracked ice—everything chilled as cold as possible.

> ". . . What does cookery mean? . . . It means knowledge of all herbs, & fruits, & balms, & spices, & of all that is healing & sweet in groves, & savoury in meat. It means carefulness, willingness, & readiness of appliance. It means the economy of your great grandmother, & the science of modern chemistry, & French art, & Arabian hospitality. . . ."
>
> *John Ruskin*

APPENDIX

WEIGHTS & MEASURES

Asparagus	20 stalks	1 lb
Bananas, skins on	3 big ones	1 lb
Beans, Green, fresh	1 qt approximately	¾ lb
Beans, Dried	1 cup	½ lb
Bread Crumbs	1 cup	2¾ oz
Butter	1 cup	½ lb
Corn Meal	3 cups	1 lb
Currants, Dried	2⅜ cups	1 lb
Dates, Dried, seeded	1 cup	5 oz
Flour, Bread	4 tbsp	1 oz
Flour, Bread	3 1/5 cups	1 lb
Flour, Whole Wheat & Pastry	1 cup	¼ lb
Lard	1 cup	½ lb
Lemon Rind, Grated	1 average size	3 tsp
Lemon Juice	1 average size	3 tbsp juice
Milk, Skim	1 cup scant	½ lb
Nut Meats	1 cup	5 1/3 oz
Raisins	1 cup	5 1/3 oz
Rice	1 cup	½ lb
Sugar, Brown	1 cup	5½ oz
Sugar, Confectioners	1 cup	4½ oz
Sugar, Ordinary Granulated	1 cup	5 oz
Tomatoes, average size	4 tomatoes	1 lb
Water	1 cup	½ lb

ALL MEASUREMENTS in THIS VOLUME, & VOLUME II, ARE LEVEL.

INDEX OF RECEIPTS

Lightning Source UK Ltd.
Milton Keynes UK
UKHW011405210322
400385UK00002B/536

9 781614 274452